V O L U M

LADIES *of* GOLD

THE REMARKABLE MINISTRY OF THE GOLDEN CANDLESTICK

The Authorized Compilation by

JAMES MALONEY

WESTBOW
PRESS
A DIVISION OF THOMAS NELSON

WestBow Press books may be ordered through booksellers or by contacting:

WestBow Press
A Division of Thomas Nelson
1663 Liberty Drive
Bloomington, IN 47403
www.westbowpress.com
1-(866) 928-1240

All scripture quotes are KJV, unless otherwise noted.

ISBN: 978-1-4497-2922-6 (sc)
ISBN: 978-1-4497-2923-3 (hbk)
ISBN: 978-1-4497-2921-9 (e)
Library of Congress Control Number: 2011918739

Printed in the United States of America
WestBow Press rev. date: 10/20/2011

CONTENTS

WHO WERE THE GOLDEN CANDLESTICK?

One of the chief questions asked when people read *The Dancing Hand of God* is, who were the Golden Candlestick? They played such an integral part in my ministry, and yet most people have never heard of them; or if they have, it's a lot of strange bits of information, almost like hearing an urban legend or something. I can assure you, the Golden Candlestick was a real ministry, but they might *have* been legendary—I'll leave it up to you to decide.

I felt the Lord impress upon me to compile all of their collected works (as many as we could find—there may be a few teachings floating around out there, but any missing pieces are more than likely nonexistent anymore) when my first book came out. I knew it would be important, not only to honor those of the Golden Candlestick (GC), but to shed some light on their purpose to the body of Christ.

The last surviving original member of the GC was a lady named Dora; she was most likely in her late eighties, early nineties, when she came to my meetings in California for the last time before she went on to glory. As Dora walked up to me, she was short and stooped over from seventy some-odd years on her knees, worshiping the Lord—it was the only way she prayed. She anointed me with oil (a LOT of oil; it ruined my suit, and I don't think she cared in the slightest.) Afterward, she told me several key things. One of those was a commissioning to compile their works to share them with the next generation. Since there are no more founding members of the Golden Candlestick, the copyrights have expired with them as well, and the few people who are aware of the GC's works have taken the little bits they have; some posted on the Internet, some reprinted and offered free of charge, some for a small purchase price, and potentially mixed with other teachings. Because no one that I know of has all the teachings in one place—some are even excerpts of larger teachings—I wanted to put out an authorized collection of their complete works, as we know them, to give to posterity.

To my knowledge, by putting my collection together with Kristeen and Wade Bandelin's collection, we have the only surviving complete set in existence. Most of these are mimeographed, some are nearly sixty or more years old, very difficult to read—they're not going to last forever, so it was important to get these down all in one place. I am indebted to Kristeen and Wade, leaders of Shiloh Christian Ministries in my hometown of Idyllwild, CA. Without their gracious assistance in lending these prized possessions to me, we wouldn't have been able to compose the collection. The Bandelins are highly educated, dedicated servants to that community, intent on extending a progressive move of God's Spirit in a very difficult area that has long had strong ties to Satanism and the occult. The Bandelins, too, have honored the GC, and it reflects in the ministry they have carved into that mountain. I honor them here for that, and urge you, if you're ever in that area, to stop by the church and say hello for me. By the way, we are tithing proceeds from sale of this book to their ministry, so let's bless them!

When we compiled all of the teachings, I came to the realization one book would not be enough to contain all the writings. So we decided to split it into two volumes. Now three. So this is simply Part One, and the remaining works will follow just as quickly as we can get them transcribed. Coming soon!

OK, so let's try to shed some light on this group of ladies (and a few men) known as the Golden Candlestick before we dive into their works.

It is difficult to compose an exact timeline for their writings—they did not seem to be overly concerned about things like precise dates. Some of the writings do contain dates, but I found it nearly impossible to put them into exact chronological order. But here are a few things I do know:

The Golden Candlestick was started and led by Frances Metcalfe in the late thirties to early forties. She was the set-person, and everyone gathered around her, not really as equals; but in recognizing her gifting, they rallied around her ministry as an apostolic seer prophetess and thus entered into her vision. She drew together a group of women from Elim Bible Institute who were all feeling the Lord push them in the same direction. Namely, that they were to give up aspirations for a public ministry and to covenant with Him in high praise and worship before His Throne. In return, He would grant them unusual experiences of His presence, and through their directed intercession, birth many moves of God in the nations.

Some of these ladies had husbands, and a few men were a part of the fellowship, but it was primarily women who made up the bulk of the Golden Candlestick, many of whom remained single in order to dedicate themselves to this ministry. Frances had three children with her husband; two of which I knew, Dwight, Jr., and Jody. The daughter was actively involved in her mother's ministry; the two Dwights were not so intimately involved, although Dwight, Sr., did lead a separate Bible study.

At its inception there were approximately twenty members (another twenty or so were invited to join soon after from LIFE Bible College in Los Angeles, that Aimee Semple McPherson established, and some from other local ministry and church settings); at its height there were about eighty people involved in the ministry. Normally it averaged between forty and fifty people. All members were by strict invitation only, and the Golden Candlestick meetings were not open to the public. (Frances did travel a little, and she did set up a few other harp-and-bowl ministries, primarily in Southern California. But her own group was always kept very private.) The meetings were usually held four, five or six days a week, from about 6-7pm until one or two in the morning on average. There were periods when some meetings would go day and night, but as some members had families (including Frances) most were typically held in the evenings.

Quite realistically, these people covenanted together to form a private association, vowing themselves to the Lord's worship and intercession. Similar to the lines of St. Francis of Assisi's orders (from a purely Protestant form of evangelical, and later, Pentecostal worship, I mean, not as in the sense of Catholic nuns—but the cloistered element of maintaining worship before the Lord, and as being in a covenant relationship together. I gathered this information directly from Frances on how she perceived their covenant relationship.)

The group moved to Southern California (where they soon met the members from LIFE and the other ministries) and Frances wanted to build a home that would have a sanctuary for the Golden Candlestick. She pulled out a map, and her finger supernaturally fell on Idyllwild, CA, what was to be my hometown growing up. Many of the jobs around Idyllwild were in the construction field, which is what many of the men did, as well as logging.

In 1948 they had a home built. The basement served as the sanctuary, and the ladies themselves laid the stones by hand. There was a stone fireplace central to the sanctuary, and the entire place was lavishly decorated in royal colors of purples, crimsons and golds, as similar to the Old Testament temple as they could make it. Many drapes and hangings all in deep kingly colors covered the walls. There was an altar where they gathered to take communion, and the main piece of decoration for the room was a golden menorah, from whence they took their name.

According to Revelation 5:8, the GC began what is now commonly referred to as a "harp and bowl" ministry unto the Lord. It was not just praise and worship, but intense intercession as the Spirit directed. It was also during this time of the Latter Rain movement, that their worship, aided by the Holy Spirit, began to take on amazing new elements. At this time, they did not sing traditional hymns in their meetings; their worship was spontaneous and led entirely by the Spirit. Frances would strum a zither while everyone worshiped in tongues, and within minutes everyone was caught right up into the Spirit. A song of the Lord would come forth, given at that moment, with different members contributing to the verses and choruses—all in rhyme! Imagine that kind of coordination between fifty or more people, to sing an unwritten song with rhyme and meter before the Lord!

The songs of deliverance that came forth were just astounding. Powerful! Songs of the Bridegroom to the Bride, or vice versa. One part would sing the Lord's words, the other part would respond as the Bride, extemporaneously in rhyme.

For Frances and the GC it was important to celebrate the feasts of the Old Testament, not out of a sense of compulsion to the Law, but in reverence to the foreshadowing of the Lord and His future Bride. To them everything pointed to the centrality of Jesus, the fulfillment of the Law, and His direct connection to His Church. They recognized the revelation of Jesus in each of the feasts, and Rosh Hashanah was an important, vital day to them, leading up to Yom Kippur and into the Feast of Tabernacles. They placed high significance on natural Israel.

In fact, for several years prior to its adoption as the official flag of Israel, Frances had flown the blue-and-white Shield of David, stating the Lord had shown the flag to her (the design had been created in the late 1880s, but was not commonly known then.) When Israel was declared independent, she sent the design to the Provisional Council, who adopted the flag in 1948.

The Golden Candlestick was also a conduit for hundreds of thousands of dollars to be funneled into the Kingdom. They followed after the pattern of George Müller in the support of his numerous orphanages and schools. They never petitioned people for money, relying solely on it coming in supernaturally as they "praised" it in. Because the money just flowed through their hands like water, the Lord entrusted great amounts to them which went out to support at one point in time 100 missionaries throughout the world. The ladies understood the importance of missions, primarily through their theological education in Elim and LIFE.

In all things, the revelation of the Bride of Christ was foremost in their experiences and understanding. They maintained a strict Christocentricity in all their experiences—they were for the purpose of understanding the King more fully. Frances once told me, "How you minister to the people on earth in love is what is important to the King above." The Golden Candlestick believed in evangelism as something of preeminence to ministry expression, bringing more of a Bride to the King.

A lot of the following material came through transcendent experiences the Golden Candlestick had—I don't know of another ministry that was blessed with the same level of rapture and translation, similar to the experiences of Elijah and Philip. When I say that members (often several at a time) were transported, I mean physically—they disappeared and were taken to another part of the world for evangelistic campaigns, sometimes for several days at a time. In these instances they were supernaturally sustained, either by the people they met or through the angelic host. Often the Spirit would translate them to a country so that they might gain strategy on how to intercede for a particular district or region, how to combat hindrances to the gospel, etc. They would then bring back these reports so the whole group could pray together. In this way, great moves of God were birthed throughout many nations. All times of intercession were guided by the Holy Spirit as He brought to them seasons for specific burdens. They would simply wait upon the Lord in high praise and worship, and if the Spirit didn't lead them to intercede, they didn't intercede—focusing solely on worshiping the King. The focus was more on worship than warfare, but they had active roles in both capacities.

All of the earthly translations and rapture were separate from the translations to heaven, where many would return with sandals entwined with strange jewels, vest-like garments inset with twelve stones representing the tribes of Israel, headdresses arrayed in almost living colors, articles of clothing that would be stitched with gold thread—I mean the metal, not the color. These were regular occurrences with the ladies of gold. It is not much of a stretch to say they were as often in heaven as on earth. When Frances is speaking about seeing the stars, for example, she means from an element of rapture or even translation—not simply in the mind's eye. These kinds of transcendent encounters, although they grew in deeper expression and manifestation as the following material shows, were constant and continuous for over fifty years, starting from day one when they gathered together.

I recall seeing a door in that sanctuary, beautifully molded, emanating a golden hue. I assumed when people walked through it, it led to another part of the house. Many years later, when walking through the house in the daytime with Marion Pickard (Frances' personal assistant, and the second-to-last original member alive beside Dora) I was stunned to realize the door was not there. It was explained to me that door was a special door to heaven. I didn't bother asking further details—they wouldn't have been provided anyway.

Had I known then what I know now, I would've asked to go along with them on these translations to other countries and to the heavenlies; however, Frances assured me at the time, "You're not ready for that yet, Jim."

I'll share an excerpt from *The Dancing Hand of God* that highlights how I came to know Frances and the Golden Candlestick, but first, let me share some of the things I saw in the several meetings I attended.

The first thing about Frances, she was a very unnerving person. She had a mystical look about her, that you knew she wasn't "earth-bound," if that makes any sense. Her eyes were very penetrating and discerning. She could read you, but she wasn't "scary" or "ooky-feeling," just unsettling.

As soon as everyone began singing in tongues, the power of God fell like a heavy, thick fog. It was overwhelming. I could hear the people, but I couldn't see them. It took a few minutes for my eyes to adjust enough to see the person next to me; those who were farther away could only be made out dimly.

The ceiling was concealed in a purple, swirling cloud—sometimes feathers were whirling inside the cloud. Out of the cloud, one could often hear the audible laughter of exultant children. It truly was an open-heavens, a spiritual portal like a Jacob's Ladder. There were numerous times the four-and-twenty elders were a part of the worship. And just a consistent coming and going of the angelic host. When an angel was there, one could see them like they see a normal human being, fully manifested, no similitude (the outline or form of an angel.) They would come to worship and share information with the group. Often they wore "normal" clothes. On one occasion I saw two men in street clothes, sitting and conversing with some of the ladies before the service. When the meeting was starting, these two stood up and gave hugs to the ladies, then walked past me and disappeared. Again, when I asked what that was all about,

Frances told me, "You're not ready for that yet, Jim." Seems she told me that a lot!

There were firelights (the only word I can use to describe them) which were angels dropping down from the cloud above to the floor below. When these firelights struck the ground, one could see the angels' feet appear out of the flames. It's interesting how little details like that have stayed with me for almost forty years now.

I recall once three ladies worshiping in an angelic tongue, whose faces and torsos were concealed behind a purplish cloud—all I could see were their arms and hands outstretched. Again I remember a powerful instance where the roomful of ladies was dancing before the Lord, caught up in the Spirit, with their eyes completely shut, yet they never bumped into each other, being perfectly orchestrated by God.

When Frances would begin strumming that zither, heavenly instruments would be added to the orchestration: violins, French horns, harps, trumpets, other angelic voices, audibly, two or three octaves higher than the human voices.

Often thunderings crashed out of the cloud, and an archangel would make an audible declaration; things like, "HOW GREAT IS THE MERCY OF JEHOVAH: THE 'I WAS, THAT I AM, THAT I WILL BE!' PRAISE HIM!" And we would. It was astonishing to hear.

There was a swirling fog of gold dust, a liquid cloud I could smear with my hand, and it would whirl and swirl. I could breathe it in and feel it cleanse me inside. Often breezes would waft into the room, each one bringing a different, unique unearthly fragrance, beautifully sweet and nourishing.

All of these experiences, of course, pale on the printed page—there is no way I can give them due justice. Add to that these were all regular occurrences on a consistent basis, at every meeting, for over fifty years, and you'll begin to get an idea just how remarkable this ministry was.

For those of you who've read *The Dancing Hand of God*, this will be a bit of a repeat, but it's necessary for those of you who have not (why haven't you?) The following is an excerpt telling how I came to be connected to the Golden Candlestick:

I was seventeen. I had come down from my home higher up the mountain into the town village to collect the mail. As I was leaving the post office, an elderly lady accosted me, just out of nowhere, materializing in front of me, wagging this bony, crooked finger up in my face.

"You're the young man!" she croaked.

Ice poured down my back. I looked around, bewildered. I thought to myself, *Oh, great! What have I done now? I can't get away with anything in this dinky, little town!* There was this strange feeling that emanated off of her—it unsettled me greatly.

Now, the town I lived in was one of the major centers for mysticism and the occult in Southern California. The Hippies living up in the woods, the transient backpackers hiking around, the seclusion of the area lent itself to the "weirdoes" who wanted to escape the oppression of Los Angeles city living.

The town was a stronghold for the metaphysical sciences. And there were these really strange groups of people who'd walk around the town in white robes and long hair. Don't really know what *they* were all about. Oh, and it was a congregating point for the Hell's Angels bikers, so you can imagine what *that* was like!

Spiritism and New Age philosophy were highly prevalent, as well as satanic ritualism. Supposedly this area was some vortex or nexus point of special power or some other such junk—the point is, the Force was strong with this town . . . .

It wasn't uncommon in that situation, living under the tyranny of the occult, to see and hear weird things. Sacrificed animals out in the woods, people dressed like witches and warlocks who would walk by you with this far-off look in their eyes and proceed to "prophesy" over you, tell you what you were thinking, read your mail. You get the idea.

I was buffeted constantly by the demonic. There were times in my life that I had seen fully formed apparitions. They'd float in and disappear. You know, it's interesting to note that not always is a demon ugly and grotesque. Some of these had the ability to appear quite beautiful. (Hence, their ability to lure people into a false sense of peace.) Still, they'd move chairs, open up drawers, throw out knives, forks and spoons, scratch on the walls, pound on the doors. It was a terribly vexing, frightening way to grow up.

(Thankfully I never participated in the occult or got involved with the mystics—it was just the saving grace of God that kept me from involvement with that oppression. But living in that saturated environment has burned within me sensitivity to mysticism and the occult; something that has aided me throughout my ministry. I have a well-developed discernment when something is of a familiar spirit, versus a true manifestation of the Lord.)

"Yes, you're the one. You're the young man," this lady crooned, still waggling that crooked finger up at me. I was unnerved by her statement, but I didn't get that same sense of "ookiness" that I got from the witches and warlocks in the village. There was something *different* about her.

I remember sidestepping this woman, muttering something to the effect of, "Lady, you got the wrong guy." I hotfooted it out of the post office, and thankfully the elderly woman didn't follow me. I half-expected that whole night for some phone call to my parents about some ancient prank I'd pulled on that lady's flower garden or whatever. I kept wracking my brain, thinking, *What did I do?* I fell into a fitful sleep that night, tossing and turning, beating my pillow, with this emblazoned image of that bony crooked, wrinkled finger wiggling under my chin. *It's you! You're the young man!*

Several days later, with that nagging image still tickling my mind, a friend in the Lord phoned me up, saying I should go over to such-and-such place at such-and-such address this evening. "There are some great people there I'd like you to meet." So on her advice, I went.

Turns out this place was a house out in the sticks. *Oh, brother, where is she sending me?* I thought. I knocked on the door and waited for a few seconds, wondering what had I gotten myself into. When the door opened, guess who was standing there, beckoning me to come in?

Yep. That little lady with the bony finger.

It figures . . . .

"Come in. We've been expecting you."

Huh? Expecting me? But I screwed up my courage and followed her into the living room. There were about two dozen people (some men, mostly women) staggered around the place, looking at me expectantly. I had no idea what I'd walked into.

The lady (I found out later her name was Frances Metcalfe) began to tell me what it was they were all doing here. I'll put this in quotes, even though I don't exactly remember the order of her words, but she did say all these things in the course of her explanation.

"We call ourselves the Golden Candlestick, and there were about forty-five or fifty of us in the beginning. Some have gone home to be with Jesus now. Forty or more years ago, we were all students in seminary, preparing to go into our various ministries, when the Lord spoke to each of us and told us He had another plan for our lives. He told us that if we gave up all aspirations for public ministry and just continuously gathered together to worship Him in the high praise and deep intercession ministry . . ." [What we would commonly term today as the "harp and bowl" ministry; see Revelation 5:8] " . . . that He would take care of our physical needs, and He would use our intercessions to birth tremendous moves of

His power throughout the earth. So, since then, all of these years, four or five nights a week, from six until whenever—sometimes one or two in the morning—we just gather here and worship the Lord. Some of us work, and the Lord has permitted thousands of dollars to flow through us into the Kingdom, to support missionary works all over the world. We praise Him, we war in the spirit against demonic powers, and we share strategies from heaven to people to further His goals. We're a chosen covenant group."

She said it so simply, just stating the facts.

"Wow," was all I could stupidly offer in response.

Mrs. Metcalfe nodded and continued. "Several years ago, in a time of great intercession, one of us called out to the Lord—not in anger, but under His guidance—calling Him to remember that we had sacrificed so much, that we had given up our own ministries for this calling. We were always praying for other people, other ministries, other issues; but in all this time, we've only asked one thing just for ourselves in return from Him: that someone, a person from our hometown, would be sent forth into the world with a ministry that would inherit all of the prayers and supplications we have offered to Him. That this person would enter into all of the ministry expressions we gave up in order to minister to Him—an anointing to open His heart to the world. We had a vision of a fireball rolling down our mountain and splashing into the world around us. That's what we asked for: just one person to be that fireball."

Electricity sparked through my entire being as tears welled up in her eyes. She began to weep and stuck that finger out at me one more time.

"Jim," she cried, "*you* are that young man!"

Ladies and gentlemen, I want you to know, as she said these words, my knees slammed into the carpet, my face dropped into my hands, and I wept. This overpowering anointing smeared over me.

I couldn't move; I couldn't speak. The humbleness of that moment is not something I am equipped to describe on the printed page. I have no words, and I am not artistic enough to tell you what was happening to me. This was the defining moment of my life. Everything that had happened to me had led me up to this one moment. It's the most astounding feeling in the world to know you are not worthy of such a calling; there is nothing in yourself that is "good enough" to receive such a grace gift. But here I was, crying like a child, while these men and women prayed over me, prophesying things I would do years and years later. Dreams and visions they had had for themselves that God would credit them for my works.

So now you know why I am the way I am. See, I can't go back now. I can't turn away from the supernatural. I don't do this for me; I do it for the Lord and to honor the Golden Candlestick. They receive their continued treasure and reward for my actions here on earth. In a way, I entered into *their* ministries. You have no idea how truly humbling that is. I never want to be the cause for their sadness.

Frances passed away in the late '70s, and the ministry continued until about 1990-ish when Dora passed away. As is the case with every human being who is truly born again, eventually we all go home to be with the Lord for good. But I like to think that the fruit of the Golden Candlestick's ministry continues on in our ministry. When the GC ceased to be, it became The ACTS Group International (AGI)—that's an awesome and a sobering thought; it's a great heritage and a great responsibility.

Now, here's an important note that I really want to drive home, a clarification of what AGI stands for. I believe there is a shocking and alarming sub-movement in the charismatic, Pentecostal stream of Christianity that borders on a pseudo-spiritual, extra-scriptural overemphasis of "glory encounters" that in some instances smack of heresy and almost take away from the simplicity and centrality of Jesus Christ. I was embarrassed of some of the things I saw on YouTube in the name of freedom in Jesus Christ. None of these experiences I saw promoted repentance, marriage fidelity, holiness, getting free from sin, etc. It's like the people seek the encounters more than they seek Jesus, if that makes sense. Look, please keep the next several paragraphs in context.

While you read these encounters of the GC, you'll most likely be surprised—and you should be! These are not the everyday, "normal" encounters the typical born-again, Spirit-filled Christian has. Not everyone is called to be a Seer. God made the human mind to deal with the everyday life of this world: we work, we eat, we raise our children, we pay our taxes and balance our checkbooks. Most of us do not see portals and doorways leading to heaven. Nor should we!

Remember the words of Jesus to Thomas: "Jesus said to him, 'Thomas, because you have seen Me, you have believed. Blessed are those who have not seen and yet have believed.'" (John 20:29)

There is a principle that Jesus put forth—the Man who was *all about* signs, wonders and miracles, glory encounters, in His earthly ministry: no matter what you see or don't see, believe in Me; blessed are they who believe Me just because of who I am, and what they experience by the Holy Spirit *internally*—not just what they see with their natural eyes.

It takes a great level of discernment that I feel is sadly lacking in the body of Christ as a whole to differentiate between what is a Spirit-inspired glory encounter and what is instigated by catering to the flesh, or even the demonic. Unfortunately, we are seeing some extreme mixtures in the charismatic Church, and I don't want the encounters contained in this book to be construed that *everyone* should have portals in their basements, or be translated to the cosmos. We can focus so much on "seeing" in the Spirit, we get nothing accomplished on this earth.

And many people, let's be honest, are not at a level of closeness in their relationship with Jesus Christ to be able to discern what is truly inspired by His Spirit in many cases. It creates an embarrassment in the Church, and niche pseudo-movements centered around a fleshly, flakey experience leaving little substance or change in the partakers' lives. I suppose that sounds a little strong, but people who know me, know my heart is to draw people closer in their relationship with the Lord, and out of *that* comes the signs, wonders and miracles, not the other way 'round.

Remember the Golden Candlestick was *not* a public ministry—these experiences were for this UNIQUE group of women (and men) based on a lifelong covenant fellowship with the Lord and each other, centered around a Seer prophetess leader who was specially called by God for these experiences.

AGI is a *public* ministry. And as such, even though it is an outgrowth of the Golden Candlestick, it is a very different vehicle in expression of Christ's ministry to the world at large. Yes, we believe in signs, wonders and miracles—I write books about them! Yes, there are certain encounters—supernatural manifestations—that I believe are for the people; but if we never saw one glory expression, it would not negate our ministry's prime focus: preaching Jesus Christ, Him crucified, resurrected and ascended for the remission of sins, repentance leading to salvation, Christ-like character development based on sound doctrine, tenets of Christianity, teaching from the Word, mixed with faith, and every encounter subjected to that Word.

All we attempt to do is reproduce the works and acts of the Lord during His earthly ministry (and the subsequent ministries of the early apostles.) We strive for salvation (the greatest miracle);

healings; deliverance from demonic oppression—those things that Jesus did while on the earth.

We are rooted in the centrality of Jesus, the redemptive works of the cross, the basic simplicity of the whole gospel message, holiness unto the Lord as a walk of life.

Of course the Golden Candlestick stood for all these things too. But what I am trying to show is that even though some of these encounters you're about to read are "wild"—the extension of the Golden Candlestick (that's The ACTS Group International) is hopefully, we pray, a refinement of those experiences that is given for the people at large. So I don't expect to see reproductions in the same level of magnitude that Frances and her ladies saw in the day-to-day activities of yours and mine Christian life. Yes, we all strive for a greater expression of Jesus' power in our lives—don't misunderstand; but it is unrealistic to suppose all of us will spend six, seven hours a day, six days a week, in high praise before the Lord in order to cultivate the closeness with Jesus required for Him to entrust His people with those encounters. If and when encounters such as these do come, it is strictly by the instigation of the Holy Spirit, supported by the entire revelation of scripture (I don't mean simply chapter and verse—I mean the concepts and themes expressed by God in His Word), with massive discernment required, which as I said above, is something generally lacking in the body at large. That's not a fault-finding statement; it is a fact I believe the vast majority of us agree with.

See, if we let our search for these encounters overtake our daily lives, these experiences can actually take us away from Jesus Christ, and they can serve as a detriment, not the blessing they were intended to be.

Let me suggest to you: worship Jesus for just who He is, not what He does for you, and as you are faithful to Him and Him alone, I am convinced the Holy Spirit will break into the day-to-day activities of this life with greater supernatural encounters, visions and dreams, etc., as He wills, at least in some measure—even if you and I are never bodily transported to Zimbabwe, or wherever, to evangelize a village.

The ACTS Group International emphasizes the practicality of service to the Lord Jesus Christ, honoring the simplicity of the gospel, calling people to repentance and a holy walk unto the Lord, and then out of that come supernatural experiences, but primarily for the purpose of cleansing the sick, raising the dead, seeing the captives set free and swept into the Kingdom of God. I want the ministry the Lord has entrusted to me, growing out of the Golden Candlestick, to take the realities of those encounters they experienced and translate them into tangible works of Jesus in the everyday believer's (and disbeliever's) life: the person in need of inner-healing, deliverance, salvation, a tumor to disappear, whatever the need may be; and if we get gold dust and purple clouds, then fine. But if not, we'll still, to the best of our human abilities, by God's grace, be teaching a foundation in the Bible, preaching the whole counsel of God, and laying hands on the sick. I know that's what Frances would want.

So we honor the Golden Candlestick and their experiences, but we emphasize the basics, and discernment against the reproach of false, extremely extra-scriptural manifestations.

I've heard of some ministries trying to "re-dig" the well of the Golden Candlestick, or retrieve the mantle of anointing and authority they had. In my opinion, that's not really possible. They were a unique expression. Now that doesn't mean that God will not birth something new, something fresh, along the lines of what Frances' ministry stood for—but even the ministry God's given me, which is the direct extension of the Golden Candlestick, is not the same in expression and execution. We don't see the same things they saw, but on the other side of the coin, they didn't see the things we *do* see. That shows me there is progression in the body of Christ that builds on the foundations of the previous laborers. And, yes, there is an importance of honoring the past, of applying those previous principles—that's the point of a book like this—again, don't take any of this out of context. But I am convinced we are being further shaped, further sharpened, further refined. And I think Frances would like to know that, too!

As powerful as the experiences of the Golden Candlestick were, they by no means had all revelation. The group did not have a solid understanding of healing provision in the atonement work of the cross, found in the Word of God. They had very little knowledge of deliverance. They lacked in-depth teaching in faith—keep in mind they came from the Latter Rain movement and the Word of Faith movement started later. Frances was often in another world, physically and metaphorically. She suffered from physical limitations, that I believe had her foundation in healing been greater developed—she would've been set free from them. This does not negate their work, their importance or their special calling. But it does show that the Golden Candlestick was not "perfect" in their ministry expression or in their own personal lives. No one is, of course—but we have come a long way in the Body since the forties.

I shared the above because I want to make it clear: I may not fully understand their experiences. Some are very revelatory, metaphorical, and I don't 100% necessarily agree with *everything* presented in these works doctrinally. I believe some theological strengthening in some places was needed in their lives. (In mine as well, so it's not a critical statement.) Still, I've left their writings exactly as is—spelling errors, archaic phraseology, grammar problems, and the theological interpretations too. There are some politically incorrect statements in there—don't forget they were writing from the standpoint of the forties and fifties. I'd say in the vast, vast majority of cases, my views represent their views—but not always, so it's important to make that clear. I do wholeheartedly believe in this "Dove Company" as Frances would term it—a group of believers, as we approach the end-time ministry of the Lord, who will be used by Him in having greater supernatural rapture and translation experiences.

So, let me caution the reader, just because you and I haven't experienced these kinds of things recounted in their works, doesn't mean they're not real or correct. We should exercise extreme caution when judging the contents of their writings. We may not fully understand or even "agree" with the revelation brought out by the GC—but that is the nature of revelation originated through rapture and translation, it can be highly interpretive, but that doesn't make it "false." Again, every experience they had was to unveil more fully the King of Glory, to lead them to the centrality of Christ in all expressions—that can never be wasted experiences!

The works are worth reading, studying and enjoying. They are encouraging, uplifting and they draw one to the Lord—which is the most important thing. They may not be the "deepest" material you've ever read, but I trust in the Lord that you will be blessed by their remarkable ministry—and knowing a little bit about it should even further increase that blessing.

Shawn Bolz is a friend and colleague with a powerful ministry, who also has a unique calling in the realm of translation and rapture. He has had many encounters in being called to heaven, and he was sharing some of his testimonies of those glorious encounters when we first met at a conference. We were sizing each other up. He'd heard of me, I'd heard of him, but we didn't know each other at all. Shawn had heard of the Golden Candlestick, but he was unaware of any connection I had with them.

So I'm listening to his testimony of one of his trips to heaven, of the great cloud of witnesses, and a particular room in heaven.

He was talking about the 400-500 people on earth now who are called periodically to go to heaven, and of the lady up there who is in charge of that group of people. He suddenly stops and turns to me and says something to the extent of:

"James, that reminds me. Do you know who Frances Metcalfe is? She told me that I was supposed to say hi to you, her spiritual son."

Imagine my shock. I was floored! I think that's fitting for her to be in charge of the people on earth now being translated and raptured to heaven. And as you read this book, you'll understand why.

THRU RAPTURE INTO TRANSLATION PART ONE

Frances Metcalfe

"By faith Enoch was translated that he should not see death; and was not found, because God had translated him; for before his translation he had this testimony, that he pleased God." (Hebrews 11:5)

"For the Lord Himself shall descend from heaven with a shout, with the voice of the archangel, and with the trump of God: and the dead in Christ shall rise first: then we which are alive and remain shall be caught up together with them in the clouds, to meet the Lord in the air: and so shall we ever be with the Lord." (1 Thessalonians 4:16,17)

"Behold, I show you a mystery; we shall not all sleep, but we shall all be changed." (1 Corinthians 15:51)

The revelations set forth in this booklet were given during experiences of "rapture," beginning in January, 1942, and continuing for several months. Guided by the Holy Spirit, I have made an earnest attempt to interpret these heavenly experiences in earthly language. Needless to say, the *testimony* falls far short of the *reality.*

Since the first edition was mailed out in 1943, we have received letters from other Christians, in many parts of the world, who testify to similar experiences and rejoice in the testimony recorded on these pages. By many reliable witnesses, the Holy Spirit has confirmed the word given to us that "rapture"—meaning "to be caught away or transported in the spirit"—is preparatory to the even greater experiences of *transport* (in the body), and *translation.* All three of these experiences are recorded in the Word of God, and are among the promises given to the full overcomers in the Latter Days, or the Time of the End. A body is being prepared "as it hath pleased Him," as revealed in 1 Corinthians, 15th chapter, whose blessed privilege is to be changed and caught up *alive*—made like unto Christ, our glorious Head. Foretastes such as this booklet records are becoming more numerous as the time of the Consummation draws near.

This was the Lord's doing, and it is still marvelous in our eyes! With all praise and glory unto our Lord Jesus Christ who has revealed Himself unto us and has shown us things to come, kindling our love, reviving our hope, confirming our faith, I offer this testimony to you.

—Frances Metcalfe

RAPTURE

Rise up on wings of the Dove,
Rise up at the call of love,
Rise up, up, up, up—
Up! To the courts above!

Why will you tarry here in darkness,
Why will you wonder, sad at heart,—
When Jesus has bidden you, "Rise up,
My love, and come with Me apart?"

Rise up, earth's chains are broken!
Rise up, the heavens open!
Rise up, up, up, up—
Up! The Lord has spoken!

Why do you linger in unbelief,
Why give place to doubt and fear?
Why is your spirit still reluctant
His will to do, His voice to hear?

Rise up! What more can He say?
Rise up! 'Tis the dawn of the day!
Rise up, up, up, up—
Up! My love, and come away!

Angels are hovering all around you,
Waiting to bear you to the Throne:
Heavenly songs float down through the spheres
To woo you in tender, loving tone.

Rise up, in joyous surprise,
Rise up, through the beckoning skies;
Rise up, up, up, up—
Up! As a bird homeward flies!

Blessed is the one whom God has called
To His high and holy dwelling;
Yes, blessed is he who thus is stirred
By the voice of Love impelling.

Rise up, through ethereal spheres,
Rise up, your redemption nears.
Rise up, up, up, up—
Up! Your King appears!

Winter has departed now at last,
Flowers are appearing on the earth;
And all creation is awaiting
A restoration and new birth.

Rise up, out of earth's dark night,
Rise up, to the courts of light;
Rise up, up, up, up—
Up! Take your rapture flight!

OUT OF THE EARTHLY

In January, 1942, the Lord began to speak to me in the most vivid way about *rapture*. For many years a little company of us had been hidden away in a ministry of intercession and worship. During this time the Holy Spirit had led us continually, and had blessed us with true prophecy and many revelations about the great End-time plan of God. We all were preparing our hearts for the glorious day when our Lord would pour out the promised rain of His Spirit in double portion, and send us forth to work the "greater works" in His Holy Name.

It was, therefore, a great surprise to me when our Lord indicated that this earthly prayer ministry was being terminated, and that I was to enter into *rest* and be taken into another realm. I was puzzled at His Word and wondered if I were going to die. One night, as I was engaged in earnest prayer with a few others, I was suddenly rapt in the Spirit: I had the sensation of passing up and up and on into the third heaven!

"The universe is thy inheritance in Me," the Lord said. "Thou hast possessed an earthly inheritance in My Kingdom, but now thou shalt spy out and possess a heavenly inheritance by faith."

He revealed that Satan and his rulers would be cast down out of the heavens, and their seats of authority would be given to the overcoming saints. I had a strong impression that I was standing on a high and very steep pinnacle. To my surprise I found myself looking at the starry heavens from *above* them! The myriads and myriads of heavenly worlds spread out before me overwhelmed my spirit. I felt that at any moment I would faint, so I leaned upon the Lord, trusting Him to sustain me upon this pinnacle. I was conscious of angelic beings and of ethereal sights and sounds, but I could neither see them plainly nor hear them distinctly.

Then, as suddenly as I was taken up, I was set down again upon the earth! "There is a path which no bird knoweth," the Spirit said. "You shall be given the wings of a dove, and shall fly away and be at rest."

I saw that hitherto I had been an "eagle-saint," a prayer wait-er and warrior. I was now to be changed into a "dove-saint." (The doves typifying the company who shall ascend and descend and finally be translated.) The following Scriptures were illuminated to me:

"Oh, that I had wings like a dove! for then would I fly away and be at rest." (Psalm 55:6)

"Though ye have lien among the pots, yet shall ye be as the wings of a dove covered with silver, and her feathers with yellow gold." (Psalm 68:13)

This portion had been spoken to me many years before. It is found in the prophetic 68th Psalm—an inspired song containing a profound revelation of the Latter-Day. As one commentator has written: "It would take the Pentecostal gifts of tongues to properly interpret this superlative song of David." Our little company has often sung and danced in the Spirit to its transcendent strains. Many think David sang it as he danced before the Ark when it was being returned. The ninth verse reveals the Latter Rain. This is followed by the giving of the Living Word to a great company who publish it. There is mention of a people once cast down in servitude and bondage who arise as pure doves, as free as a bird! If you read on you will see a picture of mighty conquest in which angels participate.

Again the Spirit spoke to me in the tender words of the Bridegroom to the Bride:

"O My dove, that art in the clefts of the rock, in the secret places of the stairs." (Song of Solomon 2:14)

And again:

"Who are these that fly as a cloud, and as the doves to their windows?" (Isaiah 60:8)

The Spirit also reminded me of Noah's ark and the dove with the olive branch—a type of those hidden away in Christ, during the present storm, who shall come forth with the everlasting Gospel of true peace.

"How beautiful upon the mountains are the feet of them that bringeth good tidings, that publisheth peace . . . that saith unto Zion, Thy God reigneth!" (Isaiah 52:7)

I was also reminded of the descent of the Holy Ghost, in the form of a dove, upon our Lord at His baptism in the Jordan River. At that time the Father spoke out of heaven:

"This is My beloved Son, in whom I am well pleased." (Matthew 3:17)

I saw that the dove was a symbol of *Sonship*, of *purity* and of *sacrifice*—as well as of the *Holy Spirit*.

I pondered these Scriptures for many days, and the Lord caused me to see that the "Dove" company is the "Bride" company—the "Son" company—the *raptured* and finally *translated* saints. I was shown that whereas I had previously *glimpsed* into the heavenlies, I was now actually to be *taken* (by the Spirit) into celestial realms. "How can these things be?" I asked, as did one of the old. After much prayer the Lord gave me a revelation which was *new* to me. This was presented to me in many ways and was verified consistently. It was this:

Rapture and *translation* are two entirely different things! The meaning of the word "rapture" is—"to be suddenly caught away or transported in the spirit." This does not involve a transportation of the *body*. St. John, according to the Greek text, was "rapt" in the Spirit when he received his revelation of Jesus Christ. His body was on the Isle of Patmos, but his spirit was taken into the heavenlies. St. Paul was rapt in the Spirit and taken to the third heaven. Daniel was rapt and fell as dead, when he was given the amazing revelation of Jesus Christ and "the time of the end." Isaiah, while in the Temple, was rapt and saw the Lord "high and lifted up." Moses was rapt in the Mount. And Ezekiel was rapt again and again.

All through the history of the Church, the saints have been given experiences of rapture. Savonarola was often rapt while preaching, and would sit motionless for hours seeing visions in the Spirit. St. Francis and many of his brotherhood were rapt and taken into heaven. They communed with angels and saints, and were given revelations of the Lord and of His sufferings and glory. St. Catherine of Sienna was rapt in the Spirit frequently, even in early childhood. She foretold the Reformation, and also saw revelations concerning "the great world-wide crusade of the latter days in which the Bride would arise, clad in beautiful garments, and the glory of God would fill the earth." Many of her experiences seem to be typical of the works which are to be wrought to the days just ahead.

George Fox of the Quakers once was rapt for many days, and his body was altered in appearance in the most supernatural way. The Holy Spirit reminded me of these things which I had previously read in brief. I had not been greatly impressed by them, supposing they were purely individual revelations. Now I saw that these raptures were *types* and *signs* of experiences which lie ahead for *us*.

About a year later, after having entered into rapture, I investigated other reports of such raptures, and found that the Holy Spirit had dealt with me in ways so similar that I was amazed. I was filled with rejoicing at the witness given to me in reading of those who were raptured in days gone by.

That which St. Paul experienced, as one born out of due time, is the perfect type and pattern of the sons of God. They will be given a *revelation* of Jesus Christ—a face to face, beyond-the-veil experience—before they are physically translated. They will be caught up in the spirit and will commune with angels, prophets and apostles, as well as with Jesus Christ Himself. They will be shown the things which have been, the things which are, and the things which are to be. They will be able to say, as St. Peter said after the Transfiguration:

"We have not followed cunningly devised fables, when we made known unto you the power and coming of our Lord Jesus Christ, but were eyewitnesses of His Majesty . . . when we were with Him in the holy mount. We have also a more sure word of prophecy; whereunto ye do well that ye take heed." (2 Peter 1:16,18,19)

Likewise, St. John could say:

"That which was from the beginning, which we have heard, which we have seen with our own eyes, which we have looked upon, and our hands have handled of the Word of life; (the Living Word). That which we have seen and heard declare we unto you." (1 John 1:1,3)

Oh, what a word of authority! We shall *see*, we shall *hear*, we shall *know*, by first hand experience. And this we shall declare to the nations—a *sure word of prophecy.* Why was it not lawful for St. Paul to tell of his revelation of Jesus Christ and of the mysteries revealed in the third heaven? Because these things were sealed up *until the time of the end.* The Revelation and Appearing of Jesus Christ is now *at hand*—a *secret* appearing and revelation to His prepared saints, before His open appearing. This is foreshown in the first three chapters of The Revelation, when Jesus Christ appeared unto John on the Isle of Patmos. In chapter one, verse ten, we read: "On the Lord's day I found myself rapt in the Spirit." (Moffatt) The entire Apocalypse was given to him by revelation while in the state of rapture, that is, caught away in the Spirit out of his natural senses, his mind being quickened and illuminated by the supernatural power of God.

After *rapture*, the next step is *transport*. We shall be taken from place to place in the *body*, as Philip was caught away when he preached to the eunuch.

The last step is translation. Then we shall be caught up—body, soul and spirit—as were Enoch and Elijah. But this will not be until the consummation of the Endtime ministry.

When this astounding revelation was given to me by the Lord, He immediately challenged me, "Believest thou this?" Then He said, "By *faith* Enoch was translated that he should not see death."

My heart was so stirred that I earnestly sought the Lord that in all things I too might walk well-pleasing to Him. I laid aside all spiritual labor and sought to enter into complete rest; but it took several months and a severe illness, before I could fully do so. I did not confide this revelation to *any one*; but the Holy Spirit confirmed it by many demonstrations, Scriptures and prophecies through others. The Lord began to speak to our company about rapture, and there were manifestations of "flying" and being transported, and prophecies about translation. We were told that *to enter into translation required long and difficult preparation*: for our entire being, including our body, must be brought into *complete submission to the Spirit*. With these dealings we were given Romans 8, 1 Corinthians 15, all of Thessalonians, and many other portions of the Pauline epistles.

We also had demonstrations about the *whole burnt offering*. Those who are truly raptured are consumed with the *fire* of Divine Love. Over and over the Word in Hebrews was given to us:

"Ye are coming (come) unto Mount Sion, and unto the city of the Living God, the heavenly Jerusalem, and to an innumerable company of angels, to the General Assembly and Ecclesia of the First-born which are written in heaven, and to God the Judge of all, and to the spirits of just men made perfect, and to Jesus the

Mediator of the New Covenant, and to the blood of sprinkling, that speaketh better things than that of Abel." (Hebrews 12:22-24)

During this time the Lord instructed me about St. John the Revelator. And one night I, too, heard a voice behind me, like a trumpet, calling me to "come up hither." I saw an open door in heaven, but it seemed far-off. My heart was pained, for I felt earthbound and knew not *how* to "come up."

I prayed much that I might find a way out of the earth into the heavenlies. I was impressed about Nathanael, the pure-hearted. He recognized Jesus as the *Son of God* and as *King*; and Jesus commended him as an "Israelite in whom there is no guile." He gave him a wonderful promise: "Hereafter ye shall see heaven open, and the angels of God ascending and descending upon the Son of Man." (John 1:51)

ANGELS FROM GLORY

Angels descending from glory I see,
Down through the open portal;
A wonderful word are bringing to me,
Sent from the King immortal.

Angels from glory are winging,
A message divine they are bringing,
"The King bids thee come up higher," they say,
"Now rise up, beloved, and come away."

My heart completely He's captured,
Soon to His Throne I'll be raptured;
Caught up in a moment, I shall arise
To meet Him in Paradise!

The Holy Spirit gave me this song as a promise. He revealed that throughout the ages this "door" in heaven has been opened at certain times to certain chosen ones. Jacob saw this "stairway" or "ladder," and the angels ascending and descending. The prophets at times looked into these heavenly realms: but now, in the End-time, oh, praise the Lord, this door is to be opened to an *entire company.* It is to be opened wide for a short season to a few firstfruits of that company. Then it is to be opened to the entire Sons of God—Bride company. Each one is to be taken up the "golden" stairway, up into the third heaven, some to higher realms, and some to the very Throne. By the way of *rapture* they are to have access to the heavenlies. They are to see and commune with the angels and saints; and are to see Jesus, *beyond the veil*, face to face, being changed into His likeness, fully united with Him. They are to be commissioned and sealed, and then sent forth for a short ministry. The pattern for this is found in the life of our Lord. He was brought up out of death, and ascended, after He also descended. He was seen by many and ministered for forty days before He was taken up again to remain at the Throne.

The Lord also revealed much concerning *Enoch.* Later I was given the Book of Enoch to read, and I found it was profitable. In it I learned that Enoch was raptured many times before he was actually translated. The marvelous revelations given him concerning God's plan—even unto the end of this age—and his knowledge of heavenly movements, enabled him to enter into the End-time privileges—and to experience the consummation of translation!

Every son of God is to have these privileges. They are to know as they are known. As I learned of these things, my heart hungered for the fulness of the revelation of Jesus Christ—the secret revelation to be given to the Ecclesia. I earnestly sought the Lord and prayed that I might be prepared to "rise up and come away." I prayed that I might be like Nathanael, pure in heart, without guile. "Blessed are the pure in heart for they shall see God." The old hymn, "Blessed Assurance" was often brought to my mind, especially this verse:

> "Perfect submission, perfect delight
> Visions of rapture now burst on my sight;
> Angels descending bring from above
> Echoes of mercy, whispers of love."

Then the Spirit again gave me a portion of Isaiah which had been impressed upon me for many years. This prophecy refers to the time of the Lord's appearing in the midst of His people:

"Now will I rise, saith the Lord; now will I be exalted; now will I lift up myself . . . . The sinners in Zion are afraid, fearfulness hath surprised the hypocrites. Who among us shall dwell with the devouring fire? Who among us shall dwell with everlasting burnings?" (Isaiah 33:10,14)

Yes, truly, our God is a consuming fire. He is even now sifting in our midst, purifying the sons of Levi. (Malachi 3:3) Isaiah gives the pattern for those who are to be raptured:

"He that walketh righteously, (in the righteousness of Christ by the power of the Holy Ghost) and speaketh uprightly; he that despiseth the gain of oppressions (frauds), that shaketh his hands from holding of bribes, that stoppeth his ears from the hearing of blood, and shutteth his eyes from seeing evil; he shall dwell on high: his place of defence shall be the munitions of rocks (the cleft of the rock, the secret place of the stairs): bread shall be given him; his waters shall be sure. Thine eyes shall see the King in His beauty; they shall behold the land that is very far off." (Isaiah 33:15-17)

In this passage it is clearly revealed that our walk, our talk, and our every action, must be guided by the Spirit. Our feet, our tongues, our hands, our eyes, our ears, must be cut off from every worldly and evil use. As St. Paul so perfectly expounded this truth:

"As ye have yielded your members servants to uncleanness and to iniquity unto iniquity; even so now yield your members servants to righteousness unto holiness." (Romans 6:19)

How difficult to shut our ears completely to the hearing of blood, in the midst of a world at war; and to shut our eyes to the seeing of evil, in the midst of this evil day. But I saw in this Word that I must deliberately "tune out" the world realm, and "tune in" the heavenly realm. The promise to those who, by His grace, enter into this complete rest is indeed glorious.

THINE EYES SHALL SEE THE KING

Who shall ascend the Hill of the Lord?
Who shall stand in His Holy Place?
Who shall appear before the King,
Beholding Him face to face?
He whose heart has been yearning
For a glimpse of that far-off land,
Whose spirit is quiet, waiting,
To move at the King's command.
Blessed is that one who approaches His dwelling,
Summoned by the voice of His love impelling!

During this time of preparation I found that my heart and mind seemed often caught away, so much so that I could hardly realize that which was taking place about me, even though I still had the full care of my home and three small children. I also noticed at times a new sensation of quickening in my physical body. Often I felt so light that it seemed that I could fly away in a moment. These ecstatic times passed—and fiery trials closely followed. I found that all my heart, my soul, was longing for heaven, longing for Jesus, longing to leave the earth. I was no longer led to intercede. Indeed, I seemed helpless to pray unless I was anointed; but I was conscious of a constant, close union with the Lord. I experienced an inner hunger similar to that which I felt while seeking the baptism of the Holy Spirit. So often then I had cried, "My heart and my flesh cry out for the Living God!" It seemed that again my flesh was crying out—this time for full *redemption.* About this time the Spirit gave this song:

THE PATH TO PARADISE

Once, a dying thief prayed, "Lord, remember me,"
As he looked in Jesus' tender eyes;
And Jesus answered him, while in bitter agony,
"Today thou shalt be with Me in Paradise."

Beyond the burning stars, up through the whirling spheres,
I have heard a hidden pathway lies;
And sweet angelic songs are falling on my ears,
As I look up and catch a glimpse of Paradise.

I often sigh and yearn, in tender reverie,
For that heavenly land beyond the blue;
And then my soul is stirred to holy ecstasy,
For I know that some day I shall dwell there too!

Today my spirit cries, like one so long ago,
"Dear Lord, wilt Thou remember me?"
And Jesus, bending near, whispers clear and low,
"My Kingdom, dear one, I give to thee."

Show me the path to Paradise,
Out of earth's darkness bid me rise;
I know my Lord is waiting there,
Walking in God's garden fair.

Angels are softly calling me,
With heavenly love enthralling me,
So I would climb the stairs beyond the skies—
The path to Paradise!

Often the Spirit came upon me in such a new way of "transport" that I seemed to be passing out of my body. But, as eager as I was to be caught up, I found that my body offered quite a resistance, similar to the resistance most of us felt in our bodies when we first sought the baptism and the Holy Spirit began to move upon our members. I saw the heavens opened one day, just a little "slit" as it were.

"Heretofore," said the Lord, "you have had glimpses into this realm." (At the time of baptism I had been caught up, and had heard the heavenly choir; and at other times there had been some experiences along this line.) "But now the heavens are opened wide to you." At this, I saw the heavens actually roll back, much as a curtain on a stage is parted. The glory of the realm supernal blinded me! I was given glimpses of the New Jerusalem, and the stairway or "ladder" leading to it. I was also permitted to see various angels, and to know their ranks. I became conscious of them about me day and night. Prior to this time I had seen a few angels, but only at rare intervals, and then very dimly. Twice the Archangel Michael had appeared and had spoken to us concerning the Time of the End. How I loved this noble Prince among angels, Captain of great hosts! How concerned he is about the "Woman" and the "Man-child," and what a great part he is playing now—gallant warrior! When I saw him and his hosts, I was like the prophet who saw the heavenly hosts—glad that I was on the Lord's side!

It was revealed to me that I would be enabled to see and to converse with the angels, and to understand heavenly mysteries. The Lord also spoke to me about passing over death; about death being swallowed up by life; about the *reign of death* which is coming upon the earth; and about the glorious *reign of Life* which is to be given to the sons of God. I saw some coming out of their graves, as they did upon the day of Jesus' death. (Matthew 27:52,53) I also saw that some of the early saints are going to be *out-resurrected* from the dead, ahead of the general resurrection, and are going to *appear* in the earth. Later, I found that in the prophecies of the early Fathers this had been proclaimed. I saw that St. Paul and St. John, among others, were to appear again in the earth during this brief supernatural ministry. Indeed, I saw much of which I had not previously heard.

Jesus said, "I have told you many earthly things and ye have believed; now I show you heavenly things." The Spirit continued to inspire me to sing new songs. This one became a daily prayer:

MY ADORABLE KING

Heavy with darkness, the world lies waiting,
Waiting for You, my adorable King;
And my heart is waiting and longing too,
And sighing, even as I sing.
I look up to the stars with their silvery lights aglow,
Somewhere up there You are looking down, I know,
And Your heart answers mine in an ecstasy divine—
As my song takes wing.

Each day I wonder how long it shall be
E'er You appear, my adorable King,
And often I ponder the mystery
Of the rapture that happy day will bring,
When I rise and take flight to Your palace of light—
Oh, hasten the day, my adorable King!

THROUGH THE VALLEY OF THE SHADOW

Alas, between me and the glorious experience of going up into the heavenlies, lay the dark vale of death. I hadn't counted upon death. I had only seen the bright and promising aspects of the upward call. But soon I found the cohorts of darkness and death concentrating around me, seemingly set for my destruction, determined to take their prey.

At the beginning of April, a little over two months after the first of the "rapture" revelations, I found the Lord dealing with me in great solemnity. A new awe and fear of the Most High God began to permeate my heart. He suddenly seemed to become veiled and mysterious, and His ways were most strange. He spoke to me often about death, and I found that it was not so easy to draw nigh unto Him at this period—for invariably He would speak to me of it. I discovered that my heart—so eager to hear the *good* things, the *bright* things of God—was most reluctant to hear *dark* sayings. During this examination, for such it proved to be, the Holy Spirit by the living Word cut through my entire being like a two-edged sword. I had the very real experience of seeing my soul and spirit divided asunder; my whole inner being was opened and cut as a burnt offering is quartered and examined.

"I must have a lamb without blemish," the Lord said, "a whole burnt offering." (We know certainly that Jesus is the only spotless and perfect Lamb, and that only by His grace can we become "lambs of God.") I found every innermost thought and motive was likewise brought into divine scrutiny. Needless to relate, I was greatly humbled in spirit, and saddened to discover that after all I was not such a complete *living sacrifice* as I had imagined myself to be. I was even more unyielded to God in the matter of becoming a *dying sacrifice.*

Finally, by the grace of God, I reached a place of complete resignation to the will of God. I was loath to die, leaving unfulfilled all the wonderful promises which the Lord had given me about the End-time ministry. I was saddened when I considered the many precious saints who, though they were given revelations and promises regarding the End-time and the Rapture, are now in their graves. It was a great trial of faith, for the Lord had spoken so long and so frequently about this ministry that to be cut off in the body seemed a crushing blow. Yet, in that hour I saw, as Abraham saw, that God could raise one again from the dead to fulfill His Word, were that necessary. I reached the place of being entirely willing to "wake" or "sleep" in Him.

I saw that *some* who are in this sonship calling, and yet have been dead for some time, will be raised as *signs*. I was given a most marvelous revelation of the resurrection power of our God. I was also shown that the resurrection of the dead holds many unheard of mysteries. Over and over I sang this song:

> "I know that my Redeemer liveth,
> And on the earth again shall stand;
> I know eternal life He giveth,
> And grace and power are in His hand."

"I am the resurrection and the life; he that believeth in Me, though he were dead, yet shall he live: And whosoever liveth and believeth in Me shall never die." (John 11:25,26)

On this Word I took my stand, as I had done many years before when the Lord first spoke it to me. May God give us Bethany faith! "Believe and thou shalt see the glory of God." Several years previously, one who was precious to the Lord lay at the point of death. He had given up hope, but asked for prayer. When I looked at him my heart despaired for his life. Suddenly it seemed that

Christ was embodied in me, and it was no longer I, but Christ, who stood before this dying man. It was clearly an act of intervention. Within my heart I heard an almost audible voice saying, "I am the resurrection and the life." And immediately life and healing were manifested in this brother! The Lord spoke again at that moment: "He that liveth and believeth in Me shall never die; believest *thou* this, also?" I said, "Yes, Lord, I believe it." And from that moment I began to look for translation rather than death.

Oh how my heart yearns for the day when our God shall be openly vindicated in the earth: when the dead shall be raised, the sick healed, and His mighty signs follow—in a greater way than at present. But all this is by *Faith.* I had not realized what a *perfecting of faith* I needed, to be prepared for rapture and translation. I had supposed that it would just *happen* when the time came! But now I knew that it required a *tried faith.* I saw too that to live until the change takes place might be more to His glory, than to die and be clothed upon from above with my house from heaven. Yet I was willing to enter the grave, if He so willed.

After many sufferings and crosses I found a deep rest in faith, but I had no outward consolation or inward feeling whatever. (Hebrews 4:9, 10) I mention all this in detail because I am given by God to see that all who enter into the *experience of rapture* and *translation* will be somewhat similarly tested and tried. And the last enemy to be overcome is *death.* The full overcomer is to inherit all things, even immortality, thus escaping the grave.

Think what a privilege is ours! But it is one thing to have the *revelation* of these great truths; it is another thing to enter into the *experience* of them. Only by His intervention and supernatural working of the Spirit, administering great grace to us, can we be in this number. Again and again I have reached the place where I could not possibly *stand,* let alone go forward another step. Always, when undergoing such a trial, the Spirit has led me to humble myself before God completely, confessing my weakness and inability to go on, with the definite assurance that Christ within me will steadily press on, since I *will* it so. The Father has willed it, the Son has secured it; the Holy Ghost will administer it. All that remains then is for me to will it, too, and yield to Him, believing that He will do it ALL; and *praise God He always does!*

One night I was taken in the Spirit to the top of a large mountain and was shown another peak opposite it. The Spirit told me to step from the one peak to the other. I was about to do so, for it seemed only a step; but, looking down, I was filled with horror, for in the valley lying between was *the grave*, and in it the forces of death were marshaled! "How shall I cross over, Lord, into this heavenly hill?" I asked.

"To die is to go down into the valley," He replied. "To be translated is to be supernaturally transported into heaven." Then He showed me how Elijah was translated, and about the symbolic meaning of "crossing Jordan." "You must cross over death; you must pass over, as the children of Israel once passed over in *flood season* and possessed the land." Is it not wonderful that, when floods of death shall be sweeping the earth with destruction, a whole company is going to pass over death without being *touched* by it!

The Spirit works out many things in our natural bodies, and His divine truth becomes embodied in us as we live under the sway of the Spirit. I can never feel that anything the Holy Spirit does is "just a demonstration," an entertainment to be enjoyed and then dismissed. If the Spirit of God demonstrates a truth in us, it becomes alive, and is established in the earth in us. We regard it as more than *teaching*—it is *reality!* When Jeremiah and Ezekiel enacted their prophecies in strange signs and wonders in the earth, these signs and symbolic actions became the *Living Word of God* to Israel. Just so, this experience of crossing Jordan was a real one to me—painfully, sorrowfully real. Is it not wonderful that in our day a few priests shall be able to turn back the flood for a great company, by the power of God? Amen! I believe it! But here is another truth that is hard to receive; for I saw that although the priests were the *first* to step in, they were the *last* to leave! (So even now, though I passed through death and have been taken on into the heavenly realm, I must still stand as a priest in the path of that flood.) (Joshua 3:15-17)

After this, my body daily grew weaker. Many forsook me in the Spirit, not understanding these strange new dealings of the Lord, wondering why, after having faith for divine health for seven years, I no longer had health or strength to do my duties. Those closest to me were sorrowful, feeling that I was to be taken from them. One was even led to anoint me for burial, somewhat as Jesus was anointed. She could not restrain her tears. All this occurred at the Easter season when thoughts of the Cross and Passover were in the minds of us all. How very real became the betrayal, the smiting, and crucifixion.

Then, one night, the Holy Spirit anointed one to "lay me out" for burial. This was almost too much to take! The powers of darkness came upon me like a flood, attempting to upset my faith and turn me against the works of the Spirit, which seemed cruel and far-fetched. In my despair I cast myself upon the Lord.

"Are you one who is glad to enter with Me into My power, and yet is unwilling to enter with Me into My death?" He asked. "To run from the Holy Spirit when He works hard things within you is to flee from Me. How privileged you are to enter into these, My sufferings. I must have a Bride who fully understands. I am letting you actually suffer these things and enter into them with your mind, your heart, and your *body*. This is a complete offering unto Me, and is well pleasing in My sight. I am writing My Word upon your heart and mind; I am deeply engraving it in them with the penpoint of suffering, burning it in with the brand of Divine Love." (Galatians 6:17)

Then the Lord showed me a large chalice. "The cup I drink, are ye able also to drink it?" He asked. I remembered when He had questioned me in a similar way after I had been baptized with the Holy Ghost. Then I had answered, as the disciples did, "Yea, Lord, we are able." I had little dreamed what it might mean. I felt that I *had* drunk it; but now I saw that it was more than spiritual suffering and death to self. It was an *actual* death—as a sacrifice. I hesitated, knowing that I dared not trifle with so sacred a matter. "By Your grace, Lord, I will drink this cup with You," the Spirit moved me to answer. I took it from His hand with trembling and raised it to my lips. I tasted of it, expecting it to be very bitter; but, to my amazement, it became as the most mellow and delicious wine!

Then He smiled and seemed about to laugh openly with joy. "This is the cup of *full salvation*," He said, "I drank all the bitterness of death, so that you might drink of My Divine, everlasting life. This is the cup of redemption."

Nevertheless, I grew weaker each day. Finally, in the first part of May, my heart grew so weak and faltering that I could barely move about. I could not breathe freely, and panted for breath most of the time. It seemed that the very breath of life was being taken. The forces of death were constantly about me night and day. I began to realize the full significance of overcoming death. I seemed to be walking in a region of thirst, darkness and pain. All anointing and blessing were removed. Just before I became completely bedridden, the Lord sent several precious sisters who were from the Middle West. I knew them only by correspondence. One of these prophesied that the Lord was about to do great things and to show me unusual favor. (I was so ill at the time that I could scarcely notice or remember her words, but this is the substance of the message.)

On the night following their visit, I was suddenly moved upon by the Spirit. Going to the piano I began to play and sing under inspiration. The theme of the song was, "Take Me Into Your Garden."

This title reminded me of one given earlier in the season—which spoke, not of a garden of love, but of a garden of Gethsemane. I had been led to sing it often during the dark weeks:

> Come, watch one hour with Me in dark Gethsemane,
> Come, pray with Me alone, for thou art all My own;
> No need to feel afraid, in nothing be dismayed;
> Soon I will take thee to My Throne.

This was the new song I sang in such weakness that night:

TAKE ME INTO THY GARDEN

Thou hast a hidden garden, Lord,
Where Thou dost wait for Thine own,
Bidding them come apart and rest
Sweetly with Thee alone.

Each flower reveals Thy loveliness,
Each tree speaks of Thy great care;
Under the sheltering bows I would sit,
Finding deep solace there.

Songbirds are singing up in the trees,
Caroling songs of Thy love;
Fragrance is born on every breeze
Straight from the courts above.

Take me into Thy garden, Lord,
See! I stand at the gate;
Open wide now the golden portals,
Lest I enter too late!
Lead me gently upon Thine arm
Into a place apart;
Take me into Thy garden, Lord,
Take me into Thy heart!

Then, suddenly, came complete collapse! All strength was gone. There was rapid palpitation of the heart, and all food made me ill. Breathing was difficult; in fact, every breath had to be snatched with labor. I mention these details only to show how very *real* this condition was. I want to make clear that none of this was *imaginary* in any sense of the word. The Lord had dealt with me for years about the subjection of the imaginations of my heart and mind. (So often the revelations of the Spirit are leavened and confused with error because our own imaginations are active.) In all this experience, while under anointings, my imagination was held in check by the Spirit; and at times when my mind tried either to *reason* or *imagine*, I was instantly reproved by the Spirit. Also, in writing or telling of these experiences, I was warned not to *add* to that *which actually occurred*. It would be so easy to do this. The human mind can scarcely recall or recount any incident without embellishing it in some way; but the Lord wants our testimony to be given in the white light of *truth*. Therefore, if any mistake is made, let it be known that it is not willful on my part. In the recounting of our spiritual experiences, to add or to alter them in any way is a grievous thing—our witness must be true.

The point is that I was really ill, dangerously so! I grew steadily worse and was engulfed in the most terrible spiritual atmosphere I had ever experienced. To say that it was a "waste howling wilderness" can best describe it. It seemed to be the very valley of the shadow of death. I believe it was just that; and that I tasted in part, at least, of the sufferings of some Saints as they are about to die, when Satan makes his last terrific attack upon their souls. I was seemingly forsaken by God, and also by those who were close to me in the Lord. It is true that they prayed. But they received no special anointing or light. They seemed to be in another world.

Diabolical forces centered upon me; and the days were like months, so intense was the suffering. I could not pray, praise, or converse; but I was conscious of complete committal unto God, and a rest of faith in which there was *no fear.* I knew that I was completely in God's hands, beyond all human aid, and that to seek such would be absolute folly. "I wound and I heal; I kill and I make alive," saith the Lord. Had I not declared with Job, "Though He slay me, yet will I trust in Him"? Was it unreasonable that He should call upon me to *demonstrate* it?

Two days and nights passed. Then God sent a dear sister and her husband to pray for me. They had not known of any of His recent dealings with me, so I was loath to receive them. I wanted nothing, *no one*, but the Lord. I knew that all my hope and help lay in Him. Nor did I want His will hindered by anyone. I was ready to live or die. It seemed to me that to depart and be with Him was greatly to be desired; yet to desire it unduly was selfish, if I wanted to escape suffering. I believe that the final end of all divine dealing is that in all things, at all times, we have no desire but this: "Father, Thy will be done." It is not enough to *know* the will of God; it is not enough to *know* and *do* it; He requires that overcomers *know* and *do* and *delight*, by grace, in His perfect will in *all things.*

So these dear ones prayed and were truly anointed. Afterward, they confessed to me that they saw death written on my face, and were greatly shocked. But for all their prayer I felt no moving of God whatever. I seemed to be already dead. They left, and I steadily became worse. By bed time that night I was fighting for every breath. If you have ever been smothered, you can understand what this struggle was. I was so very bad by this time that I saw my husband could not bear it; therefore, I asked him to call some close prayer partners to pray for me; but he misunderstood me and phoned the brother and sister who had called during the afternoon.

It was at this point that *intervention* had begun! This brother and sister had retired for the night. The sister had fallen into a deep sleep at once, and was given a glorious dream-vision. She dreamed she was singing in the Spirit in a power, beauty and glory she had never known. Her final words were, "Oh, I am drunk with the *new wine* of the Kingdom!" With these words she awoke, so heavily anointed that she knew she must arise and pray. While asking the Lord to show her for whom to pray, she heard the phone ringing. It was my husband asking her to pray for me. Both of them prayed, and within a few minutes I fell into a sleep such as children enjoy, and I awoke in the morning greatly refreshed.

This sister came to see me the next day. She was in the Spirit and declared that the Lord had revealed that I was to go to her house, and that the Lord wanted to bless me greatly; but that I was also in great danger from the forces of the enemy, who wanted to cut off my life. She saw me covered with beautiful flowers, being borne up in the arms of the Heavenly Bridegroom. But I still remained desperately ill. I was reluctant to make a move out of God's will; however, by the next night I was at rest in her home, so rapidly did the Lord move. She and her husband were led to hide me completely from all friends, which they successfully did for a month. The Lord truly took me away, far from all others, and made this house to me the *King's House* and the *King's Garden*!

When I left my home it seemed that I would never return again. Everything that occurred impressed me that I was going to die. All circumstances and feelings were combined to undermine faith. I seemed to be in a state which my mother described to me shortly before her death many years ago. She said, "I am neither on earth nor in heaven. Oh, that I might depart and be at rest." It was so strange to be in suspension—to lie thus between life and death, with only a hair's breadth between.

I am led to go into detail, for each step reveals God's intervention dealings, and though the personal pronoun has to be used—since this is a testimony—I beg you to regard it as an impersonal demonstration of divine Truth. The following night proved most difficult. Once, shortly before this, the Lord had drawn very near and whispered, "I am the Lily of the valley." And I had answered, "Yes, Lord, Thou art the sweet Lily of the valley." Then He repeated the statement with a most poignant addition, "I am the Lily of the valley—*of the shadow of death*."

All that night I seemed to be in that valley; but, praise God, I knew that the Lily of that valley was there with me, though He spoke not a word. Since that time the Spirit has shown me how much it pained my Lord to see my suffering, and yet be unable to speak; but the Father is preparing a Bride for His Son, and often must subject her to extreme tests to bring her up to the standard which He has ordained. Ah! How our loving Savior longs to sympathize and comfort us! Bless His dear name! The night passed, and I grew worse during the day. Finally, I felt that I should permit my husband to call a doctor, for his own satisfaction.

I feel that this was in order, for it established several things: first of all, that I was really very ill; secondly, that though this illness was indeed serious, the cause for it could not be found *in my body*; and thirdly, that all the doctor could do was to give drugs which I did not feel led to use, and which would have only slightly benefited me. He was very puzzled, asking if I had suffered a severe shock or *heart break*.

One translation of David's word, "Thou hast enlarged my heart," is, "Thou has *dilated* my heart." This is exactly what the Lord was doing in me; for the heart is the first organ to be changed in the creation of the *new body within*. It is also significant that in the Song of Solomon 6:12, we read: "Or ever I was aware, my soul made me like the chariots of Amminadib." Nearly all commentators have believed that this refers to rapture or translation, since Elijah was taken up in the "chariots of Israel." And we have "seen" these chariots at times. Adam Clarke commented that one reading of the original text indicates this meaning: "Suddenly, *my heart was in rapid palpitation*."

This doctor, who was not a spiritual Christian, unknowingly spoke God's word to me concerning my illness. He said, "I can't find the cause for this in your body anywhere, and I am convinced that just one thing has brought you into this state, *you have hitched your wagon to a star that is too high*." He also said, "It will appear that you are going to die, and no doubt the suffering will be such that you will want to die, but I am convinced that you will not die." When he said this, I sat straight up in bed, instantly improved. Even he had been obliged by God to testify to *rapture*, although he knew it not!

By the next day I was a little better and was able to eat a very little. But still no word from God was whispered to my heart. It was just one week from the day I had fallen ill when He manifested Himself, yet to me it had seemed a long time. Shortly after sundown, while lying in my bed, I became conscious that my hand was knocking on the wall. At first, the anointing was so faint that I did not recognize it as such. But louder and louder grew the knock! "Knock and it shall be opened unto you," the Spirit said within my heart. I did not understand His meaning, but I knocked, and the Spirit took up the intercession in another language. Then I saw a great door, and it was in heaven. As I knocked, it opened. It did not swing, but seemed to roll up as a heavy curtain. Then He said:

"I am He that openeth, and no man shutteth; and shutteth, and no man openeth . . . . I have set before thee an open door, and no man can shut it: for thou hast a little strength, and has kept My word, and hast not denied My name." (Revelation 3:7, 8)

I was stunned—amazed—and wondered what this might mean! I felt strength coming into my body, so I arose and went into the living room and told the sister, with whom I was staying, that we must all pray together; however, I did not tell her what had occurred. She and her husband were delighted that I was better, and they praised God.

As I lay up on the couch, all strength again left me. A most delightful and wonderful heavenly atmosphere filled the room. My outward senses were held in suspension, and I was filled with an interior joy and light impossible to describe. Then, suddenly, He appeared—the *King* in all His beauty! He swept in and seemed to fill the entire room! So ravishing was this sight, and so clear, that I felt I would swoon with delight! He appeared as described by the Shulamite in The Song of Solomon—and He was dressed in kingly robes! So majestic was His beauty, thus crowned and robed, that my heart melted into a new fervor of love. I saw His golden sandals, white undergarment, the royal purple tunic of a velvety substance, with jewels inset; and finally, to my surprise—as He turned—His cape or train, of finest *ermine*. It was very long, reaching from one end of the room to the other. The vision lasted about ten minutes, gradually fading from my sight. I turned and faintly heard the sister praying for America and the soldiers. I realized that they had not seen the Lord. It was so real to me that I was astonished! The sister seemed drawn to me, but I felt that I must not be touched. I seemed to be out of my body.

She approached to pray for me; but, instead, suddenly cried out, "Knock and it shall be opened unto you," repeating it again and again. Then, in demonstration, she knocked and said that she saw a large golden door which opened to her. She burst forth in joyful praise and was radiant in the Spirit. She cried out, "Oh, I see the King, the King in His beauty." She described and praised Him. The description was identical, even to the ermine train! We both rejoiced for some time. Another sister, while praying for me at the same hour, also saw the door opened. "She hath prevailed," the Spirit said, "and from henceforth the door into the heavenlies is open to her and to the company who are to enter in with her." He also gave her the verse in Revelation 3:8, which He had given to me.

I retired in great joy. Henceforth this house was to be to me "The King's House." Had He not appeared to my joy? Had He not shown me His beauty? Was I not ravished anew with love, and lifted by Him out of death into new life? Yes, I knew that I was in His House, and in a bridal chamber, as it were, being prepared for holy union. A new day had dawned for me; yet little did I dream of all the glories and blessings and revelations which He would give me during the following weeks. How unworthy I feel now as I consider these divine favors, but I recall that they are all for *the Bride*, of which I was just a representative member, being shown in advance wonderful things to come.

Just a year before this rapture, the Holy Spirit had given me a song which was prophetic of my sojourn in the King's house. It began now to ring in my heart:

DWELLING IN HIS PRESENCE

Oh, how rich is my condition, how blessed is my state,
For the King has brought me to His chambers fair;
In the secret of His presence He has hidden me away,
Oh what rest and rapture I am finding there!

Without the storms are raging, the night is growing dark,
So I dare not leave this peaceful hiding place;
For my King says, "Stay, beloved, I will hold thee to My heart,
Thou shalt evermore behold Me face to face."
In this holy habitation I have found a perfect rest,
For no harmful, hurtful thing can enter here.
And the King Himself assures me, bids me lean upon His breast,
While with tender hands He wipes away my tears.

Dwelling in His presence, walking in the light,
Feasting on His love, robed in garments pure and white.
O my soul is thrilled with rapture, a rapture all divine,
For I know that I am His and He is mine.

IN THE KING'S GARDEN

Through "The Valley of the Shadow" the King took me to the gate of the King's Garden, and on to the Door of the King's House. There in His majestic Presence I found *rest* and *rapture*! How perfect was His plan! How wonderful His ways, which are so much higher than our ways that we cannot comprehend them, but stand amazed! Amazing grace, amazing love, amazing wisdom! Oh, our King is matchless, wonderful! "How marvelous, how wonderful, and my song shall ever be; how marvelous, how wonderful, is my Savior's love for me!"

How true to Divine Pattern have been all His dealings with me! But most surprising to my own mind was this rapture. He is always doing *unexpected things in unexpected ways*. How often we have quoted: "Eye hath not seen, nor ear heard, neither hath entered into the heart of man, the things which God hath prepared for them that love Him." (1 Corinthians 2:9)

And some of us are quick to quote the following verse, which is often overlooked, "*But God hath revealed them unto us by His Spirit*: for the Spirit searcheth all things, yea, the deep things of God." How wonderful is the revelation of the Spirit of God! St. Paul further declares that we have received the Spirit of God expressly for this purpose; "That we might know the things that are freely given to us of God." (vs. 12) The Greek word translated "know" means "to behold, perceive, understand, declare." If by the Spirit we really *know* these things, then it follows that: "Which things also we *speak*, not in words which man's wisdom teacheth, but which the Holy Ghost teacheth." (vs. 13)

Yet, may I say that with all the *revelation* of these wonderful things which had been previously given to us, over a period of years, the actual experience of entering into *rapture* and the *celestial* realm and ordinances was brought to pass in ways entirely unexpected.

The element of surprise and amazement had been present in every intervention dealing. I am impressed to make this very clear. First Corinthians, chapters one and two, is the pattern for those who *experience* rapture and translation. Those who "come behind in no gift, waiting for the revelation of our Lord Jesus Christ," are instructed to become as *babes*, and as *weak*, *foolish* and *base*. The Greek word, translated in our version as "coming," is Apokalupsis, which means "appearing, manifestation, revelation." This word is a direct word of instruction to us who are being prepared to receive *His appearing*.

The true rapture experience cannot be imagined or worked up, or brought to pass through our own efforts in any way. It is an act of grace, a sovereign act of God—it is "intervention." However, Satan always imitates and counterfeits God's dealings, so he too can produce raptures, trances, and other deceptive experiences, as he has done in the past and is doing increasingly today. It is, therefore, necessary for those who are entering into these wonderful favors and privileges, and who testify of them to others, to make each step clear and plain in Scriptural pattern. I want to state that in this experience, as in all other experiences in the Holy Ghost, I followed St. Paul's word to "prove all things; hold fast that which is good." (1 Thessalonians 5:21)

The way through death into the celestial realm is a pathway beset by the fiercest, strongest, most deceptive forces of Satan. Let no one presume in these matters, nor seek these privileges unless called by God and prepared fully to do so! On the other hand, if the Lord has been pleased to bring you to the revelation of these privileges, and is preparing you for rapture and translation, do not let fear or doubt keep you "earth-bound!" You will need faith; you will need fortitude; you will need grace to take this way; but all this is amply provided in Jesus Christ, and He will do a perfect work. Whether we ascended into the highest heaven or descend into the depths of hell, or if we take the wings of the morning and dwell in the uttermost parts of the sea, even there will His hand lead us and hold us, for He possesses our reins. Our kingly father David knew the power of God, and many of his Psalms were written to instruct us in this experience. So, I repeat, all of this experience has been confirmed by Scripture every step the way.

Now, to return to the "garden." At death, a saint passes through the valley, over the "river," and is borne by angels into the celestial realm. He is given a sweet look into the face of Jesus, and is placed at rest in Paradise, the garden of God. So it was most fitting that, after seeing the King, I should be taken into His Garden to rest. I entered into *deep* rest. My body was still weak. Indeed, for many weeks I was kept in physical weakness unless I was supernaturally quickened. To this very hour I seem to have little strength in my body, and I live "by the breath of His Spirit." With small children and a home to care for, I had never been able to go away and pray or be in retreat for any length of time. All through the years the Lord has dealt with me about praying—even fasting and praying much—but always in connection with my duties to my family. I longed to withdraw and wait upon Him as many others could do, but this was not His will for me. It seemed He wanted to demonstrate His grace and intervention by often giving me the most profound revelations in the midst of my dishwashing, cooking, and other pressing duties—with the phone ringing, children crying, confusion everywhere. He had led me into the prayer of "union," where He was constantly in my heart, no matter where I was or what I was doing. Of course, this had taken years of training, and it was all to His glory and by His power.

But now, in the Garden, I was completely cut off from the world and all duties. Following His glorious appearing as King, His Presence filled the house, and He dealt in a strong way with this brother and sister. They were convinced that He was about to do great and unusual things in our midst. The sister made arrangements at once to lay down a ministry in which she had been engaged, so that she might present herself before the Lord day and night, and keep the house quiet and undisturbed by outside influences. Though engaged in secular work, the brother gave every free moment the Lord. The radio and newspaper were excluded; and all talk of natural things was set aside as much as possible. No one but my husband knew of my "Rest Home." Thus we were shut away in the heart of a big city almost as perfectly as though on a mountain top.

The Lord seemed to move in and possess the house and garden, and to put all things in Kingdom order. So real was His Presence, and so personal were His dealings and favors, that I felt I was living in the heavenlies, feasting in the King's House, and walking and resting in His Garden. This song, given later by the Spirit, expressed my childlike joy in His Presence:

IN HIS GARDEN

A wonderful joy is flooding my heart
Since Jesus has shown His love to me;
Into His garden He drew me apart,
And now His grace and His beauty I see.

Here in His garden the birds always sing,
And flowers are blooming everywhere;
Winter is over, at last it is spring,
And now His fragrance is filling the air!

We hold a communion, tender and sweet,
While walking within this sheltered place;
Sorrow is gone and my joy is complete
While Jesus holds me in loving embrace.
Jesus loves me truly, this I know,
And for my soul He gave His life a sacrifice;
Jesus loves me truly, this I know,
And His love has made my heart a Paradise.

> Let me sit in His garden,
> And bask in His sunlight,
> Let me drink of His fountain,
> And feast with Him alone;
> For Jesus loves me truly, this I know,
> And in my heart He reigns
> As King upon His Throne.

The world seemed gone forever. Human beings, including my own dear ones for whom I had grieved, realizing their need of me, seemed far removed from me. (However, needless to relate, the Father blessed my family and took care of them.) I saw that I had been born into a new realm, and that I was like a little babe—ignorant, helpless, and yet at rest. At first I could see and hear little in the heavenly realm, but gradually I became more accustomed to it.

The Sunday following the Lord's appearing was devoted to waiting upon Him. He led us to put on bright garments of praise, pin flowers in our hair, and come before Him in joy—as a demonstration that Zion was to lay off her garments of mourning and put on her beautiful, royal garments. I was too weak to pray outwardly in any way, but my friend appeared beautifully arrayed as a King's daughter, and was immediately anointed with singing and dancing. We were given a vision of the King's Court, with His daughters appearing before Him in praise!

"Let the children of Zion be joyful in their King. Let them praise His name in the dance: let them sing praises unto Him with the timbrel and harp." (Psalm 149:3, 4)

The 45th Psalm was again quickened to us—"The King's Wedding March," as some have called it—and many portions of the Song of Solomon. He revealed Himself as the "Solomon" of His Ecclesia, and spoke of His virgins, His queens, and *His choice one.*

For many years He had been "opening" to me the Song of Solomon in which, as He told me, are hidden the deepest mysteries of the Bride. But now the entire book seemed to come into new life and beauty and clarity! The perfume of His ointments filled the house. We were ravished with the beauty and glory and loveliness of the King and His Court and His royal household. He revealed His desire to "feast" with His people, and that they, as Israel of old, might know Him in "holy festivity." He spoke of the great feast set before us at His table, and He invited us to feast on His choice fruits, and to drink of the *new wine* of the Kingdom.

This is revealed in type in the first chapter of Esther. There the King gave a great feast to reveal the glories of His Kingdom. The first company HeeHe invited were "the Royal Household." They were given to drink from golden vessels, each diverse from the other. But the drinking was *without compulsion*. Our King is likewise calling the royal household to come feast with Him! He showed us that many will not come because they are so busy *laboring* for Him, and they will not take time out to rest and feast. And such are apt to condemn those who do not respond to His call. "The time is too short," they say. "We must hurry to get souls saved before the Lord comes." They are in a feverish rush of "service" and are unaware that they may be offending the King who is now sitting at the table with His own. They are saying, like Judas, "Why all this waste?" But the "Mary" company is saying, "While the King sitteth at His table my spikenard sendeth forth the smell thereof."

Others respond to the call and come to the table, but do not put on their garments of praise, nor enter into the spirit of holy festivity. These are asked to leave the table. Who would offend a King by appearing unwashed or clothed in working garments? We must be bathed and anointed with oil and perfume, and then put on our beautiful garments, to appear at His table. Of course, I refer to the oil and garments of the Holy Spirit, but the Lord required us to do this outwardly, too, and greatly blessed us for obeying. (He has dealt with us that everything we do should be done to His glory and in demonstration of the truth.) Thus the food we ate at that time had a meaning and reminded us of the Word; the clothes we wore, and on certain occasions the "ornaments" too, represented the ornaments of grace—even perfumes and flowers—*everything*, became a symbol or a token of Him.

Jesus spoke to His "inner circle" in parables which the world could not understand, but *they* did. The early Christians, hiding from their persecutors, wore signs upon their clothes which they readily understood and recognized. In Israel, nearly everything worn had significance. He reminded me of the command to write the Word of the Lord upon the door post, and upon their arms, and to speak of it while sitting at the table and walking in their houses, etc. The Word is not only being written in our minds, hearts, and bodies, but also in the outward things we do; and it is read by those who are simple and "foolish" according to the world, but "wise" in God, able to read the parables and signs and symbols of God. All the prophets *received* and often *presented* divine truth in *symbolic* form.

Oh, the wealth of the riches of God, when we reach such a place of favor and blessing that He speaks to us in *all* things, and where we, in *all* things, can reveal Him and His truth! But this is for those who are able to receive it. A few years before this time, I would have considered myself much to "advanced" for such childlike things. But He has turned some of us into little children, teaching us as they are taught. Have you ever noticed how they "act out" in their play the realities of their later life? Even so, we "act out" or demonstrate in the Spirit the *realities* of the life of the Kingdom. We "taste of the powers of the age to come." How wonderful to learn thus of our dear Father, who takes us, like a child, upon His lap, and tells us of His divine mysteries in terms of childlike simplicity which we can understand and interpret even now!

It has taken much breaking to "unteach" me to the point where I can thus learn of God. Of course I have never been very wise, nor was I well educated according to the standards of this world. How hard it must be for those who are really learned and educated to become as a little child and enter the Kingdom of God, here and now. No wonder St. Paul tells us that not many wise or mighty are called; but that the foolish and weak will be used of God to confound the wise and strong! (1 Corinthians 1:26-29) So, at the King's table, what a joyful time do the children have; but how hard it is for the learned! Some come to the table well dressed, but are reluctant about what they eat. So *new* and varied are the rich foods upon this table that they seem suspicious of them, and are afraid these rich foods will not agree with them, or might even poison them. In this case, St. Paul's rule applies very well. "Let them eat in faith, nothing doubting." When we come to the King's table it is very impolite, even ignorant, to question what is set before us. If the meat is strong, the fruits are sweet, and the dainties rich, let us partake of them with glad and thankful heart, trusting in our King who bids us dine, having provided that which is best for us. We shall find many new and wonderful foods at this table which, if eaten and *digested* and *assimilated*, will greatly strengthen and enhance the *new body* being formed within us.

Many, I am sorry to say, find the wine too strong. They only sip, then set down their vessel. But others drink deeply of both milk and wine, and experience divine inebriation, being made "drunk on the Spirit." They discover the *new wine* of the Kingdom to be the *divine life of Christ*. The wine of the sacrament represents the *human life* of Christ poured out on Calvary for our redemption—even His precious blood. And now He is pouring out *His divine life*, and it is, in essence, *divine love*. Oh, to drink deeply of this love which is better than wine, and to be divinely strengthened! Zion, ready to faint, is revived by this choice wine! But so many refuse to drink; and, since the drinking is voluntary and not by compulsion, they will not become revived and inebriated by the *Holy Elixir* of God. These are among the first to despise those who do drink deeply. Thereby their offense to the King becomes twofold.

I saw a beautiful golden platter coming down out of heaven. It was set in the center of this feast table. When I was told to look upon it, I saw twelve fruits. The Lord said, "This is the fruit of the tree of life which is in the midst of the Paradise of the Father. This fruit shall be eaten *only* by those who have partaken of everything on the table." In other words, the fruit of the tree of life is the dessert, the last course to be served! We parents often refuse to give the dessert to our children unless they have eaten the rest of their dinner. To eat of the tree of life is for the *full overcomer,* and is one of the last steps into immortality!

In the past we had been given revelations regarding the King's feast. But we had not entered into the actual experience of partaking of the feast. The above account was an actual *experience* of entering into the revelation. Therefore, it was made a *reality* to me at this time. Practically all these truths had been previously *revealed* to some of us; but when we actually *entered into* them, they took on a different meaning. Perhaps it would be more accurate to say that they were like pictures suddenly brought into the third dimension. They were made *alive*—a reality in us.

The feast continued. My whole being seemed stilled at last, and I was aware of constant union with the Lord. I was impressed over and over with the need for *secrecy* and *discretion* in regard to "secrets of the Lord." David, when fleeing to Gath, said the priest, "The King hath commanded me a business and hath said unto me, 'Let no man know anything about the business on which I sent thee.'" (1 Samuel 21:2) He asked for and received hallowed bread and a great sword!

This rapture is a "secret rapture." Jesus comes as a "thief." He hunts and digs in the field for His precious jewels and, upon finding them, He polishes and cuts them for His diadem. Even now there is much that I am not permitted to relate. Other children of God may think we are wrong in entering into such rest and rapture. If we tell them that our prayer warfare "has been accomplished"—for a time, at least—they are aghast! They seem to forget that the Bride was created by the Father primarily for the pleasure of, and love-ministry to, His Beloved Son, who is neglected and hungry for the *fruit of the Spirit* and the refreshing *wine* of her love. We become so taken up with the need of the world and the need of souls that we forget the *need of our God*. We act as if we were more concerned about souls than He is, and think that we must labor unceasingly.

Are we so uninstructed in divine matters that we do not know that souls are brought forth in the new creation by being conceived and born through those in the earth who are in *union* with God? These souls are in the "Mary" company who will bring forth the "sons of God," and the "nations that will be born in a day." Zion, Mother Ecclesia, will conceive these offspring of God in the King's House, on Zion's Hill, and not in "Babylon." Do we not realize that the King is going to give a great feast to the nations, even as Ahasuerus, who, after feasting his princes, nobles and servants, made a feast for *all* the people? Have we not realized that we shall be the "golden vessels" who carry the wine to the nations? Yes, we should go out and compel multitudes to come—by the compulsion of divine love! How can this be unless we ourselves have been partakers?

As I rested, Jesus drew very near and began to reveal Himself to me in a way so new, so close, so clear, that my whole being was drawn to Him by a divine pull. "Draw me, and we will run after Thee," cries the Bride! I was being drawn into Him—body, soul and spirit. He showed me no more of His outward beauty at this time, but began to reveal His *Heart*. Once He had shown me His pierced side and had said, "From My side sprang My Bride." Now, He laid bare His *Heart* to me. We bare our hearts only to those we deeply love. So it is with our Bridegroom. The revelation of His Heart and interior nature, His deeper affections and emotions, is so profound, so transcending, that human language cannot reveal this deep unveiling. He, Himself, will reveal His Heart unto each member of His Bride; and, as He does so, He will change each heart and bring it into full union with His own Heart.

I was so melted, so humbled, so moved by the revelation of the *sacred Heart of Jesus*, that I cried for a heart like His. Then He ministered to my heart—first binding it up, for it had previously been crushed; then He applied rare ointments, healing and strengthening it. He also enlarged and dilated it, and opened the inner chambers of my heart—the holy of holies which opens to none but our Heavenly Spouse. His glory flooded that inner chamber. His light so warmed and glowed within my heart that at times I seemed to be *all heart*. The rest of my body seemed deadened. Only those who have experienced this heart change and union can appreciate what I am trying to explain. Words are inadequate to describe it, and tend to blur rather than clarify the picture. For some time, He had been writing His New Covenant and laws on the fleshly tablet of my heart. It seemed that now it was to serve also as a tablet for the *heavenly revelation* of Jesus Christ, and that it was written there first, before it was given to my mind.

He spoke to me in flowers, and made the garden a Paradise. Each blossom carried a living word. I understood why the rose has always been the favorite flower of saints. I learned the meaning of the colors and perfumes of each tender blossom. Outside my window a rare flower—named wedding bells, or angel trumpets—swayed in the breeze, and the sound of heavenly wind-chimes ravished me. The birds sang a "song without words" to me. And each breeze carried a message. My room was kept filled with flowers. And they all seem to say, "Your Lover, the King of Creation, made me to show His love to you. I am the fair work of His hands. My perfume and color and design reveal Him!"

As I sat or walked in the garden it seemed paradisal to me, for He walked there too, wooing and courting my soul in love. I was overwhelmed! I, a commoner, a servant—to be wooed by the King! Although for seven years He had been preparing me as an "Esther," yet I still felt unprepared for such intimate, divine favor. I received Him as "My King." In my times of prayer, when He withdrew, I sought the Holy Spirit and entreated Him, the faithful Eunuch, to prepare me and make me fit for so great a King. I was helpless to do anything but to pray and seek the help of the Holy Spirit. Please do not see the personal angle of these truths, for the experience of the entire Bride Company was being depicted in me, in miniature, and my prayers were not for myself alone, but for *each precious member.* This song came with wonderful unction to me:

HEART TO HEART

I have found a sweeter communion,
Sweeter far than earth can give;
With Christ I have a holy union,
And in His presence I now live.

With everlasting love He drew me
From the depths of woe and sin;
By His Spirit He renewed me
And cleansed my heart within.

Heart to heart we talk together,
Hand in hand we walk each day;
And nothing now our hearts can sever,
Nor take this love away.

Forevermore we two are one;
Forevermore we'll dwell on high;
And heart to heart we shall commune,
My precious Lord and I.

The days passed as in a dream. At times He withdrew and permitted me to be tested, sometimes in sudden and severe ways. Except for short intervals, experiences of rapture do not lift us above temptations and trials. In fact, I am given to see that the nearer we approach the top of the Mount of Transfiguration, the higher we ascended in our flight to the Throne, the *greater* shall be the tests. Even in *rest* I found a great cross. And truly, the path to the Throne is marked every step of the way by the sign of the *Cross*! However these tests passed swiftly, and I was conscious of new overcoming power. The way is dangerous, but when God intervenes to the point where He leads us in this supernatural way, He is faithful to deliver and protect. Angels attend and defend us, and our whole battle takes on an entirely new aspect.

Since I have not dwelt upon inevitable sufferings and trials which were encountered, some may imagine that such an experience as this has been just pure bliss. But such was not the case. At times the Lord does require that Satan leave us for a season, during which we are free from testings. But it is certain that we shall be tried and measured again and again, as we move on to higher ground in the Lord. The place He has prepared for the overcomers in His "Throne Company" is exceedingly costly, and the qualifications for entering this elect number are indeed high. So we must expect tests and be watchful—and especially is this true after we have received special blessings and favors from the Lord. Above all we must trust and not fear. Having shown us such great love and favor, will He permit us to be cast down and crushed by our foes? Never! Therefore let us believe God and abandon ourselves unto Him.

When I first entered "The King's House," the sister there had said, "I believe you will be here thirty days." This proved to be the case, for on the thirtieth day the Lord told me to depart. He had begun to anoint me again, and had caught me up as in the fourth chapter of The Revelation, and had also given me some experiences similar to those in Ezekiel and Daniel. We three had received wonderful dealings, so I was loath to depart. Was all this to end as in a dream? I could not bear such a thought. I was still very weak in body, though greatly improved; but to go back to duties and labor and confusion seemed unbearable. *Wonderful Jesus!* This "dream" did not end, but proceeded step by step, from glory to glory! The gates of the "the new Eden" would soon swing open—and I would be led on and on, even to the "Mount of Transfiguration!"

THE SIGN OF THE SON OF MAN

Frances Metcalfe

The sign of the Son of Man is in the heavens,
The sign of the Son of Man is in the earth,
Proclaiming the promised day of His appearing,
When many sons shall be brought to glorious birth.

Bethlehem's bright star emblazoned in the skies the glorious announcement of the first advent of our Lord Jesus Christ, and its afterglow has illuminated the centuries, shining even unto us and causing us to rejoice in its light. We, too, "have seen His star in the East and have come to worship Him." But today an even more resplendent sign is rising in our far horizon, proclaiming His second coming—**the sign of the Son of Man**. Perhaps you are among those who have been wondering, waiting, longing to know more about what Jesus meant when He spoke to His disciples of the end of the age, and of its climactic portent: "Then shall appear the sign of the Son of Man in the heavens . . ." (Matthew 24:20) Or, it may be that you are among the blessed ones who have already caught a glimpse of His sign and have risen to follow it with joy. In either case, this message is directed to you, and, indeed, to all who "love His appearing."

There can be no reasonable doubt that the star which led the Wise Men was not illusionary, but **real**, and that it was seen for an indefinite period of time by many witnesses. However, it is evident that very few of them understood its meaning. And fewer still found their way to the manger of the little Son of God. But the Magi did! They not only "beheld the star with joy," but rose to follow it with an indefatigable zeal. They knew that merely to **see** the sign did not suffice, that its real purpose was not only to attract their attention, but to inspire them and direct them to a God-appointed destination and destiny. So they followed it on and on, over many a dangerous and wearisome road until—after a disheartening delay in Jerusalem where they lost sight of it—they came at last to **"the house"** and found **"the young Child and Mary, His mother."** (Matthew 2:11)

Likewise, in this latter day, those who behold His sign know that the time of His appearing draws near. "The wise shall understand." (Daniel 12:10) And, like the Magi, they shall "rejoice with great joy," and follow it over a lonely, hazardous way, through hardships, heartaches and delays until, at last, they too shall come to a "house" (a greater house built of "living stones"), and to a "child"—**the man child**, and a "mother"—**the woman clothed with the sun.** (Revelation 12)

THE TWO IRREFUTABLE SIGNS

At the time of the Incarnation, two amazing and unique signs were given by God, whereby all men might know that Jesus was truly the Son of God, the Messiah, the long-promised Savior. Likewise, at the time of His Second Coming—His multiple incarnation in His many-membered body—two equally amazing and unique signs are to be given by God, according to the Scriptures. Many of the Lord's people do not know what these signs are, and if they were to see them would not understand their rightful meaning. But His Spirit-taught, Spirit-led people need not be ignorant of them. And they aren't! In assembly after assembly, to heart after heart, the Holy Spirit has been speaking of these signs and giving fore-glimpses of them. At the same time, Satan has been using these very signs as a means of introducing all manner of deceptions and false teachings. He has influenced some to claim that they are Christ, come again in the flesh, and countless souls have been led off into deception and darkness.

Therefore it is of great importance that we know how to discern God's signs in heaven and upon earth, and also that we interpret them according to the clear teaching of the Word, rather than by the vain interpretations of men or the evil indoctrinations of Satan. For it is only as we discern and understand them that we shall be able to follow them on to their fulfillment.

It will help us to understand the two great second advent signs if we fully comprehend the meaning of the two outstanding signs of His first coming. We all know that the Bible is the perfect blueprint of God's plan, and that it will never be abrogated nor altered. In the very beginning of the Book, the plan of the Incarnation was announced, (Genesis 3:15), but to Isaiah was entrusted the filling in of the blueprint. This great prophet, who spoke to Zion in particular, reiterated the two miraculous signs which were long prefigured. The first—**a virgin mother!** ("Therefore the Lord Himself shall give you a sign; behold, a virgin shall conceive, and bear a son, and shall call His name Immanuel") the second—**a divine Child!** ("For unto us a child is born, unto us a son is given: and the government shall be upon His shoulder: and His name shall be called Wonderful, Counsellor, The mighty God, The everlasting Father, The Prince of Peace.") (Isaiah 7:14; 9:6)

In addition to these signs there were many lesser ones which surrounded the birth of Jesus. Some of them were revealed centuries before they occurred. As the "fulness of time" drew near, the signs increased: To Zechariah, serving in the Temple, there appeared a dazzling being—an archangel, no less!—with an astounding word. To Mary, the annunciation of the greatest favor ever bestowed upon a woman . . . a great overshadowing . . . an unbelievable commitment! To Elizabeth, an unexpected conception . . . a visitation . . . a great exultation! And there were still others, appearing at the time of Jesus' birth: Angels, the glory of the Lord, the shepherds, heavenly voices, the brilliant star, the Magi—we are all familiar with these, and yet they never lose their wonder. But these supernatural manifestations are not nearly so vital to us as **The Virgin Birth and The Divine Son.** Upon these two "signs" rests the structure of our Christian faith. To ignore them, to doubt them or to misunderstand them, is to miss the way into "the new birth" and the Kingdom of God.

Just as certainly as these two signs of His birth were perfectly fulfilled and made manifest, and have been universally accepted by true believers in every generation, so shall the signs of His second advent appear in heaven and upon earth, and, in turn, shall have their perfect fulfillment—to the glory of God the Father. Already some with anointed eyes have beheld "previews" of these portents, and have been given foretastes of their glory. So, while it is true that many, many signs of the end of the age are around us, we center our attention upon the two which are most vital to our faith, namely:

THE SUN-CLOTHED WOMAN AND THE MAN CHILD

We find these two signs prefigured in many portions of the Scripture. For instance, in Jeremiah: "The Lord hath created a new thing in the earth, a woman shall compass a man." (Jeremiah 31:22) But their clearest depiction is in the twelfth chapter of The Revelation: "And there appeared a great wonder (sign—original text) in heaven: a woman clothed with the sun, and the moon under her feet, and upon her head a crown of twelve stars . . . And she brought forth a man child who was to rule all nations with a rod of iron." (Verses 1-5) This chapter of the Bible has captured widespread attention. And many are asking, "Who or what is this woman? Who or what is the man child?"

It is quite likely that more false teaching centers around these two figures than around any other portion of the Scripture. This prophecy is hard to understand. Consequently, dozens of interpretations of it are being promulgated today. It is therefore necessary for us who desire to know the **Truth** to "prove all things" in this matter, and "to hold fast" only "that which is good" and Biblically sound. But this does not mean that we should blind our eyes to these glorious signs, nor that we should refuse to accept any light which the blessed Holy Spirit sheds upon them.

Jesus warned us of these dangerous deceptions, saying that they would "deceive the very elect, if it were possible." The apostles also told us what to expect in these treacherous latter days. So, when we hear that Christ is already come, and "Lo, He is here!" or "Lo, there!" we do not hasten out to meet Him. And when we hear of "a manifested son" or "sons," we remember that the plain teaching of the Word shows us that the sons of God will be manifested **together**, and that, while many are being prepared for this calling, **no one has yet come to the fulness of the stature of Christ.** We are not confused by anyone who claims to be "the woman" or "the man child," for we realized that while it is true that some of us are being given **foretastes** of this blessed estate, we must not mistake these **earnests** for the fulness. Nor do we look for these figures in **individuals.** A careful, prayerful search of the Scriptures will convince us that "the woman" and "the man child" **are symbolical** rather than **literal** figures, and that they are **composite** rather than **individual.** The "corn of wheat" that fell into the earth and died is going to be raised in multiple form. The one little virgin-bride and mother will appear as a great company—a Virgin Bride—The Mother from Above, in whom shall be formed the many sons of God. Two companies, yet one; one, yet two. In this, the duality of the nature of Christ is revealed—Son-Bride, Father-Mother, all in all! Then shall we see and fully understand.

THE SIGN OF THE SON OF MAN

Some Bible students have failed to differentiate between the appearing of Jesus as being the **Son of Man**, and His appearing as the **Son of God**. But the Scriptures in the original text reveal that the former is referred to by the word **epiphaneia**, which means appearing or manifestation; whereas the latter is called the **parousia**, which means personal presence, in a physical aspect. In such passages of Scripture as 1 Timothy 6:14; 2 Timothy 1:10; 4:1, 8; Titus 2:13; and others, epiphaneia is used, depicting the **appearing** of Jesus. The parousia is referred to in 1 Thessalonians 2:19; 5:23, etc. Jesus will first appear in the members of His Body as the **Son of Man**. The second phase of His appearing, called the parousia, will be as the **Son of God**. (" . . . this same Jesus, which is taken up from you into heaven, shall so come in like manner as ye have seen Him go into heaven.") Thus we see that Jesus is going to appear **to** His own, **in** His own, and finally, **with** His own—in great glory and power. And we know that "when He shall appear, then shall we appear with Him in glory." And we shall be called, "the sons of God." (1 John 3:1)

THE HEAVENS DECLARE THE GLORY OF GOD

Frances Metcalfe

The heavens declare the glory of God and the firmament showeth His handiwork. Day unto day uttereth speech, and night unto night showeth knowledge." (Psalm 19:1, 2) These sublime words of David express what millions of mortals have felt as they walked out under the stars on a clear night and gazed upon them with wondering eyes. "There is no speech nor language where their voice is not heard. Their line is gone out through all the earth, and their words to the end of the world." (Psalm 19:3, 4) Yet, sad to say, few men have been able to **understand** their strange speech or to **hear** their ethereal voices. Few have been able to trace out their "line" and grasp the significance of their "word." However, we know that since the days of Adam, Enoch, Job and the Patriarchs, and on through the times of David, Daniel and the Magi, there have been some who did decipher their message and interpret the language of the spheres. To them the starry heavens were a great scroll unrolled by the hand of Elohim, the Creator, and as they studied and pondered it night after night, day after day, many of His hidden purposes and truths were disclosed to them. "For the invisible things of Him from the creation of the world are clearly seen, being understood by the things that are made, even His eternal power and Godhead." (Romans 1:20)

> This prospect vast, what is it?—Weighted aright,
> 'Tis nature's system of divinity;
> 'Tis Elder Scripture, writ by God's own hand;
> Scripture authentic! uncorrupt by man.

We who are living in the twentieth century look upon the same stars that taught these holy men of old, and find blessed comfort in the thought of this unchanging testimony of the glory and truth of God. We, like they, long to know their burning message. The more we look at them and ponder their significance, the more difficult it becomes to express the awe we feel. We turn again to the inspired Singer of Israel who spent so many nights under the stars tending his sheep, worshiping and singing unto the Lord: "When I consider the heavens, the work of Thy fingers, the moon and the stars, which Thou hast ordained." (Psalm 8:3) Ordained! Yes, we feel it . . . know it . . . thrill to it—since the foundation of the world, the moon, the stars and the planets have had an ordained ministry to man!

In our desire to understand this ministry of the stars we search for means to that end. Who can teach us their unknown language? It may occur to us to turn to astronomy, a science making wonderful progress in our modern day. We may secure any number of books on the subject, and wade through their amazing teachings. We may visit planetariums and observatories and marvel at the new instruments and telescopes that bring the stars into ever closer observation. We may thrill to the new discoveries the scientists are making at Palomar and other places. But for most of us this knowledge is far too difficult to comprehend—we are staggered by the startling array of technical data presented to us. To know the relative sizes and positions of the stars, to trace their orbits through the skies, is stimulating to the **mind** of man, but provides little satisfaction for his seeking **spirit.** He still wonders just how all this relates to God and to His plan for the world and each individual in it.

To this all-important question it is impossible to find the answer in modern astronomy. If we studied it extensively we are apt to become overwhelmed by the relative unimportance of the world and its people, as compared with the magnitude of billions of heavenly bodies. And under stress we cry out: "What is man that

Thou art mindful of him? And the Son of Man that Thou visitest him? For Thou hast made him a little lower than the angels, and hast crowned him with glory and honor. Thou madest him to have dominion over the works of Thy hands; Thou has put all things under his feet." (Psalm 8:4-6) Marvelous! Wonderful! Our Father considers man more important than all the magnificent stars and celestial worlds. They are the **works** of His hand; but man, made in the **image of God**, was created for eternal glory and dominion over all His works. The redeemed sons of God are the true "stars" which shall shine forever in His heavenly Kingdom! (Daniel 12:3)

When it becomes evident to us that astronomy is not able to interpret the hidden message of the stars to us, we leave the astronomer to his instruments and turn, if we wish, to the astrologer with his elaborate charts and systems of sky-reading and forecasting. Astrology is a very old study. Some consider it a true science, while others deem it a pseudo-science. Still others regard it as of Satanic origin. It may seem to hold great promise when we first investigate it; but sooner or later we find it disappointing. Its main interest and purpose seems to relate to the natural sensual man, seeking to further his material interest and well-being. There is little in it to feed the spiritual man, the "new creature in Christ Jesus." Some Christians are interested in it and are attempting to live by it, taking their guidance from "the influences and indications of the stars." It distresses us that so much emphasis is put upon the natural birth time. Where does the Second Birth figure in these matters? We surely cannot let our lives be guided by the stars rather than by the Holy Spirit and the Word of God. In our search for the true interpretation of the stars we find we must leave astrology also and search yet further.

Where, then, shall we turn for a genuine spiritual interpretation of the heavens? This is a question multitudes of Christians are asking. As never before, those who are led by the Spirit are longing to know what the stars are saying. If it is true—as eminent authorities tell us—that there are more significant configurations in the heavens now than at any other time since the birth of Christ, then we, the children of God, have right to know what these mean. Did not Jesus say: "And great signs shall there be from heaven." (Luke 21:11) And in Acts we read: "And I will show wonders in heaven above." (2:19) How shall we be able to read these signs without an interpreter, a teacher? This is the cry of many of the saints. It was the cry of my own heart for many years. I believe that the Holy Spirit has given me an answer to this question. And I feel He is leading me to share it with you. In order to do so I shall have to relate His dealings with me along this line, as they were extended over a period of several years.

It was in 1934 that the Holy Spirit began to teach me about the meaning of the stars. I had been given some intimations of this even when I was a child, and had frequently gone out at night to look up into the sky and ponder the mysteries it held. Sometimes, I felt a great awe coupled with fear, and I was pained that the stars seemed so cold, so remote, so utterly unrelated to me. However, in 1934 I was awakened to their meaning in a rather dramatic way. After spending several weeks attending some very spiritual revival meetings in Los Angeles, where we resided at that time, I was taken into a new high plain of communion with the Lord. It was a "mountain-top" experience, as we say.

During these meetings I had spent much time in prayer and fasting, and had experienced a wonderful physical healing. I seemed to be completely renewed, both physically and spiritually. And I had re-consecrated myself to the Lord as fully as I knew how to do so. Shortly after these meetings closed, my husband and I were led to go to a Bible Conference conducted by a fundamentalist minister to whose radio Bible teaching we listened frequently. This conference was held in a rather secluded spot on Catalina Island, just off the coast of California. It meant four full days and nights away from the countless duties and cares of a busy household and small children—four days and nights which I could dedicated entirely to the Lord.

We set sail for the island with much joy and anticipation. Upon arriving we found that our camp had no electric lights, radio, newspaper or telephone. We were separated from the world in a realistic way. Part of the day was scheduled for classes and conferences. I discovered that one of the studies was called, "The Gospel in the Stars." My heart leapt within me when I read those words, and you may be sure I enrolled for that class. In four short sessions our teacher managed to prepare my mind for the blueprint of the starry heavens, showing how the various constellations or "signs" in the stars reveal the **entire Gospel story.** Beginning with Virgo, the sign which represents the Virgin and the incarnation of Christ, he traced all the signs around the sky to Leo, the Lion of the Tribe of Judah, displayed in the ultimate triumph of areas, the Lamb. I sat amazed, drinking in these truths and witnessing to them with abounding joy.

At night we would take our cots outdoors and sleep under the stars, after we had watched them as long as we could keep awake. How close, how intimate, how very friendly they seemed since I knew what they were trying to tell the world—they were declaring the glory of God, not only in His **handiwork**, but in His **Son**! "For God, who commanded the light to shine out of the darkness (at the creation of the world) hath shined in our hearts (when we were re-created), to give the light of the knowledge of the glory of God in the face of Jesus Christ." (2 Corinthians 4:6)

This Word, always very precious to me, became illuminated with starry glory. Over and over I sang, "Face to face shall I behold Him," not only in the sky, but "far beyond the starry sky. Face to face in ALL His glory, I shall see Him bye and bye." To add to our inspiration, the meteors put on a fiery display. Since this occurred in the month of August, there was nothing unusual about "falling stars," but it seemed to us like a special manifestation of God's glory. I was thrilled beyond words to discover that the stars were not only evangelical, but pentecostal as well! At last I could understand their unknown tongues, at least to a degree.

In 1942 the Holy Spirit continued His teaching about the stars in a very definite and consistent way. During the early part of that year I was frequently led to go out under the stars to worship the Lord and to ponder His glory revealed in the celestial luminaries. Sometimes my attention would be drawn to some certain star, and I would find myself almost rapt as I entered into a mystic communion with it. It seemed I could hear its unique ethereal song. My mind had little understanding, but I felt an exquisite inner enlightenment, as though the star had shed heavenly light into my soul. I did not even know the names of the stars, but I began to learn a little about their appearances and positions. And I took comfort in the realization that I knew the One who "telleth the names of the stars; He calleth them all by their names." (Psalm 147:4)

It suddenly became very real to me that the **Holy Spirit** was the only true interpreter of the stars. I could rely upon Him to teach me about them, just as He had interpreted and taught me God's written Word. The Word in Job became very alive to me: "By His Spirit He hath garnished the heavens." (26:13) I searched for the original meaning of the word "garnished" and found that its Hebrew root signifies "to clothe, to adorn, to make fair." The same Spirit that breathed upon the waters at the creation of the world, also clothed and garnished the heavens. I called upon the Holy Spirit with all my heart, asking Him to reveal the glory of God in the starry heavens, and to write their message upon my heart. (For other references in Job see 9:9 and 38:32.)

From that time on I received frequent impressions about the stars. These seemed to be imparted to me much like the time exposure of a picture. My heart was the "plate" upon which the impression was made, but the picture was not immediately developed. The imprint was not clear enough to reach my conscious mind. I was impressed, moreover, with the realization that the stars and planets followed their courses within invariable precision according to the laws of God. There is a beautiful revelation of this in the nineteenth Psalm. David must have purposely coupled the first six verses, which deal with the movements of the heavenly bodies, with the last eight verses, which deal with the perfect law of God—His Word. There is no greater demonstration of unfailing observance of Divine Law than that which is manifest by the stellar universe. Recently it has been our privilege to watch man walk on the moon. We have marveled at the perfect precision of the movements of the heavenly bodies. And we realize that it is because of this precision that man has been able to chart his courses into outer space and safely time his return flights to the earth. It would be permissible to say, "Thy kingdom come, Thy will be done on earth, as it is in the (starry) heavens."

Although we have the solar calendar, we take our actual time from the stars, and it is their timing, which does not vary, that governs our chronometers. In 1942 I learned about the amazing star-clock in the northern skies, revolving around the north star, the star that indicates the strange vacant space in the north where God's throne is supposed to be situated—a space into which no instrument of man has been able to penetrate! If you want to find God's great clock in the northern sky it is not difficult to do so. And when you once learn the position of the stars, you can tell time within a few minutes by observing their relation to one another. All time moves in cycles or circles. Man's instruments for telling time are circular in form—clocks, watches, chronometers. God's instrument is circular also. He has placed in the northern skies a pole star, often called Polaris, and it is the center of the dial of His great clock. A radius extending 40 degrees in every direction from the North Star marks the outer rim of the crystal, and the Big Dipper, Ursa Major (Big Bear) forms the hour hand. This hour hand makes one complete circle around the face of the star clock in exactly 24 hours, never varying a second. (Sun time does vary.) It marks the yearly cycle just as accurately. Our chronometers are set by this star-clock.

Man used to use sundials, hourglasses, and other crude means of telling time; but today even the poorest man may possess a watch which can be set to perfect time each day. Oh that man's heart and spirit might be as easily adjusted to God's heavenly time! Solomon rejoiced that God had given him not only wisdom but knowledge also. Included in this knowledge was perfect knowledge about God's times.

"For it is He that has given me an unerring knowledge of what is, to know the constitution of the world and the working of the elements; the beginning and end and middle of periods of time, the alternations of solstices and the changes of the seasons, the cycles of the years and the positions of the stars." (Wisdom of Solomon 7:17-19, Apocrypha)

At this time—in 1942—many portions of the Word were quickened to me. One Scripture was impressed often: "And God said, Let there be lights in the firmament of the heaven to divide the day from the night; and let them be for **signs**, and for **seasons**, for **days**, and for **years**." (Genesis 1:14) Also references in Job, Daniel and The Revelation were especially emphasized. I longed to understand them better and wondered if the Holy Spirit would give me any added tangible help. Then, one day, I was impressed to go to the Public Library. When I entered I was drawn toward a certain section and, as I looked to the Spirit for guidance, I found my hand reaching out and taking hold of a green book. At the same time I felt a quickening within which increased as I read the title: THE GOSPEL IN THE STARS or Primeval Astronomy, by Joseph A.

Seiss, D.D., LL.D., published by The Castle Press of Philadelphia. (We do not have copies of it available.) Glancing through it I discovered that not only was the **Gospel** written in the stars, but also the entire **End-time** or **Latter Day prophecies** were all there too. Wonderful! I rejoiced and gave thanks. I knew that it was put into my hands by the Holy Spirit and that it would afford me much help. As I began to study it, God's words to Job seemed to be applied to me: "Canst thou bring forth Mazzaroth (the signs of the Zodiac) in his season, or canst thou guide Arcturus with his sons?" (Job 38:32)

I was convinced that these signs of the Zodiac when interpreted, not by modern astronomy, or astrology, but by primeval Biblical astronomy, do indeed reveal God's Word and plan. I recommend Dr. Seiss's book to any of you who want to make a study along this line. It is an unfailing source book of authentic information. He is a sound Theologian, as well as an inspiring and well-informed writer. From the beginning to the end it will thrill you with its disclosures. It reveals the signs of the Zodiac as they relate to Israel and were displayed upon their standards. It has a chapter devoted to the Advent Star the Magi followed. And it takes up many other matters of interest.

In the years that have passed since we began to study the stars from a Biblical standpoint, we have found in ever-increasing richness in their meanings. Living here on a mountaintop, we have been given ample opportunity to enjoy the brilliance and beauty of the stars undimmed by city lights and smog. There have been frequent signs in our skies, displays of special glory, as we have walked under the stars on innumerable nights. One night as several of us walked and worshiped, the heavens were revealed to be like a most beautiful curtain hanging between the earth and the Holy of Holies of the Heavens. Just as the veil of the Temple was wrought with great skill and artistic handiwork, hanging there in majesty before the Ark and the Shekinah glory of God, veiling it from profane eyes, so the starry heavens are a curtain veiling the eternal glory of God which lies just beyond them. On that curtain, symbolically inscribed with great beauty, are written the eternal mysteries of God. We may read these **now**! We shall see His open glory **later**! It seemed to us that every star was eager to make known its message unto us, and that one of the gifts of the Holy Spirit to be given in this Latter Day was that of wisdom and knowledge of how to read the stars aright. "Praise Him, ye stars of light! Praise Him, ye heaven of heavens!" (Psalm 148:3, 4)

WHAT EVERY NEW CONVERT SHOULD KNOW

John H. Bostrom

You have now accepted the Lord Jesus Christ as your personal Saviour. You have been born again—born of God. The burden of sin has gone. The peace of God reigns in your heart. The joy of divine forgiveness is yours, as well as everlasting life. Since your name is now recorded in the Lamb's Book of Life, you are no longer under condemnation, but are justified by faith in Christ.

Now that you have been born from above—born of the Spirit—God has become your Father, and all the children of God, the world around, have become your brothers and sisters in Christ. All relationship with the devil has been severed; his hold upon you has been broken by the power of the risen Lord.

You have been redeemed at infinite cost—the precious blood of Jesus—and now you belong to God, and have become His prized possession. All of the divine promises are yours in Christ. You are an heir of God, and a joint-heir with Christ. (Romans 8:17) Now you have begun to really **live**!

All of this has taken place upon your acceptance of Jesus Christ as your Saviour and Lord. However, by taking this step of faith and obedience, the devil has been aroused. He is your avowed enemy, and because Christ has broken the chains of sin which held you captive to him, you may expect him to cause you considerable "rough going."

Permit me to make a few suggestions, the following of which will tend to smooth the rough places, and help you to walk in this new and living way.

SHOULD DOUBTS COME

Satan may try to get you to doubt your conversion. He may tell you that you just **think** you are saved, or that you do not feel any different now than you did before, and that, therefore, you have experienced no change of heart. Should this occur, look to Christ for whatever protection you need to ward off the fiery darts of the evil one. You should also know what God has said in His Word, for the use of the Bible will be very helpful in resisting the enemy of your soul. Jesus quoted from the Scriptures when He was tempted of the devil.

Remember this—the devil is a liar. Jesus said so. (John 8:44) So when he comes with disturbing thoughts, pay no attention to him whatever. You have no reason to doubt your conversion. The Bible says, "Whosoever shall call upon the name of the Lord shall be saved." (Romans 10:13) You called—so claim God's promise.

Jesus said, "Him that cometh to me I will in no wise cast out." (John 6:37) You came—and since He did not cast you out He must have taken you in.

God's Word declares that the one who confesses and forsakes his sins shall have mercy. (Proverbs 28:13) Again, "if we confess our sins, He is faithful and just to forgive us our sins, and to cleanse us from all unrighteousness." (1 John 1:9) God says that if you confess, He will forgive and cleanse—and He always speaks the truth.

Salvation is a matter of faith—not feeling. Even though you may not **feel** so much different after you have surrendered your heart to the Lord, rely on His Word: "But as many as received Him, to them gave He the power to become the sons of God, even to them that believe on His name." (John 1:12) Your feelings may change like the weather, but God's Word is immutable!

NEVER CONSIDER TURNING BACK

If the adversary of your soul cannot get you to doubt your salvation, he will endeavor to turn you back from following Christ. Temptations may come to give up your profession of faith, and go back to the beggarly elements of the world. These will come to you in various forms through your eyes, your ears, for the sense of taste, the sense of smell, and the sense of touch. Your former worldly friends (?) may invite you to join their crowd and make merry.

But let me urge you to avoid placing yourself in positions which are apt to become embarrassing. Shun evil companions whose company will tend to drag you down. Seek rather the association of believers whose fellowship will have a tendency to strengthen you in your new Christian experience.

"Have no fellowship with the unfruitful works of darkness, but rather reprove them." (Ephesians 5:11)

"Wherefore come out from among them, and be ye separate, saith the Lord, and touch not the unclean thing; and I will receive you, and will be a father unto you, and you shall be my sons and daughters, saith the Lord Almighty." (2 Corinthians 6:17, 18)

"Be ye not unequally yoked together with unbelievers." (2 Corinthians 6:14) This means that since light has nothing in common with darkness, and since righteousness and unrighteousness cannot mix, we are not to have close association or intimate friendship with those who do not love our Christ or live for Him. God's people are a separated and holy people.

A few more Scripture passages right here will not be amiss:

"No man can serve two masters: for either he will hate the one, and love the other; or he will hold to the one, and despise the other." (Matthew 6:24)

"Love not the world, neither the things that are in the world. If any man love the world, the love of the Father is not in him. For all that is in the world, the lust of the flesh, and the lust of the eyes, and the pride of life, is not of the Father, but is of the world. And the world passeth away, and the lust thereof: but he that doeth the will of God abideth forever." (1 John 2:15-17)

"Know ye not that the friendship of the world is enmity with God? Whosoever therefore will be a friend of the world is the enemy of God." (James 4:4)

"Follow peace with all men, and holiness, without which no man shall see the Lord." (Hebrews 12:14)

HOW TO MEET TEMPTATION

Temptation is not sin. My dear mother used to say, "We cannot prevent the birds from flying over our heads, but we can keep them from building a nest in our hair," which simply means that we cannot prevent temptations from coming to us but we can keep from harboring them in our minds. Suggestions to do evil will come, but do not entertain them. If you do, you will be apt to yield. Always remember that if you never take the **first step** back into sin, you will never take the **second step.**

You will have many battles, to be sure, but if you look earnestly and constantly to Jesus for strength in the hour of temptation He will make you more than a conqueror. (Romans 8:37) "Fight the good fight of faith." (1 Timothy 6:12)

Rejoice because your name is written in heaven, that Christ dwells in your heart by faith, and that since He has won the victory over the adversary, you share in His triumph. "For the joy of the Lord is your strength." (Nehemiah 8:10) You are to reckon yourself dead to sin but alive unto God. It is not your human struggles or strength that prevails against the enemy and enables you to live the Christian life, but it is letting Christ live His life in you. Be assured that "He is able to keep that which" you "have committed unto Him against that day." (2 Timothy 1:12)

"Yield not to temptation,
For yielding is sin;
Each vict'ry will help you
Some other to win;
Fight manfully onward,
Dark passions subdue,
Look ever to Jesus;
He'll carry you through.

Ask the Saviour to help you,
Comfort, strengthen and keep you;
He is willing to aid you;
He will carry you through."

"There hath no temptation taken you but such as is common to man: but God is faithful, who will not suffer you to be tempted above that ye are able; but will with the temptation also make a way to escape, that ye may be able to bear it." (1 Corinthians 10:13)

"Blessed is the man that endureth temptation; for when he is tried, he shall receive the crown of life, which the Lord hath promised to them that love him." (James 1:12)

QUESTIONABLE THINGS

Things of a questionable nature will sometimes arise, and you will wonder whether or not you would be committing sin were you to do such-and-such a thing. On this point, the advice of the mother of John and Charles Wesley is quite helpful. She said, "Take this rule: whatever impairs the tenderness of your conscience, obscures your sense of God, or takes the relish off spiritual things, that thing is sin to you, however innocent it may be in itself."

Furthermore, although some things may seem harmless in themselves, the doing of them will take valuable time away from other things that are really worthwhile. As you read your Bible and pray, God will give you wisdom to discern between good and evil.

What Jesus said when explaining the parable of the sower and the seed, is worth noting here: "And that which fell among thorns are they which, when they have heard, go forth, and are choked with cares and riches, and pleasures of this life, and bring no fruit to perfection." (Luke 8:14)

IF SIN OVERTAKES YOU

A child of God has no business sinning. The Bible says, "Likewise reckon ye also yourselves to be dead indeed unto sin, but alive unto God through Jesus Christ our Lord. For sin shall not have dominion over you. How shall we, that are dead to sin, live any longer therein?" (Romans 6:11, 14, 2) You have turned your back on the world, the flesh, and the devil.

However, should you in an unguarded moment yield to the tempter, do not give up in despair, thinking that it is impossible for you to live the Christian life. Nothing would please the devil more than for you to abandon all hope or expectation of living victoriously.

Should you fall into sin, humble yourself before God at once, petitioning Him for forgiveness, and get up and go on your way, being more watchful and prayerful than ever, and keep on the alert for the wiles of the adversary. There is no sense in staying down just because one stumbles. Here is God's gracious provision: "If any man sin, we have an advocate with the Father, Jesus Christ the righteous." (1 John 2:1)

INCONSISTENCIES OF OTHERS

It is deplorable indeed, but a fact nevertheless, that occasionally those who claim to be converted act in an unchristian manner. Should you see such inconsistencies in the lives of professing Christians, do not let them disturb you unduly. Fix your eyes on Jesus, and pray that God will help you keep **your** conduct on a par with your claims.

You may see hypocrites, but rather than allow them to diminish your love and your zeal for God and His kingdom, they should serve as a challenge to you to let the world know that although there are worthless imitations of Christianity, there are also genuine God-fearing, righteous living, and Christ-loving men and women in this wicked and perverse generation.

EXPECT OPPOSITION

Now that Christ dwells in your heart by faith, you are indeed rich. In fact, you are a child of the King! However, do not expect everyone you meet to congratulate you because of this step of faith and obedience to God that you have just taken. True, there are those who will admire your stand, and will be glad to help you in any way they can, but there are others who will be apt to ridicule you because of your identification with Christ and His church.

But, remember, now you are on the Lord's side, and He is on your side, and Christ within is greater than all the enemies that are without. He has given us this encouraging word: "Greater is He that is in you than he that is in the world." (1 John 4:4)

God will give you grace and strength in the time of need, so that with firmness, and yet with love, you can declare in no uncertain terms your fidelity to your Lord and Master, and endure the bitterest of persecutions that may come to you as a Christian. Never flinch. Do not deny your Lord. Be true to Him at all costs.

"For it is better, if the will of God be so, that ye suffer for well doing, than for evil doing." (1 Peter 3:17)

"If ye be reproached for the name of Christ, happy are ye; for the spirit of glory and of God resteth upon you: on their part He is evil spoken of, but on your part He is glorified. But let none of you suffer as a murderer, or as a thief, or an evil doer, or as a busybody in other men's matters. If any man suffer as a Christian, let him not be ashamed; but let him glorify God on this behalf." (1 Peter 4:14-16)

"Yea, and all that will live godly in Christ Jesus shall suffer persecution." (2 Timothy 3:12)

"Blessed are they that are persecuted for righteousness' sake: theirs is the kingdom of heaven. Blessed are ye, when men shall revile you, and persecute you and shall say all manner of evil against you falsely, for My sake. Rejoice, and be exceeding glad: for great is your reward in heaven: for so persecuted they the prophets which were before you." (Matthew 5:10-12)

CONSTRUCTIVE SUGGESTIONS

Having dealt with what you must guard against, let me now mention briefly a number of things that you should do.

Always allow God the first place of your life. Jesus said, "Seek ye first the kingdom of God, and His righteousness; and all these things (temporal necessities) shall be added unto you." (Matthew 6:33)

Take as your motto the first four words of the Bible: "**In the beginning God.**" Seek to know and to do His will, and bear in mind that your chief aim in life should be to glorify the Lord.

READ THE BIBLE

A new life has been begotten in you by the power of the precious Holy Spirit, and you need food to sustain that life. That food is the Word of God. Read your Bible. Study it. Jesus said, "Man shall not live by bread alone, but by every word that proceedeth out of the mouth of God." (Matthew 4:4) Just as you need physical food in order to sustain physical life, so you need spiritual food to maintain spiritual stamina.

Be equipped with the "the sword of the Spirit, which is the Word of God," (Ephesians 6:17) when you go out to make battle against the forces of evil.

Then, too, the Bible tells us how to live. "Thy Word," says the Psalmist, "is a lamp unto my feet, and a light unto my path. The entrance of Thy words giveth light; it giveth understanding to the simple. Thy word have I hid in mine heart, that I might not sin against Thee." (Psalm 119:105, 130, 11)

"Let the word of Christ dwell in you richly in all wisdom." (Colossians 3:16)

PRAYER-THANKSGIVING-PRAISE

Of vital importance to the Christian is his prayer life. Jesus said, "Men ought always to pray." (Luke 18:1) In another place we read, "Pray without ceasing." (1 Thessalonians 5:17) Yes, "prayer is the Christian's vital breath, the Christian's native air."

> *"What a Friend we have in Jesus,*
> *All our sins and griefs to bear!*
> *What a privilege to carry*
> *EVERYTHING to God in prayer!"*

There is nothing too great and nothing too small to take to the Lord in prayer. If you need employment, pray. If you need money for bills, pray. If you need bodily healing, pray. If trials oppress you and burdens stress you, pray. If you want just the right words to speak to a sinner to win him for the Lord, pray. Whatever the need, take everything to God in prayer.

"I exhort therefore, that, first of all supplications, prayers, intercessions, and giving of thanks, being made for all men; for kings, and for all that are in authority; that we may lead a quiet and peaceable life in all godliness and honesty. For this is good and acceptable in the sight of God our Saviour; who will have all men to be saved, and to come into the knowledge of the truth." (1 Timothy 2:1-4)

> *"Oh, Thou by whom we come to God,*
> *The Life, the Truth, the Way!*
> *The path of prayer Thyself hast trod;*
> *Lord, teach us how to pray."*

Although you should never neglect your prayer life, when speaking to God do not always ask for something. Notice the apostle Paul's exhortation: "In everything by prayer and supplication **with thanksgiving** let your requests be made known unto God." (Philippians 4:6)

Our loving heavenly Father wants us to bring to Him our many needs, but at the same time He desires that we thank Him for what He has already done, for what He is doing right now, and for what He will do. Thank Him for pardoning grace, and for all other spiritual, physical, and temporal blessings. Be deeply appreciative of all the goodness of God.

"In everything give thanks; for this is the will of God in Christ Jesus concerning you." (1 Thessalonians 5:18)

"Giving thanks always for all things unto God and the Father in the name of our Lord Jesus Christ." (Ephesians 5:20)

Not only should you thank Him, but also **praise** the Lord. Give Him the worship and adoration of your heart. Give God the glory and honor that is due Him for His mercy that endureth forever, and for all His mighty deeds. He, and He alone, is worthy of praise.

"Because Thy lovingkindness is better than life, my lips shall praise Thee." (Psalm 63:3)

"By Him therefore let us offer the sacrifice of praise to God continually, that is, the fruit of our lips giving thanks to His name." (Hebrews 13:15) In this verse we see that it is not enough to have praise to the Lord **in our hearts**, but there should be an audible expression.

The Psalmist, especially, tells us to praise our God. He says, "Let everything that hath breath praise the Lord." Someone has said that the only Scriptural excuse for not praising Him is to be out of breath.

"In **prayer** we are occupied with our needs: in **thanksgiving** we are occupied with our blessings; in **praise** we are occupied with God Himself."

Then, let me suggest that in addition to making requests, and thanking and praising our Lord, after you have worshiped and adored the One who is altogether lovely, tarry in His presence. In other words, when you get through talking, wait quietly before the Lord. Let Him speak to your heart. You will, no doubt, find that what He says to you is worth far more than all you have said to Him. This is, indeed, true communion, and as a result of this divine fellowship, you will be strengthened to go forth into the world and live for Jesus. Take time to wait on God.

"They that wait upon the Lord shall renew their strength; they shall mount up with wings as eagles; they shall run and not be weary; and they shall walk and not faint." (Isaiah 40:31)

CONFESS CHRIST TO OTHERS

Then there is the matter of testifying or witnessing for Jesus. This should be done unhesitatingly both in public and in private, as opportunity affords. Never be ashamed to own your Lord.

"Ye are my witnesses, saith the Lord." (Isaiah 43:10)

"For with the heart man believeth unto righteousness; and with the mouth confession is made unto salvation." (Romans 10:10)

"Whosoever therefore shall confess (acknowledge) Me before men, him will I confess also before My Father which is in heaven. But whosoever shall deny Me before men, him will I also deny before My Father, which is in heaven." (Matthew 10:32, 33)

"Whosoever therefore shall be ashamed of Me and of My words in this adulterous and sinful generation; of him also shall the Son of Man be ashamed, when He cometh in the glory of His Father with the holy angels." (Mark 8:38)

The Bible also tells us that we overcome the adversary by the blood of the Lamb, and by the word of our testimony. (Revelation 12:11)

Wisdom should be used in witnessing for the Lord, looking to Him for the right words to speak at the proper time, and trusting Him to make them a blessing. Always keep in mind that you are witnessing for Him—that you are speaking for Him, and not for yourself. Never push yourself to the fore, but rather give Christ

Jesus the preeminence in everything. We have nothing whereof to boast. We are what we are by the grace of God.

Tell the world what Christ has done for you, what Jesus is to you, and what He will do for others if they will come to Him and trust Him, and tell it with the thought of winning others to Jesus. "He that winneth souls is wise." (Proverbs 11:30)

WATER BAPTISM

As soon as possible you should be baptized in water.

Jesus said to His disciples, "Go ye therefore, and teach all nations, baptizing them in the name of the Father, and of the Son, and of the Holy Ghost." (Matthew 28:19)

"Repent, and be baptized every one of you in the name of Jesus Christ for the remission of sins, and ye shall receive the gift of the Holy Ghost." (Acts 2:38)

Here we see that water baptism is a Christian ordinance that should follow repentance. It is an outward sign of an inward work of grace. **Before** conversion it has no special significance whatever, but **after** the heart has been cleansed from sin, it speaks of our identification with Christ in His death, burial, and resurrection.

"Therefore we are buried with Him by baptism into death: that like as Christ was raised up from the dead by the glory of the Father, even so we also should walk in newness of life." (Romans 6:4)

BE FILLED WITH THE HOLY SPIRIT

"And be not drunk with wine, wherein is excess; but be filled with the Spirit." (Ephesians 5:18)

This glorious experience is more than a privilege, for you cannot be what God would have you be, or do what He would have you do, without this enduement of power. Jesus, Himself, did not attempt His earthly ministry until the Holy Spirit came upon Him, and you, too, need this divine enablement for the accomplishment of the will of God in your life, as well as for service to others.

"But ye shall receive power, after that the Holy Ghost is come upon you: and ye shall be witnesses unto Me both in Jerusalem, and in all Judea, and in Samaria, and unto the uttermost part of the earth." (Acts 1:8)

ATTEND CHURCH SERVICES

Although nothing can take the place of private devotions, it will prove very helpful if you will frequent the house of God. In fact, there is no satisfactory substitute for attending church. Both private devotions and public worship have their place in the Christian's life. In the Bible we are admonished not to forsake "the assembling of ourselves together." (Hebrews 10:25)

Now that you are a child of God, you will find delight in worshiping with others of "like precious faith." Both pleasure and benefit will be derived from faithfully attending church services where the gospel of the Lord Jesus Christ is preached in its fullness and in the power of the Holy Spirit. In this way you will receive from divinely inspired messages, the soul food that you need to grow in grace and in the knowledge of your Lord. Then, too, in addition to being uplifted by **listening** to the sermon, music, and song, as you join in the public devotions in the spirit of worship, your soul be refreshed. "I was glad when they said unto me, let us go into the house of the Lord." (Psalm 122:1)

Then, too, the Lord's Supper is a Christian ordinance which you should observe whenever possible. "For as often as ye eat this bread, and drink this cup, ye do shew the Lord's death till He come." (1 Corinthians 11:26)

It would be well, also, for you to unite with some group of believers, so that you will not only have a church home, but also be able to take a definite part in, and share in the responsibility of, getting out this wonderful gospel message. Investigation should be made and divine guidance earnestly sought before making decision as to your church membership, for, alas, some churches are not true to God and the Bible.

CHRISTIAN SERVICE

This leads us to another thought—that of rendering definite service for our Lord and Master. We are not merely to **speak** of His goodness, but allow Him to manifest His life through us in loving service to others. Christianity does not consist in **not doing** certain things that the Scriptures forbid, but the doing of God's will: active service for the Master.

If possible, undertake some specific task for your Lord, even though it takes time, thought, and money—even though it may cause inconvenience. Do it for Jesus' sake. Let your **life** speak for Him. Dedicate your life with all its talents, to the One who gave Himself for you. Perhaps God would have you give full time service in some part of His vineyard at home or abroad. If not, do what you can as He directs and opens doors of opportunity.

Here are the words of Jesus, as recorded in Matthew 5:16: "Let your light so shine before men, that they may see your **good works**, and glorify your Father which is in heaven."

Remember that we are to be men and women zealous of good works, not in order to get to heaven, but because we have been redeemed by the blood of Christ, and now we want to show our love for Him.

"Whosoever shall give to drink unto one of these little ones a cup of cold water only in the name of a disciple, verily I say unto you, he shall in no wise lose his reward." (Matthew 10:42)

"Verily I say unto you, inasmuch as ye have done it unto one of the least of these My brethren, ye have done it unto Me." (Matthew 25:40)

CONTRIBUTE TO THE CAUSE OF CHRIST

Now that you have received Christ, and enjoy this wonderful fellowship with Him, surely you will desire to make Him known to others. Among the many ways that this can be done, allow me to mention a very necessary factor in fulfilling the great commission of Jesus to go into all the world and preach the gospel to every creature.

It takes money to carry out God's work, just as it takes money to carry on any other business, as spreading the gospel is the greatest work on earth. Much expense is incurred in carrying on the work of the Lord, and to you is given not only the glorious privilege but also the solemn responsibility of participating in this phase of the work.

"Honor the Lord with thy substance, and with the first-fruits of all thine increase: so shall thy barns be filled with plenty, and thy presses shall burst out with new wine." (Proverbs 3:9, 10)

"Lay up for yourselves treasures in heaven, where neither moth nor rust doth corrupt, and where thieves do not break through nor steal: for where your treasure is, there will your heart be also." (Matthew 6:20, 21)

"Give, and it shall be given unto you: good measure, pressed down, and shaken together, and running over, shall men give into your bosom." (Luke 6:38)

"Remember the words of the Lord Jesus, how He said, It is more blessed to give than to receive." (Acts 20:35)

If you will give systematically, generously, and even sacrificially, God will richly reward you. Many a Christian has learned by experience that to regularly set aside his tithe (one-tenth of his income) to be used in God's service, and then to give offerings above and beyond that as the Lord enables, has brought the blessing of God upon his life spiritually, physically, and temporally. Do not be afraid of giving too much to the Lord. He gave Himself for you.

"Arm me with jealous care,
As in Thy sight to live;
And so, Thy servant, Lord, prepare,
A strict account to give.
Help me to watch and pray,
And on Thyself rely;
To do Thy will from day to day,
Thy Name to glorify."

"Now unto Him that is able to keep you from falling, and to present you faultless before the presence of His glory with exceeding joy, to the only wise God our Saviour, be glory and majesty, dominion and power, both now and ever. Amen." (Jude 24, 25)

God's promise is not freedom
From trials in the race;
But power to transcend them
Through His sufficing grace.
Not rest instead of labor,
But in the labor rest;

Not calm instead of tempest,
But calm when sore distressed.

Not light instead of darkness,
Not joy instead of grief;
But brightness in the midnight,
And in the woe relief.

Not gain instead of losses,
Not ease instead of pain;
But balm upon the anguish,
And losses bringing gain.

Not strength instead of weakness
Not smile instead of tears;
Not peace instead of conflict,
Not song instead of fears.

But weakness filled with power,
And tears with radiance spread,
And peace amid the battle,
And song ere fears are fled.

—Norman F. Douty

FRUIT OR LEAVES

E. Clementine Schafer

This little booklet is the outgrowth of a vivid experience. Over a period of several weeks the Holy Spirit exercised and instructed me concerning the Beloved and His vineyard. Then, to my surprise, one morning just as I awoke, the Spirit spoke to my heart and impressed me to put this experience in writing. For, although this is a very personal experience, He made it known that many of you dear ones also are passing through similar experiences, and that this might be a source of encouragement and confirmation to you.

As I wrote, I caught a fresh vision of the heavenly Gardner who says, "My soul desires the first-ripe fruit," and I saw how patiently He is waiting for this precious fruit. I realized also how easy it is to become interested in *working* in His vineyard, and to neglect the cultivation of our own fruit. As the Shulamite in the Song of Solomon said,

"They made me the keeper of the vineyards; but mine own vineyard have I not kept." (Song of Solomon 1:6)

Each phase of this writing became a living experience to me during this time, and the desire to bring forth the fruit which our Beloved is waiting for was increased in my heart.

"Let my Beloved come into His garden, and eat His pleasant fruits." (Song of Solomon 4:16)

INTRODUCTION

When I began to put this experience into writing, something which happened many years ago kept persistently coming to my mind. About a year after I was converted, unsavory stories began to be rumored about a minister in whom I had the utmost confidence. One day while I was in the home of a friend, a couple of ladies dropped in for a while, and in the course of our conversation the minister was mentioned. One of the ladies in particular began to defend him and, among other things, she said: "Now we *know* that Brother R—is all right because many souls are saved in his ministry. And the Bible says, '*By their fruits ye shall know them*'." Like many others, she sincerely believed that if ministers were good preachers, could attract the crowds, and had converts, there was no doubt about their moral integrity nor of God's approval. I heartily agreed with her and loyally defended the minister.

At that time I was just a young girl and so naïve that had I known the truth concerning the preacher, no doubt my faith would have been shattered. But our heavenly Father who will never "suffer us to be tempted above that which we are able to bear," spared me. And by the time I learned the sad truth, my faith was strong enough to stand the shock.

Someone has said, in effect, "The exponents of Truth are often its worst enemies!" It is one of the cleverest strategies of Satan to try to hinder or defeat the cause of Christ through the blunders of those who represent Him. St. Paul deplored the unchristian *walk* of many professors of the faith in his day, calling them enemies of the cross of Christ.

"For many walk, of whom I have told you often, and now tell you even weeping, that they are the enemies of the cross of Christ . . ." (Philippians 3:18)

How often Christ has been reproached, maligned, and despised because of the manifest *lack of Christian character* in those who profess to know Him!

As I grew in grace and in spiritual understanding the Holy Spirit taught me the difference between *service* and *fruit*. Briefly, *service* is what WE DO for Christ; *fruit* is the manifestation of what *WE ARE*—what He *HAS DONE* in us! And, oh, it is much easier *TO DO* than *TO BE*! When we understand this, it is plain to see how one can *serve* God and yet be lacking in essential Christian *character*. This character is the *fruit* by which we are known. What WE ARE glorifies God much more than what WE DO for Him. Have you noticed how much the Apostles wrote in their epistles about the WALK of the believer? A great deal of refining and purifying must be wrought in us by the Holy Spirit before we can really *glorify* God by our daily walk. It is good to be a Christian, even a weak one; but our aim should be to *GLORIFY GOD* in this life. In his letter to Titus (2:10), Paul exhorts us to ADORN the doctrine of God by our conduct. This verse in Moffatt's Translation is beautiful:

" . . . To prove themselves truly faithful at all points, so as to be an ORNAMENT to the doctrine of God our Saviour in all respects."

Oh, that we might GLORIFY Him with the beautiful PRAISE OF OUR WALK!

Since the subject of this writing concerns spiritual husbandry, it might be well to consider the *cycle of seasons* through which we must pass in order to bring forth fruit. In natural and spiritual realms alike there is a time or season for all things. (Ecclesiastes 3:1) It is an established law which we accept without question.

"While the earth remaineth, seed time and harvest, cold and heat, and summer and winter, and day and night shall not cease." (Genesis 8:22)

Everything in God's vast universe follows a cycle: the sun and the moon and the stars wheel in their courses with unerring accuracy;

day invariably follows night, and night follows day; and seed time and harvest have never ceased since this Word was spoken to Noah.

> The covenant of God with men,
> Written with His rainbow pen:
> "Seedtime and harvest shall not fail,
> And though the gates of hell assail,
> My truth and promise shall prevail."

In the cycle of spiritual fruit-bearing no doubt you've recognized each one of the seasons in your own experience.

The coming of Spring, the first season, is welcomed by all. It is the season of *life in manifestation.* After the seeming desolation of wintertime when life lies dormant, it is a thrilling experience to see visible signs of life again.

"For, lo, the winter is past, the rain is over and gone; the flowers appear on the earth; the time of the singing of birds is come, and the voice of the turtle is heard in our land; . . . and the vines with the tender grape give *a* good smell . . ." (Song of Solomon 2)

Springtime is also the time of "new beginnings," and holds forth the promise of fruitfulness.

Then, when we have passed the budding and the flowering stage and have settled down to *growing*, it is Summertime. Not only *life* but also *fruit* is visible at this season. The heat may become oppressive at times, but it is necessary for ripening the fruit. This is the time of *growth*; the time of patient *waiting.*

Next comes the Autumn season, the time for the *gathering* of the fruit. There is a sense of finality about this season. If the harvest is good, it is a time of great rejoicing; if it is a failure, there is remorse, and no doubt the resolve to do better the next time. Fortunately, we pass through many cycles in our experience before the final and general harvest. This affords us opportunity for further cultivation of the fruit.

Not long after harvest the pruning time begins, and usually extends into the Winter season. The once fruit-laden branches are cut back, and there is a sense of desolation, of bareness. But let me assure you that the bareness you then feel is not *barrenness*, as you may be tempted to believe. When one is going through this season it is not an unusual thing to be criticized by those who do not yet understand God's way of purifying souls.

As an illustration, once we thought a certain tree in our yard was not only barren but also dead, and we almost made the mistake of cutting it down; but since we had just moved to that place, and the tree was an unfamiliar one to us, we decided to wait another season. To our utter amazement and delight, that seemingly dead tree burst forth into blossom the following spring! What we thought was a dead tree was a flowering myrtle which looked like a huge bouquet and was a source of much pleasure to us.

During the pruning phase of your experience many things happen to you which you cannot account for. You are filled with a sense of pain and loss. You no longer find the usual pleasure and satisfaction in your devotions. The hours seem "tedious and tasteless," as the song says. Besides all this, your bare branches soon become covered with ice and snow. This is the time to believe God, and to offer the praise of *active faith*. Passive acceptance and endurance of your state is not enough. *When you feel nothing but pain and desolation*, give God the SACRIFICE OF PRAISE, which is well pleasing unto Him. And remember, dear one, you are still joined to the Vine! You are not *barren*; you are only *bare*.

It happened that my recent pruning experience coincided with the time when the vineyards here in California were being pruned, and this increased its significance to me. I'm sure those of you who have had this trying experience will agree that its importance cannot be over emphasized, for every branch that bears fruit must be pruned for greater fruitfulness.

Ever since my conversion the Holy Spirit has constantly stressed the theme of fruitfulness, and pressing it upon my heart and mind, and giving me the desire that this fruit might be brought to maturity in my life—whatever process may be required. Now, after many years and also many "downsittings and uprisings," as the Psalmist said, this desire still burns in my heart. I am very conscious of my own imperfection and unworthiness, but I am confident that the heavenly Gardener will faithfully cultivate every branch that is joined to the Vine, and that His labor and care will not be in vain. All glory and praise belongs to Him now and forever!

Chapter One

A STRANGE VINE

Everything about the life and ministry of our Lord was unique in the truest sense of the word. He gave the world its greatest philosophy and sublimest truths; but His doctrine was not expounded from the pulpits of the Jewish Synagogues nor in the famous Temples of Religion. He taught the people as He walked along the dusty roads or through the cornfields; on the mountainside, by the sea, or in the homes of His friends. He was not clad in priestly vestments, but clothed in a seamless robe. The Words of Life that fell from His lips were not delivered with fine rhetoric, but were taught in simple parables. He used lowly and commonplace things as topics for His illustrations—"The sower and the seed," "The tares and the wheat," "The grain of mustard seed," and many others. All these had for their subjects things which were known and understood by the common people. He was loved by the poor and the outcast; but hated by the scribes and the Pharisees. He spoke with such wisdom and authority that even the unbelieving were compelled to say, "Never man spake like this man!"

During His brief ministry Jesus and His disciples frequently went apart from the multitudes for solitude and prayer. One of these retreats to which they resorted was a garden not far from Jerusalem. Just before the close of His earthly life, after many tense days in the city, Jesus and His little company started for a retreat at this garden. The road led them through fields and vineyards, outside the city walls, across the brook Kedron, to a place near Mount Olivet.

And as they walked and communed together that day amid the numerous vineyards, no doubt our Lord was reminded of *another vine* which had been planted in that very land centuries before. ISRAEL—His own people—had been compared to a *vine* which God had brought out of Egypt, and planted in Palestine, but which, instead of bringing forth good fruit, brought forth only bitter fruit. Their unbelief, rebellion, and unfaithfulness had long "grieved Jehovah at His heart," and through the prophets He had remonstrated with them. Notwithstanding, they had continued in their own ways. When He chastened them, they sought Him and inquired of Him; and He, being full of compassion, forgave them. "Nevertheless they flattered Him with their mouth, and they lied unto Him with their tongues. For their heart was not right with Him, neither were they steadfast in His covenant." Again and again Jehovah was moved with pity for them, and His anger was turned away from them.

As Jesus was thus wrapped in thought, He recalled the prophets who had been sent unto Israel, and He remembered how Jeremiah had pleaded with them:

"Yet I had planted thee a noble vine, wholly a right seed: how then art thou turned into the degenerate plant of a *strange vine* unto Me?" (Jeremiah 2:21)

Ah, Israel had become a *strange vine* because they were estranged from their God. Can we imagine anything more cruelly heartbreaking than the estrangement of those we love?

Ezekiel too had lamented for the princes of Israel when they were in captivity saying:

"Thy mother is like a *vine* . . . planted by the waters: she was fruitful and full of branches . . . But she was plucked up in fury and was cast down to the ground . . . and now she is planted in the wilderness, in a dry and thirsty ground." (Ezekiel 19:10-13)

Because Israel "had forsaken God, the Fountain of living waters," they had been carried away captives to a dry and thirsty land. What folly to think that one can find satisfaction in anything apart from the Lord after having tasted of His goodness! After drinking from the pure and living Fountain of Life it is almost inconceivable to think of drinking of the polluted waters which this world offers!

And with a song of poetic beauty Isaiah also had tenderly entreated them:

"Now will I sing to my wellbeloved a song of my beloved touching his vineyard. My wellbeloved hath a vineyard in a very fruitful hill: and he fenced it, and gathered out the stones thereof and planted it with the choicest vines, and built a tower in the midst of it, and also made a winepress therein: and he looked that it should bring forth grapes, *and it brought forth wild grapes.*" (Isaiah 5:1, 2)

Jehovah's heartbreak and disappointment were poured out through the voice of the prophet as he tried to woo them back to their "first love." Yes, His disappointment was keen. Had He not chosen them and set His love upon them? Had He not made of them a great nation—a witness and the testimony of His power and goodness among the heathen nations? Had He not delivered them again and again from the hand of their enemies? "Yet for all this they sinned still, and believed not His wondrous works."

As the inspired prophet continues his plea, it is a cry wrung from Jehovah's own heart:

"What could have been done more to My vineyard, that I have not done in it? Wherefore, when I looked that it should bring forth grapes, brought it forth wild grapes?" (Isaiah 5:4)

The poignant, sorrowful undertones in Isaiah's song-parable must have recalled to Jesus His own lament over Jerusalem which He had uttered just a few days previously.

"O Jerusalem, Jerusalem, which killest the prophets, and stonest them which are sent unto thee: how often would I have gathered thy children together even as a hen doth gather her brood under her wings, *and ye would not.*" (Luke 13:34)

Perhaps the Lord was reminded of still another prophet who had been sent unto them. Hosea's reproof was abrupt and to the point:

"Israel is an empty (barren) vine, he bringeth forth fruit unto himself... Their heart is divided... For now they shall say, We have no king, because we feared not the Lord..." (Hosea 10:1-3)

What a striking similarity between Israel of Hosea's time and Israel of Jesus' day! Israel of old—captives under the intolerable yoke of the oppressor—crying: "We have no king!" (Because they feared not the Lord.) Israel of Christ's time, also crushed under pagan rule, had seen their King come unto them, meek and riding upon the foal of an ass; but they had rejected Him in their hearts, just as their forefathers had rejected the prophets. (Because they knew not the day of their visitation!) And *very soon* they would be crying as did Israel of old, "*We have no king*... but Caesar!" This would be the public and official rejection of their King. For Jesus *had* come unto His own—"But His own received Him not."

Chapter Two

THE TRUE VINE

Because Israel as a nation had degenerated into a *strange vine*, a *false vine*, which brought forth only bitter fruit, they had been "cut off." Thenceforth, the life of the Root was preserved in David and his posterity, and the "cluster of the vine" became the symbol of the House of David.

Since Jesus was "THE ROOT AND THE OFFSPRING OF DAVID," it was a most propitious time for Him to reveal Himself as the True Vine as He and His disciples walked amid the vineyards that day.

"I am the True Vine, and My Father is the Husbandman." (John 15:1)

With characteristic simplicity Jesus here declares that HE ALONE is the Root, the Fountainhead, the Source of life and fruitfulness. Without the Vine there can be no fruit.

The Father is the Husbandman or Gardner. Under His watchcare the choicest plants are set out in His vineyard. He is responsible for their cultivation—the work of grafting, pruning, watering, and all that is necessary for the welfare and growth of the plants. All barren branches are removed lest they encumber the vines. The wall or hedge around the vineyard is kept in repair so that the wild beasts cannot break through, and He catches "the little foxes" that would spoil the vines when they have tender grapes.

CONDITIONS FOR FRUITFULNESS

1—Pruning or Cleansing

"Every branch in Me—if it bears no fruit, He (the vine-dresser) takes away; and every branch that bears fruit He prunes, that it may bear more fruit." (John 15:2, Moffatt)

The Lord makes it very plain that fruitfulness in the believer's life is *conditional.* The fruitbearing branches must be pruned if they are to bring forth *more* fruit. To one who knows nothing about husbandry, it appears to be a shameful waste to see the vine-dressers pruning the branches, cutting away every bit of superfluous growth. (Of all trees, shrubs and vines, the grapevine is trimmed the closest.) When all the pruning is finished one cannot help but wonder how the branches could ever bear fruit again! But the husbandman is not anxious. He knows the "shoots" or "suckers" cannot bear fruit. They look good, but do nothing but sap the strength from the vines; therefore he cuts them off. He wants fruit—an abundance of fruit.

The knife or pruning hook which is used in the work of pruning the vines reminds us of the Word in Hebrews (4:12):

"For the Word is quick and powerful, and sharper than any two-edged sword . . . and is a discerner of the thoughts and intents of the heart."

Is there anything sharper or more effectual than the living Word as it searches out and reveals the very motives of our hearts? One reason why many of us are not more fruitful is that we do not *ask* the Holy Spirit to scrutinize our hearts, to search out and remove the things which sap our spiritual vigor and hinder fruitfulness. And it is the hold which *self-love* still has upon us which *keeps us from asking.* Nature shrinks from the suffering involved in this pruning process; but, could we realize it, the loss we suffer by not yielding to the pruning and cleansing is incalculable!

Many cannot understand why God's people suffer such cruel and heartbreaking experiences in this life: sorrows, afflictions, disappointments, reproaches, losses, persecutions, and the thousand and one woes that beset our pathway. But when the Father reveals to us that *"all things work together for good;"* that they are for our refining so that we might bring forth the *choicest fruit*, then we rejoice and our hearts overflow with His praise. St. Paul said, "Discipline is never pleasant at the time; it is painful; *but to those who are trained by it; it afterward yields the peace of character.*" (Hebrews 12:11, Goodspeed)

2—Abiding or Union

"Abide in Me and I you. As the branch cannot bear fruit of itself, except it abide in the vine; no more can ye, except ye abide in Me." (John 15:4)

As we have seen that the branches which bear fruit are *pruned branches*, we shall now see that they are also *abiding branches.* The analogy of "The Vine and the branches" beautifully illustrates the union of Christ and the believer. As we abide or remain in union with Him, we experience the merging of our will, affections, desires, and interests. His will becomes our will; His love our love; His way our way; His pleasure our pleasure; His work our work. This merging of the human spirit with the divine is true union. Oh, what a blessed privilege to be thus united with our Lord!

"I'm only a branch, only a branch,
Only a branch in the Living Vine;
Life flowing free from His heart to mine,
I'm only a branch in the Vine."

In ourselves we are helpless to bring forth fruit, and we shall remain so until we learn this *secret of abiding*. For this fruit cannot be produced by self-effort. The natural branches do not have to "struggle and strive" to bring forth fruit! They simply remain on the vine and receive life and nourishment. *It is the life-principal in the vine communicated to the branches which produces fruit.*

Like begets like: grapevines produce grapes, and apple trees bear apples. Likewise, Christ reproduces HIS LIKENESS—His nature or character—in the believer who remains in union with Him. It is only as this fruit is manifest in us, that others can see Christ revealed in His Body.

Chapter Three

WHAT THE FRUIT IS NOT

1—Human Culture

Much that *appears to be fruit* is only the product of human culture. Our social, educational, and cultural life can lift us above the plane of the savage, but cannot deliver us from the "law of sin" that operates our members! It cannot free us from the passions and appetites of the flesh that enslave us! Unless man is *born from above*, made a new creature in Christ, he cannot bring forth the fruit of righteousness. The best that can be wrought in man by human culture, education, social and moral reforms, is only an imitation of the Christian virtues.

We all know that man by his skill can make artificial fruit so nearly perfect in *appearance* that it is difficult indeed to tell it from real fruit; but here the similarity ends. None of us would think of trying to find life-giving nourishment from a bunch of artificial grapes—it is obvious that the *life-elements* are not there. They did not grow on a branch that was nourished by the vine; they were never wet with the dew, nor kissed by the sun! They are not grapes. Thus, "man may imitate the minor moralities and the graces of Christianity, but never the fruit of the Spirit."

2—Gifts of the Spirit

The *gifts* of the Spirit and the *fruit* of the Spirit should not be confused. One is a MEANS to an end; the other is THE END. St. Paul, when writing to the Corinthians (chapter 12), enumerated the *gifts* and ministries of the Spirit, and said: "The manifestation of the

Spirit is given to every man to profit withal." He further clarified this in his letters to the Ephesians (chapter 4), where he explained the *purpose of the gifts*:

> The gifts are given—
> "For the perfecting of the saints,
> For the work of the ministry,
> For the edifying of the body of Christ:
> Till we all come—
> In the unity of the faith . . .
> Unto a perfect (mature) man,
> Unto the measure of the stature of the fulness of Christ:
> That we henceforth—
> Be no more children . . .
> But speaking the truth in love,
> May *GROW UP* into Him in all things . . ."

How plain this is. The *gifts* are given to us for the purpose of taking us through the GROWING UP period (while the fruit of the Spirit is being perfected in us), until we reach MATURITY! But, if we mistake *gifts* for *fruit*, we shall stop short of maturity and bring no fruit to perfection. There is a prevalent tendency among believers today to place the emphasis on gifts, talents, blessings, and ministries, and to forget their *purpose*. This is an indication of spiritual immaturity. If we are not maturing—that is, if we are not being made partakers of His nature, if the fruit of the Spirit is not being produced and perfected and manifested in us—then the ministry and operation of the gifts have not profited us.

"Let us therefore . . . advance toward maturity." (Hebrews 6:1, Goodspeed)

"That is what I pray for—the perfecting of your characters." (2 Corinthians 13:9, Goodspeed)

3—Service and Soul-Winning

The difference between *service* and *fruit* has already been mentioned, but I think it will bear repeating. *Service* is what WE DO for Christ; *fruit* is the manifestation of WHAT WE ARE, or what HE HAS DONE in us. And, while soul-winning can be regarded as the fruit of one's labor, it is *not* the fruit of righteousness, or Christian *character.* Furthermore, the winning of souls cannot be attributed to the labor of a single individual; whereas, the fruit of the Spirit is produced in the individual. Regarding the realm of service and soul-winning Paul said:

"I did the planting, Apollos did the watering, but it was God who made the seed grow. So neither planter nor waterer counts, but God alone who makes the seed grow. Still, though planter and waterer are on the same level, each will get his own wage for the special work that he has done. We work together in God's service . . ." (1 Corinthians 3:6-9, Moffatt)

Thank God, we are laborers together. One plants, another waters, and still another reaps; but unless God gives the increase, we toil in vain. Since this is the case, how can the planter or the waterer or the reaper take credit unto himself? It is a common mistake for those who do the reaping to think that they are responsible for the winning of the souls, forgetting that others plowed and planted and watered. Let us not forget that the laborers are on "the same level" as the Apostle said, and that each will get his own reward for his service. And let us not make the mistake of thinking that *service* is *fruit.* It is possible to render service, and yet be lacking in the fruit of the Spirit; however, *if service is really to glorify God*, it must be coupled with Christian *character.*

Chapter Four

THE FRUIT OF THE SPIRIT

Now we have said a great deal about what this fruit IS NOT. Nevertheless, culture, moral and social reforms, the gifts of the Spirit, and Christian service all have their place. For, although these are not the fruit of the Spirit, they are necessary and commendable in their proper spheres.

We read in James (chapter 5), that the husbandman is patiently waiting for the precious fruit of the earth. What, then, is this fruit?

"But the fruit of the Spirit is love, joy, peace, longsuffering, gentleness, goodness, faith, meekness, temperance . . ." (Galatians 5:22, 23)

Only nine little words are used to describe this fruit, but what a rich harvest is represented! We are given to understand that the fruit of the Spirit is not nine separate fruits, but is a composite fruit made up of these distinct parts—the nine Christian virtues or graces—and is produced in the believer by the indwelling Christ. The possession and manifestation of this fruit is *Christian character.*

THE NINE GRACES

As we define each grace of this nine-fold fruit, may the Holy Spirit give us understanding and deep heart searchings. The first of these graces is *love*; but the Spirit has led me to reverse the order and to take the last grace first. You will see the purpose of this later.

TEMPERANCE

Temperance is, "Continence, self-control, or moderation, principally with regard to sensual or animal appetites. Moderation in eating, drinking, sleeping, etc."

We are not surprised to find this grace in the fruit of the Spirit, for man is a triune being—spirit, soul, and body. Because of the indwelling Spirit, our *bodies* are called His *temple*. For this reason Paul exhorted, "Therefore glorify God in your *body*." Also, "Present your *bodies* as a living sacrifice, holy and acceptable unto God." And again, "But I *keep under my body*, and bring it into *subjection*: lest that by any means, when I have preached to others, I myself should be a castaway." (1 Corinthians 6:19; Romans 12:1; 1 Corinthians 9:27)

St. Paul knew that if the fleshly appetites were indulged *beyond their proper use*, the appetites would become master instead of servant. The *subjection* of the body is by no means the *neglect* of the body, but it is the governing or controlling of the appetites. When the body is *kept under*, the spirit has the ascendancy: it is then the master.

Jesus knew that the fleshly appetites would be a snare to us, therefore He warned us of the danger:

"But take care that your hearts are not *loaded down* with self-indulgence and drunkenness and worldly cares." (Luke 21:34, Goodspeed)

(The word "self-indulgence" is literally "crapulous headache," and means: "sick by intemperance.") This certainly is a common malady today.

Isaiah gives us a graphic picture of the Christian's walk in the following verse:

"They that wait upon the Lord shall renew their strength; they shall mount up with wings as eagles; they shall run, and not be weary; and they shall walk, and not faint." (Isaiah 40:31)

It is the ability to *mount up with wings* (to have communion and attunement with God) that enables us to run and not be weary, and to walk and not faint. But, how can we *soar* in spirit, if the fleshly appetites of our bodies have become *weights* that keep us earthbound? We can readily see that if our spiritual communion with God is hindered, our *walk* will not be victorious. Instead of being able to *run* and *walk* without weariness, we find ourselves so *loaded down* with self-indulgence that we can do nothing but stumble and drag along.

"Wherefore . . . let us lay aside every weight . . . and let us *RUN . . .*" (Hebrews 12:1)

MEEKNESS

This is defined, "Mildness: indulgence toward the weak and erring; patient suffering of injuries without feeling a spirit of revenge; an even balance of all the tempers and passions, the entire opposite to anger."

First of all, we should understand that the grace of meekness is *not*, as some think, the disposition of being easily *cowed*, of being *spiritless*. As we contemplate the life of Jesus, the meekest of the meek, can we imagine Him cringing before His enemies? There was certainly nothing spiritless about our Lord when He scathingly denounced the scribes and the Pharisees for their ungodliness. He fearlessly exposed their hypocritical inconsistencies and their self-righteousness, and called them "white-washed sepulchers," "blind guides," and "a brood of vipers."

"He was oppressed and He was afflicted, yet He opened not His mouth; He is brought as a lamb to the slaughter, and as a sheep before her shearers is dumb, so He opened not His mouth." (Isaiah 53:7)

This is Jesus—the Lamb of God. Although He fearlessly proclaimed the truth, He suffered all the injuries which were inflicted upon Himself without a feeling of revenge, without retaliation. This is *meekness*. Betrayed by Judas, He called him friend. Delivered up to be crucified, He suffered the scourging, the indignities and cruel mockings that were heaped upon Him, without a word. Dying, He prayed, "Father, forgive them; for they know not what they do."

A glimpse of Jesus as the Lamb of God, meek and lowly, melts our hearts and fills us with longing for the beauty of His nature. But this can be imparted only as we humble ourselves, letting Him break the pride and hardness of our natures, and mold us after His own adorable image. Blessed are the meek . . . the followers of the Lamb!

FAITH OR FIDELITY

The Greek word here which was translated "faith" in the King James Version, is translated "fidelity," "faithfulness," or "good faith," in other translations. Adam Clarke also translates it as "fidelity," and defines it as: "Punctuality in performing promises, conscientious carefulness in preserving that which is committed to our trust in restoring it to its proper owner, and in transacting the business confided to us, neither betraying the secret of our friend, nor disappointing the confidence of our employer."

Faithfulness, trustworthiness, loyalty! These three words are conveyed by the definition of "fidelity." What a priceless virtue! Jesus said,

"He that is faithful in that which is least is faithful also in much; and he that is unjust in the least is unjust also in much." (Luke 16:10)

It is in the little, the insignificant things that we are really proved. Sometimes we chafe under the discipline of the daily "grind," but if we would do everything as unto the Lord, the most ordinary duties and work would have meaning. "Life is a school," someone has said, "in which every duty, every opportunity, however insignificant it may seem to us at the moment, is a lesson. *The learning or neglect of these lessons means loss or gain in character.*"

The possession and manifestation of this grace is truly an ornament to the doctrine of our Saviour.

GOODNESS

Adam Clarke's definition for goodness is, "The perpetual desire and sincere study, not only to abstain from every appearance of evil, but to do good to the bodies and souls of men to the utmost of our ability. But this must spring from a good heart—a heart purified by the Spirit of God; and then, the *tree* being made *good*, the *fruit* must be *good also.*"

Many today are misled by the sophistry of this world, and have a very muddled concept of what is right and wrong. They have devised a moral (?) standard that suits themselves. "Plausible sophists who are seared in conscience," Paul calls them. When we are born of the Spirit of God and made new creatures in Christ, our conscience too is renewed; we receive the consciousness of the moral goodness or badness of our conduct and motives, together with the feeling or obligation to do or to be good. Now this faculty, if it is not obeyed, can become calloused or seared, and this is exactly what has happened to many. Paul said,

"Certain individuals have scouted the good conscience and thus come to grief over their faith . . ." (1 Timothy 1:19, Moffatt)

When we understand what "Scout" means, we can see how serious it is to neglect the warnings of conscience. Scout means: "To reject with contempt as something absurd; treat with ridicule;

flout." When we put away a good conscience we make shipwreck of our faith. Paul warned the Christians in his day of the danger of sophistry. In his letter to the Ephesians he exhorted them to avoid all forms of evil, and then said: "Let no one deceive you with specious arguments . . ." (Ephesians 5:3-7, Moffatt)

"Woe to those who call good evil, and call evil good, who make out darkness to be light, light to the darkness, who make out bitter to be sweet, and sweet to be bitter." (Isaiah 5:20, Moffatt)

The sophists, with their deceptive, subtle arguments were calling evil good, and good evil, and thereby deceiving the weak or unwary. This grace of goodness will cause us to *love righteousness* and to follow in its path. It will enable us *to recognize evil* for what it really is, and *to hate it.*

Goodness consists not only of the moral qualities which constitute Christian excellence; it is also benevolence; kindness. This is manifest in deeds and acts of kindness—feeding the hungry, clothing the naked, comforting the sorrowing, relieving the distressed, alleviating pain and suffering—not for reward nor for the praise of men, but because of the goodness of the heart—His goodness wrought in us.

"This too is my own earnest endeavor—*always to have a clear conscience in relation to God and man.*" (Acts 24:16)

GENTLENESS

Gentleness is, "Softness of manners; mildness of temper; sweetness of disposition; tenderness; mild treatment."

Gentleness is an unmistakable mark of Christian refinement—a noble and desirable grace.

"They are as gentle as a lamb." How often this simile is used when describing gentle souls. They are not harsh, rough, or sharp;

but have a mild temper, a sweet disposition. When some are inclined to be otherwise, the gentle ones are like oil on troubled waters.

"A mild reply turns wrath aside, but a sharp word will stir up anger." (Proverbs 15:1, Moffatt)

Even when firmness is necessary in dealing with the obstinate, it is much more effectual when coupled with gentleness. And we all have appreciated the blessing of this rare grace when it has been administered to us, for gentleness is balm to the wounded soul.

LONGSUFFERING

Longsuffering is, "Bearing with injuries or provocation for a long time with patience."

Let us ponder this. We may bear the injuries or provocation for a *long time*, and still not have long-suffering; but when we bear the injuries for a *long time with patience*, that is longsuffering. Then, by defining "patience" we have this definition for longsuffering: "*Bearing injuries or provocation for a long time with uncomplaining endurance.*"

At some time or other each of us has felt the need for this grace and has prayed for it, little realizing how it would be accomplished. Then, in answer to our prayer, the refining process began: there came to us an *injury* or *provocation* of some kind. But by that time, no doubt we had forgotten about praying for longsuffering, so we began to pray for *relief* from our distress. Now what was the Lord to do? Which prayer should He answer? We had prayed first for longsuffering; but just as soon as He began to answer our prayer, we asked Him to stop.

What strange and contradictory creatures we are! James said, "A double minded man is unstable in all his ways." Also, "Ye ask and receive not because ye ask amiss, that ye may consume it upon your lusts." Our first prayer was for our good and God's glory; the second one was for our own selfish purpose.

In His dealings with us, God never forces nor compels; He just makes us willing. Many times He has removed a trial or testing which was sent for our purifying because we were unwilling to go through it. How many of us have come to the place of testing—our Kadesh Barnea—only to draw back! The giants were too big for us!

But with infinite patience the Lord continues to deal with us. Under the gracious influence of the Spirit we see the beauty of His nature, and His love melts our hearts. While we are in this tender mood, He shows us that the fiery trials are sent for our purifying; and we whisper, "Have Thy way, dear Lord." Little by little, we learn the value of the discipline of sorrow and trouble, and are enabled by His grace to "give thanks in all things;" "to take pleasure in reproaches, in necessities, in persecutions, in distresses;" and to "glory in tribulations." (2 Corinthians 12:9, 10; Romans 5:3)

This grace is not wrought in us in a day, but as we continue to surrender our wills, and to rejoice evermore, the virtue of longsuffering is gradually perfected in us.

PEACE

Peace is defined as, "The calm, quiet, and order, which takes place in the justified soul, instead of the doubts, fears, and alarms, and dreadful foreboding." Also, "Harmony between persons; amicable relations."

PEACE—*with God*! Being justified by faith, we have "peace with God," through our Lord Jesus Christ. Oh, to think that we who were once enemies—our hearts hostile to Him in evil doing—are now at peace with God!

The "peace *of* God" is also our portion. "My peace I give unto you," Jesus said, "not as the world giveth." This inward peace is ours upon the condition that we commit all our anxieties unto Him who cares for us.

"Do not be over-anxious about anything, but by prayer and earnest pleading, together with thanksgiving, let your requests be unreservedly made known in the presence of God. And the *peace of God*, which transcends all our powers of thought, will be a *garrison* to guard your hearts and minds in unison with Christ Jesus." (Philippians 4:6, 7, Weymouth)

What comfort and assurance this affords the child of God when attacked by the enemy. The PEACE OF GOD—A GARRISON! When our hearts and minds are assailed by doubts, fears, alarms or dreadful forebodings, we simply commit all to Him, and this transcendent PEACE becomes a FORTRESS—impregnable against the fiery darts of the foe!

"And let the peace of God *rule* in your hearts . . ." (Colossians 3:15)

"Let the *ruling principle* in your hearts be *Christ's peace*, for in becoming members of one body you have been called under its sway." (Colossians 3:15, Goodspeed)

Because this ruling principle of His peace has sway in our hearts, we will also do all within our power to live peaceably with men. "Blessed are the peacemakers: for they shall be called the children of God."

JOY

Joy is the "exultation that arises from a sense of God's mercy communicated to the soul in the pardon of its iniquities, and the prospect of that eternal glory of which it has the foretaste in the pardon of sin."

It is the occasion for *great joy* when the sinner is pardoned of his sins. There is JOY in heaven in the presence of the holy angels; there is JOY in the hearts of God's children because another name has been written down in Glory; and there is JOY in the heart of the forgiven one because it is *his* name!

JOY is one of the first emotions which a believer feels when he receives the witness that his sins have been forgiven. Multitudes testify that it was the JOY they saw manifest in the Christians that drew them to the Lord. When David sinned he lost the joy; when he repented he besought the Lord to restore it unto him, and said, "Then will I teach transgressors Thy ways; sinners shall be converted unto Thee." He knew it was useless to try to convert sinners unless he himself had the JOY OF SALVATION.

Now this JOY in the believer's heart is not dependent upon pleasant circumstances, surroundings or environment. JOY is in inner state produced by the Spirit as we remain in union with Christ. And our capacity for joy depends upon our capacity for suffering.

> "Oh joy that seekest me through pain,
> I cannot close my heart to Thee;
> I trace the rainbow through the rain,
> And feel the promise is not vain
> That morn shall tearless be."

In this song George Matheson beautifully expresses the truth that, "Weeping may endure for a night, but joy cometh in the morning." Our joy is made richer and fuller because of sorrow. The longest night of sorrow will end; but while it lasts it is refining our nature, and increasing our capacity for JOY. For this reason we can *count it all joy* while we are going through the testings.

As chief of the praisers, David incited the worshipers of the Lord to offer unto Him the SACRIFICE of JOY to *sing* for JOY; *shout* for JOY; *leap* for JOY; *dance* for JOY.

"FOR THE JOY OF THE LORD IS YOUR STRENGTH!"

LOVE

Love is, "A strong personal attachment; ardent affection; desire for, and earnest effort to promote, the welfare of another."

Adam Clarke defines it as, "An intense desire to please God and to do good to mankind; *the very soul and spirit of all true religion*; the fulfilling of the law, and that which gives energy to faith itself."

LOVE COMPARED

"I may speak with the tongues of men
    and of angels but if I have no love,
I am a noisy gong or a clanging cymbal;

I may prophesy, fathom all mysteries
    and secret lore,

I may have such absolute faith that I
    can move hills from their place,
    but if I have no love,
I count for nothing;

I may distribute all I possess in
    charity,
I may give up my body to be burnt,
    but if I have no love,
I make nothing of it." (1 Corinthians 13, Moffatt)

These are strong words! It seems inconceivable that one could "speak with the tongues of men and angels," and not have love; or "have the gift of prophecy, and understand all mysteries, and all knowledge, and have all faith . . . and have not love." But to think of one giving *all his goods to charity*, and *his body to be burned . . .* !

Nevertheless, we know it is true. For we have heard eloquent oratory that chilled our souls; and have seen the manifestation of gifts and talents—prophecy, tongues, interpretation of tongues, singing, etc.—which left us untouched and unprofited. But on the other hand, how often we have been comforted, encouraged—yes, even transported with holy delight to the heavenlies, by the ministry of the Spirit through the gifts and talents when they were administered in LOVE!

Since LOVE is "*the very soul and spirit of all true religion*," it is understandable why gifts, charities and sacrifices are NOTHING without it. For, as the body without the spirit is dead, so *religion without love* is dead also.

All are not gifted to speak with the tongues of men and of angels, but we can understand and speak the language of LOVE—if we will!

LOVE DESCRIBED

"Love is very patient, very kind,
Love knows no jealousy;
Love makes no parade,
Gives itself no airs,
Is never rude,
Never selfish,
Never irritated,
Never resentful;
Love is gladdened by goodness,
Always slow to expose,

Always eager to believe the best,
Always hopeful,
Always patient.
Love never disappears." (1 Corinthians 13, Moffatt)

"This love never fails, and is the *means of preserving all other graces*; indeed, properly speaking, it *includes them all*; and all receive their perfection from it." (Adam Clarke)

It is plain to see that LOVE is the means of preserving (keeping intact or existent) the other graces. There can be no joy or peace or longsuffering or gentleness or goodness or fidelity or meekness or temperance *without love.*

When we carefully read the description of LOVE, it is obvious that LOVE *does include all the other graces.* Love is joyful; love is peaceable; love is longsuffering; love is gentle; love is good; love is faithful; love is meek; love is temperate.

Perfection cannot be attained in any single grace *apart from the others.* We cannot decide that we would rather have JOY than meekness, or PEACE than temperance and set about cultivating and perfecting the grace of our choice. They are inseparable. Blended together, they form one harmonious whole!

Now the epitome of all this is: "GOD IS LOVE; and he that dwelleth in love dwelleth in God, and God in him." This is Christian character *in manifestation*; this is *maturity*; this is the *stature of the fulness of Christ*!

CONTINUE IN MY LOVE

"Herein is My Father glorified, *that ye bear much fruit*; so shall ye be My disciples.

"As the Father hath loved Me, so have I loved you; continue ye in My love." (John 15:8, 9)

The Holy Spirit impressed me very much with these two verses. Notice that *up to* verse nine, Jesus had been talking about FRUIT. Then in verse nine, it is LOVE. Evidently He was showing the disciples that the FRUIT of the Spirit is comprehended in LOVE—or, that LOVE *is the sum total of all the graces*. As we have already seen that *love includes all the graces* it would seem that the sudden transition from the word FRUIT to LOVE in verses eight and nine would also indicate this. We see the same transition again in verses 16 and 17:

"I have ordained that ye should go and *bring forth FRUIT*, and that your fruit should remain . . .

"These things I command you, that ye *LOVE one another*."

And now we hear Him saying to us, "Continue ye in My love." In other words "Stay in My love; persist in My love; persevere in My love; be constant in My love . . ."

"Love that no tongue can teach
Love that no thought can reach:
No love like His.
God is its blessed source,
Death can ne'er stop its course,
Nothing can stay its force,
Matchless it is."

Chapter Five

FRUIT OR LEAVES

Now we may believe in an abstract way all that has been said, and we may theorize about it, but this will not produce nor perfect the FRUIT in our lives. Spiritual maturity is not attained at once. By the miracle of the *new birth* we receive a *new nature*—the nature of Christ, although still undeveloped. Full stature—Christian character in manifestation—is attained only by the *process of growth.* As in the natural, so it is in the spiritual—the seed is sown or the vine is planted as the case may be; then comes the process of growth—"first the blade, then the ear, after that the full corn in the ear." This requires a certain period of time, the completion of the cycle.

We are often grieved because of the traits of the *old nature* manifest in us, and long for the graces of true Christian character. But how to attain this is the question. If we sincerely want to overcome our faults, they must be recognized and called by name. In this way we bring a secret enemy out into the open, and this is the first step toward victory. It is easy to recognize the sins of the "prodigal sons" who leave the Father's house; but sometimes it is difficult to discern the sins of the "brothers" who remain at home. The prodigal of whom Jesus spoke was guilty of the "sins of the flesh;" the prodigal's brother was guilty of the "sins of the spirit" or disposition. We may not be committing the sins of wantonness, drunkenness, licentiousness and such; but what of the anger, the sullenness, the discontent, and envy that was revealed in the prodigal's brother? We are exhorted by St. Paul to cleanse ourselves of everything that defiles *body* or *spirit* (2 Corinthians 7:1), and to perfect holiness in the fear of the Lord.

After recognizing and acknowledging our faults, we must deplore them and "take sides" with the Spirit against SELF; then yield to the *purifying work* of the Spirit, for He alone knows how to accomplish this work in us.

"Whatever light, whatever feeling we may possess is all a delusion if it lead us not to the real and constant practice of dying to self. We cannot die without suffering . . . He who sees in us what we cannot see, knows full well where the blow should fall . . . Pain is only felt where there is life (self-life), and where there is life, is just the place where death is needed. Our Father wastes no time by cutting into parts which are already dead . . ." (F. Fenelon)

Thus, it is by yielding to God as He purifies, purges, or prunes us that the self-life is destroyed, and the fruit of the Spirit is perfected in us. And it is left up to us whether or not we will be barren or fruitful; whether or not we have little or much fruit.

The Scriptures have reported many concrete examples of those who were *barren branches*; and although we do not like to dwell on the negative, we cannot close our eyes and pretend that barrenness does not exist. Let us not forget that although Israel as a nation was highly favored of God—though they saw manifold miracles, signs and wonders which Jehovah wrought on their behalf; though they ate angels' food, and were guided like a flock through the wilderness—they were finally cut off as a barren branch because they did not bring forth the fruit of righteousness.

"Now all these things happened unto them for examples *and they are written for our admonition*." (1 Corinthians 10:11)

We cannot afford to take our spiritual state for granted. We cannot afford to be complacent. As it was in Israel's time, so it is today. There are multitudes among the believers who appear to be fruitful, though in reality they have *little fruit*, but *many leaves*. They have not yet been cut off as hopelessly barren branches—they still have little strength—but they are blind to their true spiritual state. Some of them are in demand in certain religious circles because of their talents and personalities; and they derive a kind of satisfaction from this. But their lives are almost devoid of the *fruit which glorifies God.*

This does not necessarily mean that they are guilty of the grosser sins; but they have allowed things to come into their lives which hinder fruitfulness. However, they could still be fruitful branches if they would submit to the process of cleansing or pruning; if they let the Holy Spirit remove the things which have sapped their strength, so that new life and vigor could be imparted unto them from the Vine. How much better it would be to suffer the loss of all things than to be cut off as a useless branch! Oh, when the time of harvest comes, what will our harvest be? FRUIT or FADED LEAVES?

> "Nothing but leaves at the time of the harvest;
> No golden fruit to lay at His feet.
> The summer is ended, the harvest is over—
> Nothing but leaves, vain-glory's deceit."

FRUITFUL BRANCHES

We are glad the Bible also abounds with examples of those who were *fruitful branches*—a great multitude who lived for the glory and praise of God. A few instances may inspire and encourage us.

JOB

"Ye have heard of the patience of Job," said the apostle James. Now Job did not get this grace of patience simply by wanting or wishing for it! It was wrought in his nature by the many afflictions and testings which he endured.

Although suddenly bereaved of his children and despoiled by robbers he could still praise God and say, "The Lord gave, and the Lord hath taken away: blessed be the name of the Lord!" Then, when Satan was given permission to afflict him with "sore boils from the sole of his foot unto his crown," his wife "added insult to injury" by ridiculing his faith, telling him to "curse God and die." And, as if that were not enough, his three friends who came to comfort him decided he needed reproof, and told him he was just reaping what he had sown. (Job 4:8) "Miserable comforters," indeed, they proved to be.

Still that righteous patriarch retained his integrity, and said: "But He knoweth the way that I take: when He hath tried me, I shall come forth as gold." And after a prolonged season of refining, Job received a "double-portion blessing" from the hand of the Lord, and in his *latter days* he was more fruitful than in the former ones. His victorious life speaks to those of us who are living in these *latter days.*

JOSEPH

Joseph, likewise, is one of the most beloved characters in the Old Testament. The psalmist said of him:

"Whose feet they hurt with fetters; *he was laid in iron.* Until the time that His word came: *the Word of the Lord tried him.*" (Psalm 105:18, 19)

It was through that very ordeal, while Joseph was "laid in iron"—imprisoned and disgraced—that spiritual strength and hardness like iron entered into his soul. It is at such times that true character is formed. Someone has said, "Temptations, which cause the shallow, unstable man to fall, only strengthen the faith and perfect the character of the true Christian."

The familiar story of surpassing beauty and tenderness tells how Joseph was sold into slavery by his brethren; how he became the governor of Egypt, and was instrumental under God in saving the nation, and his own kindred also, from famine and death. Thus, as Joseph said, "God hath caused me to be fruitful in the land of my affliction." (Genesis 41:52) And later, when his father Jacob was dying, the blessing which he pronounced upon Joseph was a glorious tribute to this faithfulness to God.

"Joseph is a *fruitful bough*, even a fruitful bough *by a well*; whose branches run over the wall." (Genesis 49:22)

MOSES

Moses did not attain his spiritual height in an hour or a day. He was brought up in the royal household of Egypt as the son of Pharaoh's daughter; but the time came when he refused that honor, and chose to identify himself with his own people in their afflictions. He knew in his heart that he was a man of destiny.

However, before God could entrust to Moses the leadership of his people, he had to undergo a period of discipline and testing for forty years—forty years on the backside of a desert . . . tending sheep! What a strange way we may think for a man to receive his training—a man destined to be the leader of a great nation! But God's ways are not man's ways! Such discipline was indeed rigid for one who had been reared in luxury and ease as the son of a king's daughter; but it was the making of him: for it was afterward recorded that *Moses was the meekest man on earth*!

Time would fail to tell of the men and women of God who, down through the ages, triumphed over the world, the flesh, and the devil, and attained the stature of spiritual giants. All these, though they are dead, still speak to us by their faith and fruits of righteousness.

And in our day—if we have eyes to see—there are multitudes "unknown and unsung," whose names also are being added to the list of heroes in God's "Hall of Fame." This great company represents every tongue and tribe and nation. Among them are those who take the Word of Life to them who "sit in darkness;" those who feed the hungry, clothe the naked, care for the sick and helpless—because the love of Christ constrains them. Multitudes of these chosen ones are living in countries ravaged by war, and are victims of the cruelty of godless men. Yet, in the face of privation, persecution and torture, they manifest the Spirit of Christ, and pray for their enemies. Thousands are making the supreme sacrifice of giving their lives rather than deny Him who died for them.

Many are living apparently ordinary lives, but their conflicts and triumphs are by no means ordinary; for their days are filled with deeds of rare devotion to Christ and humanity. If we could see "behind the scenes" in the drama of their lives we would be amazed at their faith and courage in adversity; their patience and endurance in trials and afflictions; their love and loyalty in the dark hours of confusion and misunderstanding.

Yes, in all these things they are "more than conquerors through Christ." There is a quiet calm and peace in their souls that this world cannot take away. There is a light in their eyes that tells us they are looking "not at the things which are seen, but at the things which are unseen"—the glories beyond this veil of unreality. And the pure incense of love and adoration for Christ burns on the altars of their hearts, for their "affections are on things above, not on things of this earth." Truly, these shall bring forth a rich harvest of fruit for God's glory.

Chapter Six

VINTAGE TIME

In the meantime we are nearing the end of the cycle of fruit-bearing. Harvest time is coming. And while the fruit on the vine is ripening, the leaves are fading and dying. There is a certain time during the process of growth when the fruit "sets." In other words, it reaches the stage where further care and cultivation cannot improve it. The productiveness of the branches—the quality and quantity of the fruit—is then decided. Many have already reached this place in their experience. If so, there is nothing that can be done to improve their spiritual state; neither are they interested in doing so. On the other hand, if we are concerned about our state, and sincerely desire to improve it, this in itself is evidence that we have not yet become "set."

"The past is no longer ours: it is gone. Tomorrow may never be ours. But today—the living present is ours. Let us forget the past and make full use of the present." And when the heavenly Gardener comes into His vineyard to gather His fruit, God grant that there will be a rich harvest—thirtyfold, sixtyfold—yes, even a hundredfold fruit, *more fruit*, MUCH FRUIT . . . !

"For whom He did foreknow, He also did predestinate to be *conformed to the image of His Son* that He might be the firstborn among many brethren." (Romans 8:29)

Conformed to the image of His Son! This is the image in which man was created in the beginning, which was lost to the fall, and which is being restored in those who are called according to His purpose.

Conformed to the image of His Son! For this we were foreknown and predestinated. Does not your heart thrill at the very thought? Born to bear His image! Chosen from the foundation of the world "to show forth the praises (virtues) of Him who hath called us out of the darkness into His marvelous light!"

Conformed to the image of His Son! This is the possession and manifestation of the nine-fold fruit of the Spirit, the Christian virtues—Christian character in manifestation.

Conformed to the image of His Son! We know full well that we have not attained; that we have not reached the ultimate in God's purpose in us; but *we are in the process of becoming*. By His infinite grace we are being made partakers of His divine nature . . . We are growing up into Him in all things . . . We are coming unto the measure of the stature of the fulness of Christ . . . We are *being* conformed to His image . . .

Conformed to the image of His Son! This is the glorious destiny of the lovers of God . . . That we might be TO THE PRAISE OF HIS GLORY. For when the Father sees the image of His Son in us, HE IS GLORIFIED.

I WILL WORK
A WORK IN YOUR DAYS

Frances Metcalfe

With sublime imagery the Prophet-Poet Habakkuk dramatically portrays the mighty End-time work of God. "He that hath an ear, let him hear what the Spirit saith unto the church" through this inspired word. "Behold ye among the heathen, and regard, and wonder marvelously: for I will work a work in your days, which ye will not believe, though it be told you." (Habakkuk 1:5)

Like many of the prophecies, Habakkuk's vision had a partial, local fulfillment; but that the complete fulfillment occurs in the End-time cannot be disputed by those who are led of the Spirit. The Apostle Paul quotes this verse in the beginning of the Gospel dispensation, (Acts 13:41) as looking forward to a future accomplishment. Other verses which follow, plainly set the date as being just before the return of the Lord of Glory. "Let your hands be strong, ye that hear in these days, these words by the mouth of the prophets." Amen!

The revelation of Habakkuk is one that should cause God's people to greatly wonder and rejoice. Of a truth all who have been given even so much as a glimpse into the Latter Rain, End-time work of the Lord, are amazed and filled with praise. Yet strangely enough there are many who will not believe it, even though it be told to them. It is certain that so great and far-reaching is God's program that none of us have sufficient faith to believe whole-heartedly in the complete work. "Lord, we believe, help Thou our unbelief."

The first chapter opens with a crying heart. Out of the midst of a vision of terrible wickedness and violence, the prophet calls upon the Lord, "O Lord how long shall I cry . . . and Thou wilt not save?" Does that cry find an echo in your praying heart today? How quickly the Lord answers him, and us. "Behold ye among the heathen, and wonder marvelously: for I will work a work in your days." Then God gives to him a picture of judgment. A bitter and hasty nation arises which marches through the breadth of the land, possessing dwelling places that are not theirs. Not only does this army march, but their horses are described as being fiercer than wolves and swifter than eagles, flying to eat the prey! Habakkuk interrupts this horrible picture to cry out in faith: "O Lord my God, mine Holy One, we shall not die. O Lord, Thou hast ordained them for judgment; and O mighty God, Thou has established them for correction." Judgment—correction—"so far, and no farther!" God is still on the Throne!

INTERVENTION!

"Intervene," cries the prophet. "Spare the righteous." He asks for and expects an answer from the Lord. Throughout the world today, the Spirit-controlled intercessors are repeating this cry. We too ask, and we, too, expect an answer from heaven. Habakkuk was not disappointed, nor shall we be. "I will stand upon my watch to see what He will say unto me, and what I shall answer when I am reproved. And the Lord answered me." Praise His Name! The Lord still answers those who cry and watch in the prayer-tower. God's answer was not for the prophet's ears alone, but was for all who would hear. He must give the word to the people, and so too must we.

"Write the vision, and make it plain upon tables, that he may run that readeth it. For the vision is yet for an appointed time, but at the end it shall speak, and not lie." The Leeser translation, from the Hebrew, makes this more explicit. "For the vision is yet for an appointed time, and it speaketh of the end, and will not deceive." "Though it tarry, wait for it; because it will surely come, it will not tarry." How significant that the "it" is changed to "He" in the book of Hebrews, where we read in chapter 10:37: "He that shall come, will come, and will not tarry." This quotation identifies this word with the return of Christ.

In Habakkuk 2:4, we find the first utterance of the battle cry of the Reformation, "The just shall live by faith," repeated in Romans 1:17. Martin Luther was gripped by these six little words, and shook the nations with them in the 16th century. Justification by faith alone, through grace, shall likewise save multitudes in the 20th century! Descending from the height of this tremendous revelation, the prophet describes the final end of those who have dealt such death and destruction upon many nations. "Shall they not rise up suddenly that shall bite thee? . . . Because thou hast spoiled many nations, all the remnant of the people shall spoil thee." We shall soon see this word fulfilled in connection with those who have wrought great havoc. He ends the chapter with a trumpet call to the nations. "The Lord is in His holy temple: let all the earth keep silence before Him."

WRATH AND MERCY

In chapter three we come to one of the most beautiful portions in all literature. The prophet, anointed with the Holy Spirit, bursts forth with a magnificent psalm of prayer and prophecy. This prayer was recorded at the Throne of Grace and is sure to be answered! "O Lord, I have heard Thy speech, and was afraid: O Lord, revive Thy work in the midst of the years, in the midst of the years make known; in wrath remember mercy."

The one concern of the prophet's heart was that the Lord's work should not suffer loss, because of violence and judgment in the earth. This should be the consuming passion of the praying saints today, that the Gospel should not suffer loss, because of the turmoil in the earth. O, that in some way, in the midst of the years of wrath, there might come a mighty manifestation of mercy and grace. This one verse alone is sufficient authority for praying and expecting a revival in the midst of judgment. The rendering of this verse in the Leeser translation is poignant with meaning. "O Lord, I have heard Thy fame, and was afraid, O Lord revive Thy work—(here there is a break in his utterance). In the midst of the years of sorrow revive Thou it—in the midst of the years make it (God's work) known!"

Then in vision, the prophet was shown the answer to his prayer, and in this prophecy we have a picture of the Latter Rain Revival. "God came from Teman," the R.V. and Leeser render this, and to the end of the chapter, not "came," but "cometh," the future tense! "Teman" means south-land, or wilderness. God comes to His people in the midst of spiritual drought. "Who is she that cometh out of the wilderness leaning upon the arm of her beloved?" He must meet His Church where she is, and bring her out upon His arm." "And the Holy One from Mount Paran." "Paran" means to glow, to be bright and illuminated. Praise God for the wonderful light which is manifest even now to those who are preparing for the Latter Rain. "His brightness was like the sunlight, rays streamed forth out of His side." (Leeser) This closely fits Malachi's word concerning the "Sun of Righteousness shall arise with healing in His wings."

The next line is very significant. "There was a hiding of His power." A secret revelation, to His chosen ones; a mighty working of His Spirit, which is even now in operation! Hidden now, soon to be manifest! Still quoting from Leeser, "Before Him went the pestilence, and fiery bolts went forth at His feet." Pestilence with war! "He stood forward and made the earth to tremble. He looked and dispersed nations . . . the ways of the world are His. Thou didst ride upon Thine horses and Thy chariots of salvation. Thy bow was made quite bare . . . the paths to the tribes were a sure word. Thou didst cleave the earth with rivers." Streams in the desert—rivers and floods in the wilderness!

MANIFEST SALVATION!

"Thou wentest forth for the salvation of Thy people, even for victory, with Thine anointed." (Shall we be in that number?) Surely this is a great manifestation of salvation and deliverance brought by the direct intervention of the Lord, through His anointed ones! In the midst of world-wide judgment, here is a world-wide visitation of salvation! Habakkuk ends this prophecy with a song of praise. Looking forward to this triumphant work, he rejoices, even though he finds himself in a period of unfruitfulness and drought. We, too, may join in this victory song, rejoicing in the hope that in the midst of the years of wrath, we shall see the fulfillment of this prophecy, and by the grace of God, actually participate in bringing it to pass!

"Yet will I rejoice in the Lord, I will exult in the God of my salvation, for the Lord eternal is my strength, and maketh my feet fleet as those of the hinds, He will cause me to tread on the high places." Glory!

THE KING'S FEAST

Frances Metcalfe

The hour is at hand for the King of Glory to show forth to His subjects the "riches of His glorious Kingdom, and the honor of His excellent majesty." He is preparing a great feast, and will assemble His own to His table, where He will feed them upon the riches of His Living Word, and give them to drink of the new wine of the Kingdom. This feast is not a feast for those still in the highways and by-ways of worldliness and sin. It is a feast for those of His own household, His servants and subjects. It must take place before His great worldwide Harvest feast of ingathering.

The Lord's own royal line, the Kingdom saints, are now being prepared to rule and reign with Him, when the Kingdom of Heaven is openly established on the earth. They are to be given a "Preview," as it were, of the riches and power and glory of that reign. They are to "taste of the powers of the age to come." The mysteries of the Kingdom, so long hidden, are now being unlocked, and revealed to humble, simple-hearted believing ones. Jesus spoke of these as "babes," and thanked the Father that He had hidden these things from the wise and prudent and revealed them unto babes. The Spirit is now revealing these mysteries of the Kingdom to those who are willing and able to receive them. Of them this word may be truly spoken, "Blessed are your eyes, for they see; and your ears for they hear. For verily I say unto you, that many prophets and righteous men have desired to see those things which ye see, and have not seen them; and to hear those things which ye hear, and have not heard them." (Matthew 13:16, 17)

THE BANQUETING HOUSE

A beautiful poetic picture of the King's feast, is found in the first chapter of the book of Esther. The King Ahasuerus, (Xerxes) who reigned over a great and far-reaching kingdom, made a special feast for his princes and subjects. There was a great desire in his heart to reveal the riches and glories of his kingdom, and the honor of his excellent majesty. (Esther 1:3, 4) This royal feast was held in the court of the garden of the king's palace. In the Song of Solomon this court is referred to as the "banqueting house," or "house of wines."

What a privilege to enter into the king's hidden garden! The rich exotic beauty of a Persian garden is redolent with rare oriental perfumes. The rioting color of the flowers, the song of the birds, the floating strains of a beautiful melody, played upon stringed instruments, all tend to entrance the one whose feet tread the paths of the sacred, hidden, enclosed garden of the king! "The King hath brought me to His banqueting house, and His banner over me was love."

Entering the house itself we find curtains of fine linen, white and green, and blue, fastened with cords of purple silk, to silver rings on pillars of marble. The couches were fashioned of gold and silver, placed upon a pavement of mosaic marble of mother of pearl. This beautiful picture in Esther is all symbolic of the ravishing beauty and refreshing rest to be found in the King's house.

THE GOLDEN VESSELS

The vessels chosen for the king's table were of pure wrought gold. "And they gave them to drink in vessels of gold, the vessels being diverse one from another, and royal wine in abundance, according to the bounty of the King." (Esther 1:7) No other vessel is fit to receive the royal wine. How significant that in the Hebrew this reads, "The wine of the Kingdom!" God's people are fainting for the strength, and joy, and love, and life which is to be poured out in the new wine of the Kingdom. The dispensation of grace which began with the outpouring of the physical life of the Son of Man, typified by the communion cup, is to end with the outpouring of the divine life of the Son of God! The "Latter Rain" is nothing less than the effulgence of the resurrection life of the Sun of Righteousness, poured out in abundant, overflowing measure, first upon His own household and servants, and then upon the multitudes. As Jesus took the cup upon that memorable night of the Last Supper, He spoke these significant words. "But I say unto you, I will not drink henceforth of this fruit of the vine, until that day when I drink it new with you in my Father's Kingdom." (Matthew 26:29)

"But in a great house there are not only vessels of gold and of silver, but also of wood and of earth; and some to honor and some to dishonor. If a man therefore purge himself from these, he shall be a vessel unto honor, sanctified and meet for the Master's use, and prepared unto every good work." (2 Timothy 2:20, 21) The King will choose only golden vessels for the royal feast. Vessels put through the fire, melted and molded and fashioned by His own hand, thoroughly purged and prepared. For many years He has been seeking out these vessels. What suffering and tribulation these have known. What anguish and pain, what refining fires. But they have stood upon His Word. "He knoweth the way that I take: when He hath tried me I shall come forth as gold." Only those who are willing to be thus separated and prepared can be chosen to receive the wine of the Kingdom.

COME AND DINE

"And the drinking was according to the King's order, without compulsion." (Esther 1:8, Leeser) All were freely bidden to the feast, all were given in abundance according to the bounty of the King, but none were compelled to eat or drink. It is difficult for us to realize that many who come to the Lord's table will go away empty! The King enjoins, "Drink, yea, drink deeply beloved," but many will only taste and sip! Some will not heed the invitation to all, and will even despise the Lord's table, and consider it unholy.

"Also Vashti the queen made a feast." At the same time that the King was feasting his subjects, Vashti, a type of the organized worldly church, was also feasting many at her table. The King commanded that she come to His feast, but this she refused to do. Because of this she was set aside, and lost her right to reign with Him. The modern church is feeding the multitudes upon man-made philosophies and doctrines, upon stale bread, mouldy and tasteless; the wine of the Spirit is spurned. Turn from this table, and feast with the King!

The Kingdom of God is at hand! The King is even now calling us to a great feast. The vessels of gold are being placed upon the table, ready for the outpoured wine! All glory to His Matchless Name. "Thine is the Kingdom and the power and the glory forever."

ALERT!

Frances Metcalfe

Alert!" The order is issued from the commanding officer, and every man of the regiment is brought to attention. Uniform intact, weapons at hand, every man at his post. Awake and ready to go into action at a moment's notice! Danger is near, the enemy must be faced and encountered, and every man is alert, ready for defense or attack!

The Holy Spirit has issued an "Alert" command to the entire Church of the Living God. The greatest battle of the ages is just ahead, and the Lord of Hosts, the Lord Mighty in Battle, is mustering His earthly army, the soldiers of the Cross. Every man must be clad in the whole armor of God, sword in hand. The prophet Nahum, speaking in the Spirit of this day, "the day of His preparation," issued a stirring command: "He that dasheth in pieces is come up before thy face: keep the munition, watch the way, make thy loins strong, fortify thy power mightily."

> "Raise the battle cry, see, the foe is nigh!
> Lift the standard high, for the Lord.
> Gird your armor on, stand firm every one,
> Rest your cause upon His Holy Word!"

HE THAT DASHETH IN PIECES

Satan—the prince of this world, the destroyer, as this word is rendered in some translations, he who is come "to steal, to kill and to destroy," the whole earth is filled with the terror of his violence. The heavens above are made horrible with smoke and fire, and death rains from the skies; to the depths of the seas he carries multitudes of his victims; and through every land he stalks with famine and pestilence, violence and bloodshed. His time is short and his wrath is great! Outwardly we see his forces on every hand despoiling the nations; but behind that which is visible, we see with eyes of the Spirit, the spiritual forces of Satan marshalled and arrayed for Zion's war. He is out to make war on the saints and to overthrow them. Leeser's translation reads; "The destroyer is come up against thee, to enclose thee with works of siege." What a picture of the Church in this hour, surrounded, and undermined with the works of the enemy. Alert! Church of the Living God, you are face to face with the arch-enemy of the Lord Jesus Christ. You cannot, you dare not slumber in this hour. To do so is to invite certain defeat, and eternal loss in the Kingdom of God!

KEEP THE MUNITION

"Defend the fortress," in another rendering. We must sing anew this stirring song: "Hold the fort, for I am coming; Jesus signals still. Wave the answer back to heaven, By Thy grace, we will." The Church must be set for the defense of the Gospel, prepared to war a good warfare, and to contend earnestly for the faith once delivered to the saints. For the past thirty years or more, the Church as a whole has been steadily yielding ground, retreating bit by bit, appeasing, compromising, growing weaker, and more ineffectual with every passing day. But the Spirit of God has called this retreat to a dead halt! "Strengthen those things which remain." We dare not yield another inch of ground, we must be prepared at any cost to wrestle, to contend, and having done all, to stand!

WATCH THE WAY

"What I say, I say unto all, watch." Our Lord again and again commanded watchfulness in the evil day. "Watch and pray, always that ye may be accounted worthy to escape all these things which shall come to pass, and to stand before the Son of Man." "Watchman, what of the night? The watchman said, The morning cometh, and also the night." The morning of translation for the saints, the night of tribulation for the unsaved. Isaiah, called to be a watchman in his day, cried, "My Lord, I stand continually upon the watchtower in the daytime, and I am set in my ward every night." The Church at last awakening from her disastrous slumber, is commanded now to watch and pray as did Isaiah. Vigilance in prayer. The very word, "Alert," is derived from the French word, "*Alerte*," meaning to be on a watchtower or height, on a look-out. "Instant in prayer," said the Apostle Paul, be one of God's minute-men! The mid-night hour approaches, and as Paul Revere rode out into the night, sounding the alarm, calling the "minute-men" into action, so God's minute-men and women, must be ready at any moment for the call of the Spirit. "And that, knowing the time, that now it is high time to awake out of sleep: for now is our salvation nearer than when we believed." (Romans 13:11)

MAKE THY LOINS STRONG

"Stand therefore, having your loins girt about with truth." So spake the Spirit through Paul. Likewise He spake again through Peter. "Wherefore gird up the loins of your mind, be sober, and hope to the end for the grace that is to be brought unto you at the revelation of Jesus Christ." (1 Peter 1:13) Throughout the Word of God, the girding of the loins typifies a preparation for action, and the loosing of the girdle typifies the preparation for rest, or a loss of power. When the children of Israel were to be led out of Egypt, they were commanded to gird their loins, and put on their shoes. Woe unto the one who was not prepared to flee when the order came. So in this hour the Church is called anew to gird herself with God's whole Word, the Truth. Thus girded, she is ready for defense or advance.

FORTIFY THY POWER MIGHTILY

The command to the Church is to seek for a mighty enduement of the Spirit of God for the evil days just ahead. This is the hour of preparation, the hour to "seek the Lord," till He comes and rains righteousness upon us. The Lord has provided a double portion of strength and grace for his Church in the End-Time. He must finish His work in the earth, a quick work, cut short in righteousness. He must sanctify and bring forth His Church, holy and triumphant. "Who is she that looketh forth as the morning, fair as the moon, clear (pure) as the sun, and terrible as an army with banners?" Without this fortification of His Spirit, the Church would go down in ignominious defeat; with it, she shall emerge triumphant, with much spoil!

Alert! God's command to the Church, and to you as an individual, is three-fold. Be watchful and vigilant in prayer. Gird your mind with His Word, the Truth, and seek for a mighty enduement of His Spirit. "He that dasheth in pieces is come up before thy face: keep munition, watch the way, make thy loins strong, fortify thy power mightily."

LIVING THE LIFE OF PRAISE

Frances Metcalfe

INTRODUCTION

We are living in a time when thrilling new discoveries are being made almost daily. And whether these discoveries are in the realm of nuclear Science or of Biblical Archeology—the two areas of investigation which are said to be the most rewarding—the life of each of us is affected, at least indirectly, by each new disclosure.

In the realm of THE SPIRIT too, man is making wonderful new discoveries—or rediscoveries. For this is an hour of Revelation, in which Jesus Christ is increasingly manifesting Himself among men! The Holy Spirit is being outpoured throughout all the earth and among all true believers. The great Day of the Lord is drawing near!

Some of the greatest discoveries the "sons of God" are making are in the realm of God's nuclear power—the "dunamis" of the Spirit. This omnipotent power—of which the nuclear energy in the physical universe is a fitting symbol—is released and channeled into the earth by faith and PRAISE. When God is actively and fervently and continuously praised, this dunamis power is readily manifested. For praise provides a "habitation," an atmosphere, in which God can move and act.

In both the Old and New Testaments there is much instruction about praising the Lord. But each generation seems to have to rediscover this truth. In the days of Israel's greatness, King David knew the secret of this power. Not only did he practice praise himself, but he taught all Israel how to praise God. And he set apart several thousand chosen ones to be trained to minister continually unto the Lord in praise.

This power of praise was likewise known and manifested in the Christian Church, both in early and later days. It was prayer and praise that prepared the disciples for the descent of the Holy Spirit on the Day of Pentecost, and drew Him to their hearts. And in the succeeding ages, praise has again and again released this power on earth.

We are indeed thankful that, many years ago, the blessed Holy Spirit filled our vessels also, as we lifted up our hearts and voices in loving praise. And we rejoice that He has set us apart too for this high and holy and eternal ministry, even while we are still on earth. He has continued to teach us, as no doubt He is teaching you how to praise Him more perfectly, fully and acceptably. In 1952 we were inspired to write and circulate LIVING THE LIFE OF PRAISE. It has proved to be a blessing and source of edification to many who are discovering the power of praise in their own lives. Because we have received so many requests for additional copies, we have now published it again.

MAKING HIS PRAISE GLORIOUS—a companion writing which was included in the first edition—is being published separately.

We are now making astounding new discoveries in this realm of praise, and perhaps we can soon share them also with you. The Praisers of God are increasing in number and power. May you be found in that glorious number, transformed, illuminated and glorified by His Divine Power! And may we learn together how to live the Life of Praise and glorify the name of Jesus in our generation.

—Frances Metcalfe

AS LONG AS I LIVE

As long as I live it shall be a rule engraved on my tongue to bring praise like fruit for an offering and my lips as a sacrificial gift. I will make skillful music with lyre and harp to serve God's glory, and the flute of my lips will I raise in praise of His rule of righteousness. Both morning and evening I shall enter into the Covenant of God and at the end of both I shall recite His commandments, and so long as they continue to exist, there will be my frontier and my journey's end.

Therefore I will bless His name in all I do, before I move hand or foot, whenever I go out or come in, when I sit down and when I rise, even when lying on my couch I will chant His praise.

My lips shall praise Him as I sit at the table which is set for all, and before I lift my hand to partake of any nourishment from the delicious fruits of the earth.

When fear and terror come, and there is only anguish and distress, I will still bless and thank Him for His wondrous deeds, and meditate upon His power, and lean upon His mercies all day long. For I know that in His hand is justice for all that live, and all His works are true. So when trouble comes or salvation I will praise Him just the same.

—Praising God at All Times (Column X),
Manual of Discipline, Dead Sea Scrolls

"You who stand or abide in the House of the Lord, who dwell in the courts of our God, must, beyond all others, abound in thanksgiving. From you unceasing praise is expected." (Psalm 135:2)

—C. H. Spurgeon

THE UNIVERSAL CALL TO PRAISE

From the heights of the holy mountain of our God—the Heavenly Zion—a stirring call is trumpeted! Universal in scope, supernatural in glory, it rings from one end of the heavens to the other; it descends and resounds throughout the earth; it shatters every resisting force and penetrates the darkness of the ultimate depths,—IT IS THE CALL TO PRAISE THE LIVING GOD!

For generations, inspired mortals have lifted up their voices and re-echoed this call among men. They have painstakingly recorded it and preserved it in Holy Writ, translating it from the tongues of angels who sound it above, into the heterogeneous tongues of earth dwellers. In stately anthems and in fervent hymns, melody and harmony have given added beauty to its thrilling call. The 148th Psalm presents it in a most compelling and eloquent form:

"Give praise to the Lord in heaven; praise Him, all that dwell on high. Praise Him, all you angels, praise Him, all His hosts, praise Him, sun and moon; praise Him, every star that shines. Let all these praise the Lord; it was His decree that fashioned them, His command that gave them birth. He has set them there forever and given them a law which cannot be altered.

"Give praise to the Lord on earth, monsters of the sea, and all its depths; fire and hail, snow and ice, and the storm-wind that executes His decree; all you mountains and hills, all you fruit trees and cedars; all you kings and peoples of the world, all you that are princes and judges on earth; young men and maids, old men and boys together; let them all give praise to the Lord's name. His name is exalted as no other, His *praise reaches beyond heaven and earth;* and now He has given fresh strength to His people. Shall not His faithful servants praise Him, the sons of Israel, the people that draws near to Him?" (Knox Version)

As a flash of lightning flames through space and enwraps both heaven and earth in one vestment of glory, so does the adoration of the Lord in this psalm light up all the universe and cause it to glow with a radiance of praise.

Over and over the psalmist trumpets out the word, "Praise! Praise! Praise!" Energized by the Holy Spirit, David caught the vision of the *desire* of the Creator that *all His creatures* and *all His works* should praise and glorify Him. Like a prophet, the psalmist sings of that age to come in which the glory of God shall fill not only heaven, but also the earth and the entire universe.

"The praise of God ascends and descends from the heights to the depths and back again. The universe is vocal with the glory of God. The joy of the Lord becomes 'unspeakable and full of glory'—exultation which knows no bounds. Every creature is magnetized by it and drawn into the chorus. Heaven is full of praise, and earth is full of praise, and praise rises from the earth. Everything that has breath joins in the rapture. God is encompassed by a loving, praising creation. Man, the *last* in creation, but the *first* in song, knows not how to contain himself. He dances, he sings, he commands all the heavens, with all their angels, to help him; beasts and all cattle, creeping things and flying fowl must do likewise, and all deeps must yield contributions. He presses even inanimate things into service,—worshipping God and making His praise glorious."

—John Pulsford.

We cannot help but thrill and respond to this vivid picture of universal worship, when our beloved Lord shall be praised on earth as He is praised in heaven. But our joy turns to sorrow and chagrin as we realize that our world, instead of being filled with the praise of God, is tumultuous with enmity and blasphemy and cursing. What a clamor it sends up into the heavens! The cries of the afflicted, the agonized protests of the downtrodden, the shouts of the cruel, the shrieks of the tortured, the harsh words of passionate men, the sighs of the dying—all these blend into a horrible cacophony of dispraise unto the Creator.

Nor does nature praise God in the manner for which it was created. The very elements are disturbed and the seasons are in disorder. The winds, the storms, the waves of the sea, add their own lamentation to that of man. All nature is tuned to a minor key, and seems to groan and travail as it waits for the day of deliverance. (Romans 8:22) And in the animal kingdom there is continual warfare. The beasts of the field roar after their prey and take it by violence. We cannot help but cry out in dismay, "How then, and by whom, is God praised on earth?" And our hearts send back the answer in a whisper, "God is praised only by the redeemed." But this answer affords us small comfort. Without question, we know that *even the redeemed of the Lord are largely barren of the pure and perfect praise which is described in the Scriptures.* How then shall God's praise be made glorious in the earth?

All inspired teachers of the Word agree that God's *primary purpose* for man is that he *worship and glorify* his Creator and *enjoy eternal fellowship with Him.* He has instilled in man's heart a deep and seemingly unquenchable desire to worship. Some psychologists have told us that this instinct is as fundamental as the instinct of self-preservation. Man *must* worship! And God must be worshiped! Thus, man's own heart, even in the unregenerate state, reiterates the call to worship. Yet, man, estranged from God and not having the assistance of the Holy Spirit, cannot offer acceptable praise. But man can and does worship other gods, often with frantic devotion. He fashions idols out of wood or stone or precious metals and bows before them. He yields himself to evil spirits and serves them well. He often creates and sets up images in his own heart and mind, and becomes enamored with them. In other instances he makes an idol of some creature whom he loves; or, as is the practice of this day, he may turn to self-worship, deifying his own mind and nature, honoring the "god within." Needless to say, all such practices are abominations in the sight of God.

At various times statistics are published which show how many million "worshipers" now embrace the Christian faith. But where are these so-called worshipers? If we turn to the Church, as it is known to the world, we find one branch engaging in much formal worship—"Having a form of godliness, but denying the power thereof." Every day litanies are recited, chants and anthems are sung, and symbolic rites are observed; but this is not *the living praise* desired by THE LIVING GOD, unless motivated by pure and fervent love. On the other hand, in other churches, there is "worship" of another type. Hymns are sung, Scriptures are read, the Gospel is preached. Yet this worship, too, often lacks vital praise.

Where then, how then, is God to be praised by man? The Samaritan woman asked the same question centuries ago when Jesus conversed with her by the well. And no clearer answer can be found than the one Jesus uttered: "The hour cometh, and now is, when the true worshipers shall worship the Father in spirit and in truth; for the Father is seeking such to worship Him."

The Father not only *created* man to worship Him, but actually *seeks* for true worshipers—so great is His desire for such. The worship described by Jesus can be offered only by those whose entire being—body, soul, spirit, heart and mind—is united in the offering of true praise unto the True God. This means that His praise is found among the few—*the very few*—who have received His salvation by faith and have so surrendered their own wills and hearts that they can walk in the Spirit and obey the Truth. The blessed few! The Father has called them out from among earth's teeming millions to become His worshipers, and they shall walk in the light of His presence forevermore, reflecting His transcendent glory and splendor.

What then of the *great universal call to praise?* Is it to be forever ignored? Is this glorious praise never to be realized on earth? Turn to the magnificent psalms of David, and from that superb, prophetic master-singer learn of its scope and excellence. A "greater than David" is speaking—it is the voice of the King Himself! He is foretelling the Kingdom Age, during which the Father shall receive the glory due His name.

The high praise of heaven shall come down to earth and find habitation in man. The mountains and the hills shall break forth into singing, and all the trees of the field shall clap their hands in jubilation. Everything that has breath shall praise the Lord, and all inanimate things shall manifest His glory. Not only shall the knowledge of God be spread over the entire earth, as the waters cover the sea, but also every created thing in heaven and in earth, from the highest arch-angel through every grade and phase of being, down to the smallest atom, shall unite in a millennial anthem of praise.

The Call To Praise is the one universal and eternal call of the Spirit. All other calls will pass away with the dawning of Heaven's perfect day. But throughout the ages to come we shall hear and respond to the perpetual call to worship. Blessed are they who hear it while they are still on earth. Twice blessed are they who not only hear it, but also respond by giving themselves to the highest duty and ministration given to man. Most blessed are they who excel in praise—going beyond the mere practice of praise, into the LIFE OF PRAISE.

A HOLY SEED ORDAINED FOR GOD'S PRAISE

The Eternal Most High God Who "dwells not in temples made with hands," nor "gives His glory to another," created man in His own image in order that *He might indwell him and glorify him with His own nature.* He purposed to show forth through man His dominion and power. This desire of God met with frustration in the Garden of Eden, when the creatures designed for His glory become the instruments of disobedience and shame. How often was this to be repeated in the course of the human race! Sin, entering into the world, so corrupted mankind that *it became impossible for men to worship and glorify God as He had intended they should.*

In the midst of this defeat God revealed another plan: A holy seed would be preserved in the earth; from this seed would come forth a unique nation ordained for His praise. Furthermore, God would indwell this people and magnify them in the sight of all nations; and, in due time, His Son, Immanuel, would be born of them and become incarnated in them. This amazing plan was first revealed to Eve, "the mother of all living." (Genesis 3:15) As CHVH (Hebrew), she is shown to foreshadow the Wife of YHVH, the "mother" of the holy seed. Here we catch the first glimpse of the Bride of the Lamb, the New Jerusalem, of whom would be born the holy race called the sons of God. "A seed shall serve Him; it shall be accounted to the Lord for a generation (posterity)." (Psalms 22:30)

Two sons were born to Eve—Cain and Abel. Cain brought an unacceptable offering to the Lord—the fruit of his works. Abel, a true worshiper of God, brought an approved offering—a sacrifice which typified the offering of the Lamb of God. He was martyred by his jealous brother. Thus, Satan introduced into the world the conflict which had begun in heaven at the Throne of God, when Satan (as Lucifer) became jealous of the worship and praise which ascended unto God, and sought to appropriate it for himself. It was his spirit that turned Cain into a killer. Age after age this conflict has continued in the earth, and millions have sealed their life of worship with their blood.

The death of Abel did not signify the end of the holy seed. No! God's plan had been set into operation and no power on earth or in heaven could overthrow His will. This "royal line," as it is sometimes called, was perpetuated in another son, Seth, whom God soon gave to Eve in the place of Abel. The record of Seth's posterity has been carefully preserved in our Bible, and there is special significance in their names as well as their lives.

It begins with Seth—meaning *appointed* or *substituted,* as it is revealed in Genesis 4:25. This name also has the added meaning of *compensation.* The second in line was Enos—meaning *mortal man,* a term less dignified than Adam (meaning "made in God's image"), indicative of weakness and frailty. The son of Enos was Cainan which means *possessor.* The fourth in line was most significant—Mahalaleel, meaning *the praise of God!* The next was called Jared—*descending.* From Jared Enoch was born—the seventh from Adam. His name means *dedicated* and implies disciple. We are all familiar with Enoch's perfect walk with God and with his amazing translation into heaven. His son was Methuselah, meaning *man of the weapon.* Lamech was his son, his name means *youthful power* or *strength.* And finally, of Lamech was Noah born—the builder of the Ark. Noah means *rest.*

This line of patriarchs was extended over a long period of time. In them, the true worship of the true and living God was preserved. By putting their names together we can read a most wonderful and revealing message: God *appointed and substituted* mortal man (in place of man made in His image) for His *possession* and *praise.* From Seth would *descend* a *dedicated, disciplined* lineage who would walk with God. They would become His *men of the weapon,* wielding His sword (the Word), and by them the world would be judged and purged. He would manifest His *strength* and *power* in them, and would take up His abode in them and *rest* in them forever.

In the meantime, sin and corruption had so increased that it became a stench in the nostrils of God. "Every imagination of the thoughts of man's heart was only evil continually." The great flood was sent to purge the world by water, and all evildoers were destroyed. There remained only godly Noah and his family, through whom the human race would be perpetuated. Noah's first act after emerging from the Ark was an act of worship. He built an altar unto the Lord and "the Lord smelled a sweet savor." He made a covenant with Noah and set His rainbow in the cloud as a sign; as long as the earth remained it would not again be destroyed by water, nor would the seasons of the year fail.

Centuries passed. God's praise was only a hidden song in the midst of corruption and idolatry. The knowledge and worship of the True God were rare and confined to the few—the very few—in whom His holy seed was preserved. From among these God selected Abram and called him out from among his people. He led him forth into a *new land* and a *new life,* bestowing upon him a new name, "The father of the faithful!" The Lord appeared unto him, and Abram built an altar and worshiped Him in spirit and in truth. "He staggered not at the promise through unbelief, but was strong in faith, giving glory to God." (Romans 4:20) One version reads: " . . . his faith won strength as he gave glory to God."

Abraham was a Praiser! To him God renewed His covenant concerning His holy seed, promising to give him a son—a son of promise. When Abram first heard of this he laughed in his heart, because of his advanced age. Sarah, too, laughed aloud in unbelief—for which the Lord reproved her. But in due season their mouths were filled with laughter and rejoicing when they held their son in their arms, calling him Isaac, meaning *laughter.* "Then was our mouth filled with laughter and our tongue with singing." (Psalms 126:2)

God's plan to enlarge the holy family into a holy nation began to take form when Isaac's son, Jacob, was born. It was he whom God chose to become the father of twelve sons. In turn, they would father the twelve tribes of Israel. Jacob also was given a new name and was led into a new land.

As Jacob, he was a *deceiver* and *supplanter* of his brother; as Israel, he became a *prevailing prince* of God. His sons bore prophetic names, and their lives foreshadowed events far in the future. The first was called Reuben, meaning *behold a son!*

The second son was Simeon—to *hear* with intelligence, implying *obedience.* Following him was Levi, meaning *joined or attached.* Jacob's fourth son's name bears a striking similarity in meaning to that of the fourth in the line of Seth, Mahalaleel, meaning *praise.* "And Leah conceived again and bare a son: and she said, *Now will I praise* the Lord: therefore she called his name Judah (praise); and left bearing." How eloquent are these simple words!

Here is the *first open declaration of praise* in the Bible! And it is highly significant that it burst forth from the lips of Leah when Judah was born. Well might she rejoice and rest! She must have sensed, to a small measure, the prophetic significance of this son—Judah! From him there would descend a tribe which was destined to give the world some of its greatest and noblest men—men who would be known and celebrated among the nations. Upon this tribe would the favor of YHVH rest, and they would become His sanctuary in the earth. They would praise and worship God in the midst of the heathen nations, and make His great name known unto all peoples. One of their sons, the illustrious David, would capture the very music and praise of heaven and bring it down into the earth. David, the chief singer of Israel! A poet and prophet whose words are more widely known, cherished and quoted—to this very hour—than those of any other man. "In Judah is God known." Indeed!

Eventually, the promised Messiah would be born of this tribe—the Lion of the tribe of Judah! He would be the actual Judah (praise) of God, manifest in flesh. He would declare the Father's name unto His brethren, singing aloud of Him in the midst of the Church. (Hebrews 2:12) This unique Son of God would be the firstborn of many brethren; He would father a new race of sons, and—at last!—in them would the pure and perfect praise of God find its eternal dwelling place. They would become the epitome of His manifest glory. Rejoice, O Leah! Praise thy God, O Zion!

Eight additional sons were born to Jacob, and their names continue to unfold God's plan. The fifth son was Dan, whose name means a *judge.* Then came Naphtali—the *wrestlings of God.* And Gad, meaning a *troop* or *company,* followed. Then Asher—*happy* or *blessed.* The ninth son was Isaachar—*reward.* After him came Zebulon, meaning *dwelling* or *habitation.* The eleventh son was born of the beloved Rachel. "Rejoice, thou barren!" This son of her deepest desire and fervent prayers was named Joseph, meaning *increase* or *fruitfulness.* Of the eleven, Joseph alone lived a life of true worship and obedience unto God. The last son was Benjamin, the favored—*son of my right hand.*

Putting these names together—as in Seth's descendents—we find another prophetic proclamation. It is as though God said: "Behold, a Son! He shall *hear* My voice and *obey* it, and shall be completely *joined* (united) unto Me. He shall *praise* Me in the earth and shall become My manifest glory. I will make Him a *judge* and a warrior who shall *wrestle* with evil and overcome it. He shall lead forth a *company*—a *troop,* who shall be blessed and favored of Me, and they shall be His reward. I will make them My *habitation* in the earth. Great shall be their *increase* and *fruitfulness.* He shall be called the Son *of My right hand,* and shall reign forever."

In spite of the glorious promise revealed in the *names* of Jacob's sons, we are shocked to find that the record of their *lives* is most inglorious.

This favored family, designed for everlasting fame and honor, gave little praise to God; on the contrary, their shameful deeds made them notorious even among licentious pagans. How evident it is that unless God's children become a glory and praise to Him, sooner or later they are certain to become a shame and a reproach.

So, in the case of Jacob's sons, God again found a way to circumvent human failure and sinfulness.

The story of how He did it is one of the most stirring dramas in all literature—the tale of Joseph and his brethren.

Joseph was a true worshiper of God, offering unto Him the praise of his *life* as well as that of his lips. By his faith and obedience he overcame the power of sin and found favor with God. His life portrays the life of the Son of God. In every phase of it—his calling, his visions, his cruel betrayal and suffering, the years of testing, and his final promotion and power—he manifested a spirit of "sonship." Compelled to live in the midst of an exceedingly sinful heathen people, his faithfulness to God was openly manifest—dangerously so! Again and again he risked his life rather than deny his faith. He endured a long and trying imprisonment in Egypt, and showed such grace through it all, that he won the hearts of his jailers. As a reward for his faith and obedience, God gave him favor in the eyes of his enemies. *Because he was not overcome by sin in his own life, he was able to overcome every obstacle from without.* He praised and honored God openly in the midst of a people who worshiped their own gods with fanatical zeal.

Even when standing before Pharaoh—who was himself considered a *god*—he boldly declared the name of Elohim and manifested His Spirit! As a result of this, Pharaoh gave unprecedented honor and authority to Joseph. Great was Joseph's reward and glory, but he took none of it unto himself. His *name*—"a fruitful branch that ran over a wall,"—and his *life* both pre-figured Jesus in a glorious way—"My Servant, the Branch."

After reviewing the shocking and disappointing record of the royal line whom God had appointed unto eternal glory, it is a joy to find such a one as Joseph. How our hearts leap with love and praise at the very thought of him! What pleasure and satisfaction God must have found in him! Through him were "much *people preserved alive.*"

In him was culminated a cycle of time—a harvest time. Both good and evil had come again to fruition. In Joseph, God reaped a harvest of praise and righteousness. We greatly rejoice in this. But we are saddened when we consider the greater harvest of disobedience and sin! The works of the flesh had come to full fruition in the royal line—the "holy seed." In mercy, God preserved them alive in the midst of judgment and famine, but they were obliged to leave their own land—The Promised Land—and go down into Egypt where they would soon become captives and slaves. Four hundred years of servitude and affliction lay before them before God would again intervene to deliver them.

Joseph's dying words confirmed the testimony of his life: "God will surely visit you, and bring you out of this land unto the land which He swore to Abraham, to Isaac, to Jacob." Thus ended the earthly cycle of Joseph's life of obedience and faith—a life that was a living praise unto God.

He who praises God with his life shall have praise of God. (1 Corinthians 4:5) This word proved true in Joseph's day. It still holds good in ours! "Whoso offereth praise glorifieth Me."

ISRAEL—A HABITATION OF PRAISE

The Living God "dwells between the Cherubim"—according to the declaration of the Scriptures—and "inhabits the praises of Israel." As Creator, He has provided a *special atmosphere* for every living thing. Likewise, He has chosen a *special atmosphere for Himself.* A fish must have water in which to live and swim; a bird must have air in which to fly; and man ceases to breathe if he is deprived of oxygen. These elementary facts afford a key to a great mystery—the secret of the *immediate presence and revealed glory of God.* He desires, yes, requires, His own medium of expression—a special atmosphere in which He lives and moves and has His being. It is true that by His Spirit He is everywhere present in the entire universe, and that the emanations of His life and power reach out to the uttermost extent of His domain. But let us consider well this arresting fact: *The Hebrew word* shekinah *means "The divine manifestation through which His presence is felt by man."* The Bible reveals that *God's direct presence and His shekinah glory are manifested on earth only when His people provide for Him an atmosphere of pure and fervent praise,* similar to that high praise which continually surrounds His throne. Our God lives and moves in the midst of PRAISE. So pure, so exalted, so holy is His nature, that any other atmosphere is unfitting and dishonoring to the Great God and King of Heaven.

It was in order that He might take up His dwelling on earth among men that He chose Israel, a people dear unto Himself, and ordained them for His praise. By a series of strange and marvelous dealings, He made known unto them—and the world—that He does indeed "inhabit the praises of Israel." (Psalm 22:3) He was not content to dwell with one man or with one family. No! There must be a *holy nation, a* people prepared for His glory. He never lost sight of this purpose during the long years of His dealings with Abraham, Isaac, and Jacob and his sons. Their failures and sins did not annul His will nor diminish His relentless desire for a people with whom He could commune, and in whom He could be manifested to the world. Through Joseph, an obedient son, He preserved the others alive in the time of famine. But even Joseph could not save them from the punishment for their sins. They and their descendents had to leave their own peaceful "holy land" and dwell in Egypt, "the underworld," the land of darkness, sin and idolatry.

"And Joseph died and all his brethren, and all that generation. And the children of Israel were fruitful, and increased abundantly, and multi—plied, and waxed exceeding mighty, and the land was filled with them." And the Egyptians set over them "taskmasters to afflict them with their burdens . . . and made their lives bitter with hard bondage." Did God permit this because He saw that before they would willingly worship and serve Him, they must first be purified in the furnace of affliction and broken upon the wheel of slavery and bondage? Would their forced and bitter obedience to Pharaoh (a type of Satan) help to teach them how to obey their true Master, the God of Love?

Surely the mystery of human suffering and bondage is bound closely with the mystery of iniquity and rebellion. How strange that man of his own accord will not worship nor obey his Creator! And even more appalling is the fact that the very children of God, His own chosen sons and daughters, find it so hard to yield to Him until they have been subjected to much suffering and crushing. It was in mercy that God permitted Israel to be afflicted, in order that He might bring them forth "as the Lord has affirmed . . . His peculiar people," making them "high above all nations which He hath made, in *praise* and in *name* and in *honor.*" (Deuteronomy 26:18-20)

It thrills our hearts to find that the true worship of God was preserved during the four hundred years of bondage, at least in the hearts of a faithful remnant. Among the sons of Levi, God found one upon whom He could lay His hand, singling him out for special honor. His name was Amram, meaning *an exalted people.* He married a favored daughter of Levi whose name had an even greater significance—Jochebed, *whose glory is Jehovah,* (although this Name had not yet been openly revealed.) She proved to be both fearless and faithful, and lived up to her high name. Of these two, Moses was born, the son of Israel—who was to become their deliverer, prophet, leader and law-giver. Pharaoh, fearing the increase of the Israelites, had ordered that all male children be thrown into the river as soon as they were born. But Jochebed did not obey this order. At God's direction she hid Moses three months; then prepared a tiny ark in which he was preserved alive in the midst of the river of death. She appointed Miriam, his sister, to watch over him. God intervened and caused the daughter of Pharaoh to save his life and to bring him up as her own son.

It is to the everlasting glory of God that Moses, when he came to manhood, "refused to be called the son of Pharaoh's daughter; choosing rather to suffer affliction with the people of God, than to enjoy the pleasures of sin for a season." How great was this sacrifice! As the son of Pharaoh, the riches and power of Egypt were at his disposal, as well as honor and every pleasure known to man. As an Israelite, he became a castaway, a slave, risking his very life by incurring the ruler's displeasure. Moses' every attitude and action gave praise and honor unto God. No wonder God highly exalted him before them all, giving him honor and glory above all the sons of Israel! It is evident that those who honor God are honored of God; those who exalt Him and humble themselves are sure to be exalted in due season; those who praise God do receive the praise of God. Yet, no man dares give glory to God merely for this reason. *To purify man's praise, God seemingly subjects those who especially honor Him to special humiliations and sufferings.* Moses was destined to high honor, but it was to be in the far-distant future. Ahead of Moses lay a lifetime of servitude and testing. There was no immediate indication of the favor of God. He led Moses in the path he had chosen—that of "suffering affliction with the people of God."

"When Israel was a child, then I loved him, and called My son out of Egypt." At length God's appointed hour dawned—"the acceptable year of the Lord, the day of His vengeance." God visited Moses on "the backside of the desert," in Horeb, the mountain of God. And He appeared there to him in the burning bush. (Exodus 3) How sudden was this visitation! How mandatory the word that was spoken! Moses was commanded to bring forth the children of Israel, even unto the holy Mount, where they might *sacrifice* to the living God, and *serve* Him with devotion. One meaning of the original text is "be in bondage to," and another is "worship." The great purpose of God in delivering Israel was that they might become His servants—love-slaves—and His worshipers. Furthermore, God revealed unto Moses His high and Holy Name which had hitherto been veiled—YHVH—I AM THAT I AM. He promised him that in this Name great wonders should be wrought, such as had never been wrought in the earth before (nor since!) "I will stretch out My hand and smite Egypt with all My wonders." He also performed signs for Moses, blessing his simple shepherd's rod and making it the "rod of His strength."

"And afterward Moses and Aaron went in, and told Pharaoh, Thus saith the Lord God of Israel, Let My people go, that they may hold a feast unto Me in the wilderness." The word "feast" is "*chag*" in the original. It refers to a solemn procession, celebration or dramatization of some great event. With elaborate feasts the heathen worshiped their many gods, observing festal days with great ceremony and wild demonstrations. This is the *first* instance of the Lord calling His people to a *feast,* and it is clear to us that it was a holy feast, a memorial feast of communion which was to have prophetic meaning and eternal significance. This feast was to begin with the Passover, the *Lord's Supper.* God set the table for this feast, just as He later set the table in the wilderness; yes, and as He will set it for the Marriage Supper of the Lamb. Blessed are they who are bidden to the feast of the Lord!

We all know how great the struggle with Pharaoh proved to be, and how he hardened his heart again and again, refusing to let the Israelites go. It was only after a series of strange and terrifying miracles had been wrought by Jehovah, accompanied by severe judgments, that Pharaoh gave the word of their release. By the observance of the Passover feast all Israel passed through judgment and death, in a type. Then they were led forth through the Red Sea, a type of baptism, and came up on the other side of the sea a *free people, a holy people,* in the sight of the Lord. Suddenly their hearts overflowed with praise. "Then sang Moses and the children of Israel this song unto the Lord."

"I will sing unto the Lord, for He hath triumphed gloriously; The horse and his rider hath He thrown into the sea."

This paean of praise is one of the greatest uttered by mortal tongue. (Exodus 15:1-19) An entire race sang together at their birth (as a nation), as the morning stars sang together at the creation. The author of the Book of Wisdom attributes this song to the "wisdom of God." He declares that upon this occasion God opened "the mouths of babes" as described in Psalm 8. So ageless and universal is this song that it shall be sung by the redeemed when they stand beside another "red sea"—the sea of glass mingled with fire, where, with harps of God in their hands, they shall sing "the song of Moses and of the Lamb." (Revelation 15)

"The Lord (YAH—Jah—the vehement form of Jehovah) is my strength and my song, and He is become my salvation: He is my God and I will prepare Him a habitation. (In the original text this reads, "habitation of praise.") My father's God, and I will exalt Him."

It will enrich our own praise if we read this superlative song again and again; if we sing it and ponder it and make it our very own. We also have come up out of Egypt and the bondage of sin; we have partaken of the Passover, and have passed through the sea of baptism. In newness of life we have begun our pilgrimage to the New Land. Our mouths, too, have been filled with singing. And Moses' song becomes our song as we join in the chorus of the redeemed. With Miriam, we take up the timbrel and go forth in the dance of praise, for He has turned our mourning into dancing, and has given us the garment of praise for the spirit of heaviness. We find our own voices shouting in exultation:

"Who is like unto Thee, O Lord, among the people? Who is like Thee, glorious in holiness, fearful in praises, doing wonders?"

In the midst of this high praise we become aware that YHVH is moving mightily, as in the days of the wilderness journey. *The more we praise Him, the more we sense the awe and majesty of His presence.* We become aware of His wonders taking place around about us! Yes, "Great is the Lord, and greatly to be praised in the mountain of His holiness."

"Thou shalt bring them in, and plant them in the mountain of Thine inheritance, in the place, O Lord, which Thou hast made for Thee to dwell in, in the sanctuary, O Lord, which Thy hands have established. The Lord shall reign for ever and ever."

How glorious, how conclusive, how exalting is this grand finale of the Song of Moses! He was singing of a greater Mount than Horeb—Moses had glimpsed the Heavenly Zion of Hebrews 12, the Throne and Sanctuary of YHVH, the City of our God!

Surely no other nation had so auspicious and glorious a birth as triumphant Israel. Their darkness was swept away in the dawn of an apocalyptic day. As a joyous company, they set their faces toward the Holy Mount of God. It would give us satisfaction to picture them journeying on their way in radiant faith, praising and giving thanks unto God. But such is not their odyssey. Three days later, we find them at the waters of Marah, *murmuring in unbelief!* How could it be that their exultant praise died down as suddenly as it had flamed? How is it that this same thing goes on happening *today* in the midst of spiritual Israel? O that Israel had praised the Lord! O that *we* would praise the Lord! *It takes more than miracles, more than salvation and the baptism in the Spirit, to produce a people who will provide a continual atmosphere of praise for the Lord.* The Father seeketh such! He desires a dwelling place among them, for He is the God who inhabits the praises of His people.

"They shall abundantly utter—a boiling-up or bubbling-up like a fountain of holy fluency in praise! Open your mouths; let the praise pour forth; let it come, rivers of it. Stream away! Gush away, if you possibly can. Say something greater, grander, and more fiery still. You cannot exceed the truth. You have come to a theme where your most fluent powers will fail in utterance."

—C.H. Spurgeon

THE WAY TO THE MOUNT OF GOD

The way to the Mount of God lies through "a waste howling wilderness!" Peril *and* pain, hunger and thirst, weariness and strife, accompany those who set their faces toward the Holy Hill of YHVH. Without faith, obedience, and divine guidance, no one can hope to scale its cloud-crowned crest. The children of Israel were the first to make this pilgrimage. Their journey from the Red Sea to Sinai, and thence on into Canaan, was the most portentous in the history of mankind. Although it took place nearly four thousand years ago, it impresses us in some mysterious way as being up-to-date, as though it had been projected from the distant past into our own century. And although we can recall only a few of the names of those two million or so wayfarers, at times they seem to be "close kin" to us, as, in spirit, we trace their steps and live their experiences. We, too, hear the summons to the Mount! We, too, partake of the Passover Lamb! We, too, pass through the Sea, beholding the Cloud! And we lift our voices in the triumphant chorale of praise! All this is but the beginning. The Holy Spirit has revived and re-emphasized their story to succeeding generations, in order that all believers in the True God might profit by its spiritual significance and its tragic lessons.

It shocks us to discover that for some reason men have gone on *following the example* of the Israelites, rather than *heeding the warning* of their ignominious failures along the way. The seeds of unbelief and disobedience, which they sowed in the wilderness, continue to bring forth a harvest. But it is a harvest of sin and reproach rather than of righteousness and praise. Indeed, *we* need to give careful heed to their example lest we too are numbered among those who fall in the wilderness, failing to fulfill "the *high* calling of God in Christ Jesus!" We, too, have left Egypt and set out for the Mount of God. We, too, must keep "a feast unto the Lord." Our Mount is not *Sinai*—"the mount that might be touched," but *Zion,* the heavenly Jerusalem. Our feast is not a consecration of the Covenant of the Law, but the feast of high and holy love and praise—the consummation of the New Covenant. Our fellow-travelers are not ignorant and rebellious Israelites, but redeemed and Spirit-filled sons of God. Awaiting us is an innumerable company of Angels and saints, whose praise shall blend with ours at the Marriage Supper of the Lamb. If, without due preparation and testing, the children of Israel were unable to ascend the earthly Mount of God, where He appeared in the bush as a *fire that did not consume,* how shall we, in an unperfected state, expect to go up unto the Heavenly Mount where He is manifest in far greater power and glory as *A Consuming Fire?* (Hebrews 12)

The Journey of the children of Israel began with a mighty manifestation of glory. Jehovah brought them forth from Egypt with a mighty hand and an outstretched arm! All of them witnessed the wondrous miracles wrought by God in a reign of judgment and death. All passed under the cloud and through the sea. All were filled with praise and song. We know these facts are true, not only because they are accredited by history, but also because they have been re-enacted in our own lives, at least to a degree. We are spiritual Israelites, chosen to become His present-day habitation of praise, and their experiences are typical of our own. Surely God, who is able to make a dry path through the sea, is well able to level a straight and smooth highway through the wilderness, or to transport His children to the Holy Mount in some supernatural way! Such thoughts must have been in the minds of the Israelites when they started out, just as they occur to us today. We, too, are inclined to thirst for the supernatural, the spectacular, and to expect God to make the way easy for us. But God's ways are not our ways! In His wisdom He has deemed it necessary to try men's hearts and to prove and scourge every son whom He accepts. (Hebrews 12:6) Even our blessed Lord did not escape the fiery trial of suffering, for it is written, "Yet learned He obedience by the things which He suffered." Our Father knew that the Israelites could never become His living Temple, until they had passed through a purifying of their faith, and had been exercised sufficiently to grow up into mature sons of God. Wherefore He did not release them from their bondage and immediately set them on high. First they had to pass through trials in the wilderness, and make their way to the Mount through testings. Even as you and I.

Their way led through MARAH . . . ELIM, THE WILDERNESS OF SIN, REPHIDIM, MASSAH-MERIBAH and finally to the DESERT OF SINAI at the foot of THE MOUNT. With a little insight we can trace our own pilgrimage by these landmarks. We may find the route similar, but—Praise God!—*the manner and the spirit of our journey* lies within the province of our own will. If we wish, we may follow the example of the Israelites and make each move miserable by our murmuring and complaining. We, too, can doubt and find fault, turn back and limit the Holy One of Israel, yes, and even provoke Him. (Psalm 78:40, 41) Or, we may take the Davidic way, *the Kingdom way,* rejoicing and singing as we journey toward the Holy Hill. Then shall the wilderness blossom before us like a rose and re-echo with songs of praise. Even in the valley of Baca (weeping) we shall find a well of joy! (Psalm 84:5-7) But we must make the choice between the way of unbelief and the way of triumphant faith. Can rejoicing keep company with complaining? Will fretting and trusting journey together? What part has rebellion with praise? Some of us have supposed that we can praise and rejoice part of the way, and yet indulge in grumbling, fault-finding and fear, the rest of the time. We have risen up to praise God loudly in the midst of the assembly; but after the Spirit has lifted, and we again face the tests, we have turned to repining and doubting, thus annulling our meager offering of praise. "What? Does a fountain give forth both sweet and bitter waters? These things ought not so to be!" (James 3:10) If we are seeking to *live the life of praise,* let us purge ourselves of all thoughts, words and deeds which are incompatible with praise. We should exercise ourselves to do all things "in the name of the Lord Jesus, giving thanks to God and the Father by Him." (Colossians 3:17) Then the way to the Mount will become a *joyful* pilgrimage. We shall go from strength to strength and appear before God in Zion!

From the Red Sea to Marah was but a three-day journey. However, it was ample time for their supply of water to run low and for the Israelites to become weary. We can imagine how disappointed they were when they found the waters of Marah brackish and bitter. They had been accustomed to the sweet and salubrious waters of the Nile, which were famous for their refreshing goodness. And no doubt they were somewhat dazed by the sudden contrast between the recent supernatural happenings and the drastic down-to-earth struggle with reality. (We, too, have known such experiences of "let-down.") Things had not turned out quite as they had expected; so they began murmuring. In the original text the rendering is stronger: "They complained obstinately." Moses cried unto the Lord and He heard the cry. God showed him a tree and told him to cast it into the water. When he obeyed, the water was immediately sweetened. In addition to this blessing, the Lord gave them a special promise of health, providing they would obey Him. Thus the bitter waters became a healing stream. Many interpreters of the Word have believed that this tree typified the Cross of Christ. The Targum says: "The Word of the Lord showed him the tree ardiphney, on which he wrote the great and precious Name (YHVH) and then threw it into the waters." I believe the Holy Spirit reveals the tree as Christ—our TREE OF LIFE—by whose death we are crucified unto self and sin and by whose resurrection we rise to walk in newness of life. We learn to come with joy to the waters of Marah.

"The waters of Marah He will sweeten for thee. He drank all the bitter in Gethsemane."

The next resting place along the way was an oasis of blessing. Praise God, He still provides such refreshing for His weary travelers! Elim—the place of the twelve wells and the seventy palm trees. Here was given to them a prophetic picture of the twelve tribes and the seventy elders. God was not testing His people in vain. He was sifting out those who were to become the spiritual burden-bearers and rulers of His people—just as He is doing today. Elim was also a place of vision, for Mount Sinai could be seen in the distance. It is disappointing that there is no record of any praise or thanksgiving offered there unto God.

Adversity and prosperity alike test our faith and obedience.

They had been away from Egypt one month when they left Elim for the wilderness of Sin. No doubt their provisions were getting low, so their complaining began to increase. Soon "the *whole* congregation murmured against Moses and Aaron." They even lamented and wished they had died in Egypt with full stomachs. How typical of God's people today! Not only have we savored the waters of worldly pleasure, but at times we lust for the flesh pots of Egypt as well!

We crave the *feast* but abhor the *fast.* O for a people who will be willing to fast and *praise!*

Not because of their complaints, but because of Moses' and Aaron's faith, God intervened. We all know the wonderful story of

His visible glory appearing in the cloud, and of the quail and the manna. Here was another beautiful type of Christ, the Living Bread of Heaven. With these blessings, however, God provided further tests of obedience and, sad to relate, disobedience and greed were added to their lamenting and com—plaining. We have no record of thanksgiving for "this table set in the wilderness."

Thirst followed hunger, and at Rephidim they "chided" Moses because of it. Here again the original text is strong: "They turned upon, or wrangled" with him; in fact, they were about ready to stone him! It seems that with each new test the Israelites became more openly unbelieving and rebellious. *Miracles* have never wrought *grace* in human hearts. Miracles are intended only as *signs,* pointing the way to *salvation.* Nothing but the pure grace of God can produce a broken and a thankful heart. But even grace cannot operate in opposition to human will. God commanded Moses and the elders to go to "the rock in Horeb" and to smite it. Enough water poured forth to quench the thirst of that vast multitude! It is said that this rock is still recognizable, and that it has deep channels which attest to its once fountain-like state. It was another type of Christ—the Rock whence the Water of Life flows freely. Moses named this place Massah—meaning temptation, and Meribah—meaning strife, "Because there they *tempted* the Lord, saying, Is the Lord among us or not?"

Their woes increased in proportion to their sins! "Then came Amalek and fought with Israel."

Again God showed forth His power to deliver them. Joshua was chosen to lead the warriors, and Moses stood on the hill, uplifting his rod—Aaron and Hur assisting him by supporting his arms. When the rod was lowered, the battle went against them, but when it was uplifted, it brought victory. At sunset Israel had prevailed. "And Moses built an altar" and there he called on the name of the Lord, Jehovah-Nissi—the Lord my banner.

It was not until the third month after leaving Egypt that they departed from Rephidim and came to the Desert of Sinai" . . . and there Israel camped before the Mount." How arduous and inglorious had been their journey! It is safe to suppose that the Lord had intended to lead them through the wilderness in a triumphant procession. (Psalm 68:7-17) How glorious their way might have been . . . The Lord's arm outstretched in power; their arms and voices uplifted in praise! The magnificent anthem sung at the Red Sea could have become a "Hallelujah March," setting the tempo for their hearts and feet as they moved onward unto the Mount. Who knows but that they would have entered Canaan as the redeemed are to enter Zion, "with singing and everlasting joy." Instead, they stumbled along in blind unbelief, murmuring and complaining every mile of the way. We shudder when we think of their utter failure; but what of us who have a tendency to stumble along in much the same manner, *imitating* rather than *detesting and avoiding* their example?

"Now this took place as a warning for us . . . *and it was written down for the purpose of instructing us whose lot has been cast in the closing hours of the world.* So let anyone who thinks he stands take care in case he fails." (1 Corinthians 10:6-13, Moffatt) O that Israel had hearkened unto the Lord and walked in His ways! Their day of opportunity has long since passed; ours is passing swiftly. Let us arise and go up to the Mountain of the Lord's house with shouts and songs of highest praise. "Great is the Lord and greatly to be praised in the mountain of His holiness."

"You have come to Mount Zion, the city of the Living God, the heavenly Jerusalem, to myriads of angels in festal gathering, to the assembly of the first-born registered in heaven, to the God of all as judge, to the spirits of just men made perfect, to Jesus who mediates the new covenant, and to the sprinkled blood whose message is nobler than Abel's. Therefore let us render thanks that we receive a realm unshaken; and in this way let us worship (praise) God acceptably—though with godly fear and awe, for our God is indeed a consuming fire." (Hebrews 12:22-24, 28, 29, Moffatt) "By Jesus Christ therefore let us offer the sacrifice of praise to God continually, that is, the fruit of our lips giving thanks to His name." (Hebrews 13:15)

Quotations from C.H. Spurgeon:

"Singing is the fit embodiment for praise, and therefore do the saints make melody before the Most high God. Their harp may be unstrung for a little season, but soon they will be sweeping its harmonious chords, flying on the wings of music to the third heaven of adoration."

"We cannot be too firm in the holy resolve to praise God, for it is the chief end of our living and being that we should glorify God and enjoy Him forever."

"Praise ye the Lord! Let his character be extolled by you, and let all that He has revealed concerning Himself be the subject of your song; especially let the holy and incommunicable name of YHVH be the object of your adoration. Do not merely admire Him because He is God; but study His character and His doings, and thus render intelligent, appreciative, fervent praise."

"If others are silent, you must not be. You should be the first to celebrate His name."

"The vocal expression of praise in sacred song is one of our sweetest delights. We were created for this purpose, and hence it is an unfailing joy to us. It is a charming duty to praise the Lord, All pleasure is to be found in His worship. The mind expands, the soul is lifted up, the heart is warmed, and soon the whole being is filled with delight when we are engaged in singing the high praises of God. When in any occupation goodness and pleasure unite, surely we should perform it without stint."

"The Holy Spirit invites, entreats, urges and commands all men to praise and magnify the Lord. Praise ye the Lord! This exhortation can never be out of place, speak it where we may; and never out of time, speak it when we may. Those who are nearest to the Lord should lead the song, and all who dwell in His courts should join in heartily. Keep not your worship to yourselves, but let it fall like a golden shower from the heavens on men beneath."

"Praise is the occupation of the godly, their eternal work and their present pleasure."

MAKING HIS PRAISE GLORIOUS

Frances Metcalfe

MAKING HIS PRAISE GLORIOUS was originally published in multigraphed form more than ten years ago. It had a limited circulation as a supplement to LIVING THE LIFE OF PRAISE, which had been published in a similar form. During the intervening years, the Holy Spirit has been greatly stressing the purpose and power of praise in the life of the Christian believer and the Church. So we had an increasing number of requests for these two writings. Already LIVING THE LIFE OF PRAISE has been widely circulated in a compact printed form. And now we are glad to present its sequel.

We believe you will find this booklet of special interest because it is a compilation of experiences, revelations and instructions shared by individual members of the Golden Candlestick Fellowship.

It has been our joy for many years to dedicate ourselves to living the Life of Praise. And for us the words of the Psalmist have rung out with no uncertain sound: *"Sing forth the honor of His name. Make His praise glorious . . . Make the voice of His praise to be heard."*

PREFACE

The Lord first began to speak to me about praise some thirty years ago. But even before that time I had experienced a special delight in the beautiful anthems of praise which we sang in the Baptist Church choir. I memorized these and often felt an ecstatic joy as we used them in worship. Since most of these anthems were taken from the Psalms or prophets of the Old Testament, I began to realize that praise was very important in the worship of the Hebrews and the Early Christian Church. As these inspired songs took root in my heart, my whole attitude toward the Lord began to change. I sensed a new hunger for His presence, and began to seek Him daily, earnestly, consecrating everything in my life to Him in a new way. Then, one day, as I was waiting upon the Lord in prayer, the words from an old hymn began to ring within me, almost like a chime:

> "Take my moments and my days
> Let them flow in *ceaseless praise.*"

My mind was illuminated with a new concept of serving the Lord—by offering unto Him ceaseless praise! Such a thought was revolutionary to me, for I had always considered daily prayer and faithfulness in the tasks of the Church to be my appointed service. How could anyone live a life of ceaseless praise on earth? I had never heard or dreamed of such a thing.

Then the Spirit began to bring Scriptures to my mind, reinforcing this new calling. "By Him (Christ) therefore, let us offer *the sacrifice of praise* to God continually, that is, the fruit of our lips, giving thanks to His name." (Hebrews 13:15) I was really staggered by the thought that the praise God desired was not only an *inner attitude* but an *outward manifestation* involving my tongue and lips; "I will bless the Lord at *all* times: His praise shall *continually* be in my *mouth.*" (Psalm 34:1) Blessed are they that dwell in Thy house: they will be still (always) praising Thee." (Psalm 84:4) These and several others lingered in my mind for days.

Then, one day as I was quietly waiting on the Lord He reminded me of a sermon I had recently heard preached by a converted atheist. He had described the powerful effects of skillful blasphemy! He told us that he and other militant atheists were actually trained in how to blaspheme God effectually. He said that the most proficient among them could stand on a corner and blaspheme God for hours without repeating the same thing twice. As a result of this practice, they often became endued with strange, supernatural power, he reported, and many startling signs and even seeming miracles were wrought. Though I was amazed and shocked by this testimony, my only reaction was to be thankful that this man was now testifying of the grace of God in Christ, and had been delivered from such diabolical ways.

However, as the Holy Spirit reminded me of this sermon, He impressed me with an entirely different aspect of truth. First there were these questions: "How many Christians could praise God for hours without stopping? And, if they did, would not the supernatural power of God possess them and work His true signs and miracles in the earth?" My only answer was that I did not know any Christians who praised God out loud at all, except in hymns at Church. And then a sense of shame engulfed me. How terrible that God should be skillfully blasphemed, but not skillfully praised! As I considered these things, the Lord seemed to challenge me to begin to practice praise and to seek to excel in this service to God, as I had sought to be faithful in the church.

At the time of which I write, I had not received the special infilling of the Holy Spirit. But I had experienced anointings, especially when I was called upon to speak or sing before others. I had also learned that He was my Teacher and Guide, though little was said about this in our church. So now I put myself in His hands, seeking His instruction and help in obeying this new "command" from the Lord. I got down on my knees and began trying to practice praise. But I couldn't think of even one thing to say in praise of the Lord! And my mouth seemed to be sealed; it needed to be pried open! For some fifteen minutes I struggled, fearful of the sound of my own voice, most inhibited and barren of the precious fruit of the lips, of which the Scripture speaks. By this time I was almost exhausted, as though I had been at hard labor. I began to realize that obedience to this challenge was not going to be as easy as I had expected. But I resolved to continue to keep my practice time, which amounted to a mere fifteen minutes a day. What painful practices I had!

About this time the Lord began to answer my cries for help. I was asked to bring a message at our church prayer meeting. I felt impressed to speak of this call to praise, and I prepared carefully. I usually experienced liberty and lucidity in speaking; but not so on this occasion! A strange sense of bondage came over me as I arose. I felt that someone had their hand at my throat and was attempting to choke me. I coughed, lost my trend of thought, and became more and more confused as I continued. I felt that I had completely failed, and I wondered why the blessed Holy Spirit did not assist or anoint me. I was also humiliated and really disheartened. But, to my surprise, several who were present were moved on and began to praise God daily! One, in particular, had an amazing experience in praise, and carried the word on to a large prayer group she attended weekly. So the Spirit had owned the message, in spite of my seeming failure. This made it plain to me that I had come face to face in conflict with the one who wanted me to blaspheme, but not to praise. I realized now that my practice of praise was not only to be an *exercise*, but a *warfare*.

I persevered in my practice and in seeking the help of the Lord. Then, in a short time, I was present in a small private prayer meeting where the enemy was really at work. A home and hearts were being broken, and prayer seemed not to avail. Suddenly I remembered what the Spirit had shown me about the power of praise. So I began to praise. At first my voice sounded like a mere chirp, but I continued to chirp away, and gradually my voice grew strong and my praise began to rise in a flow of Scripture. (My daily practice periods were producing results!) Then a most surprising thing happened to me. The power of God took hold of me in such a way that I could not *stop* praising. Like an artesian fountain, the praise rose higher and higher. It was joyful, confident, free and wonderful! Meanwhile, the Spirit moved on the heart of the one who was rebelling against the Lord, and a great and lasting victory was won.

During the intervening years, I have continued to practice praise, not only under the anointing of the Spirit, but also as a *sacrifice*. The Holy Spirit was swift to teach me the difference between the *spirit of praise* and the *sacrifice of praise*. It is easy to yield to the Holy Spirit, as He moves in us to sing and praise the Lord. But it is most difficult to pour out praise unto the Lord when our hearts are heavy, dry, and crushed with sorrow. It is this *sacrifice* that New Testament priests are called upon to offer. In fact it is the only acceptable sacrifice prescribed for them, after they have offered their bodies as living sacrifices. This sacrifice is an act of faith, an offering most holy unto the Lord, since we praise Him in obedience to His Word, not because of what He does—or we want Him to do—but because of what HE IS. And we make this offering apart from our own feelings or supernatural enduement.

The Lord has graciously united me with a whole company of Davidic praisers. Each of these could tell you of amazing experiences in this high and holy calling. In the following pages you will find some of these recorded for your edification and blessing. We know that the Lord is preparing a great company of Praisers throughout the entire earth, and that these shall in time and in truth "bring up the Ark" of the Living God. But whether or not you have received a special call from God to this praise ministry, this book is for you, for ALL in Christ are thus enjoined: "Through Him (Christ, our High Priest) therefore, let us constantly and at all times offer up to God a sacrifice of praise, which is the fruit of lips that thankfully acknowledge and confess and glorify His Name." (Hebrews 13:15, Amplified Version)

—Frances Metcalfe

LESSONS IN THE SCHOOL OF PRAISE

"Sing ye praises with understanding."

The Spirit commanded us to *excel in praise,* just as once He had commanded us to excel in love and in the gifts of the Spirit. I found that the word "excel" meant to "go beyond, to project, to surpass, to outdo, to be choice, prime, admirable." And with this word came another . . . excelsior! It means "still higher, ever upward." *"O Lord, our Lord, how excellent is Thy name in all the earth!"* And how *excellent* should be Thy praise? O may we excel in praising and glorifying Thee!

The Spirit has been speaking to me that now, more than ever before, we are called upon to sing the HIGH PRAISES of our MOST HIGH GOD. For some of us this means *a separation from other types of ministry in order that we may be devoted to being His unique song of praise and glory in the earth.* Let those who hear this call respond quickly! High praise is like rare frankincense, costly and most desirable unto the King. With it is mixed the myrrh of the pain and sorrows that have afflicted us in times of darkness and desolation.

Not until we have descended into the depths of self-death and devastation can we be projected into the heights of heaven. Our cries are resolved into shouts of highest praise. Our very anguish and distress have but stretched and tuned the strings of our lyres, so that we are fitted to play skillfully unto the King. As we praise together our incense is blended into a fragrant, fuming cloud of glory in which our God appears in new splendor.

We have all marveled at the special anointings of the Holy Spirit which have enabled us to praise the Lord in beautiful ways. For many years now we have reveled in such movings of the Spirit, as we have assembled before him. But of late the Spirit is showing me that He seeks a *practical* praise too—a praise that extends into every function of our daily life. I caught a glimpse of the transformation which would take place in me and in each of us if we met everything, yes, every single thing, in the attitude of thanksgiving and praise; and deliberately refused to think negative thoughts and speak negative words, or even have negative feelings. I know this takes *discipline.* It means a purging of ourselves from many things which do not *seem* evil to us, and yet which are definitely not in keeping with *positive praise.*

Sometimes I have lived this way for a few days at a time, refusing any sort of thought or expression, except that of thanksgiving and praise. How great a change was wrought! But soon I would become careless again, and the tides of darkness and oppression would sweep over me. Almost before I realized it I would be giving place to thoughts from another realm. I know that the Word of God declares that all things work together for good, and that in all things we are to glorify the Lord. This includes our looks and attitudes, as well as feelings, thoughts and words. One poet said, "O may my every look be love!" Well, praise is divine love singing its highest song, so I am saying, "O may my every expression be praise!" There are many forms of praise, as I am coming to see, and we know little about them. We are limited to the lower forms, I feel. But the HIGH PRAISE shall be given to us, by the Spirit, after we have learned to *live praise out in every action of our daily lives.* At least this is the way the Spirit instructs me.

One thing most frequently stressed about praise is that it must be *pure.* The Lord has been revealing that much praise is mixed with other "ingredients," and is not holy and altogether acceptable. For instance, many of us have praised in a more or less mechanical way. We come together, and we have many things on our minds; maybe we are troubled in spirit or in heart. But we know that Holy Ghost people should begin every gathering with praise, so we praise along with the others, repeating any phrase that comes to our minds. Our attention may not be upon it at all—*"sounding brass, tinkling cymbals!"* Then, too, we may praise very fervently because we want the Lord to *do* something for us, such as heal us, or answer some urgent prayer, supply some material need, or give us a special blessing. Such praise is like a sort of refined "bargaining" with the Lord. God is to be praised primarily because He is *deserving of praise;* because His Word declares that He is to be praised, regardless of whether He answers any of our prayers or not. Our praise must be divested of thoughts of reward and enrichment. For several days the Spirit directed me not to ask or even think of receiving anything from Him as I praised. I found that this was a sort of exercise. I had not realized how much attention I was giving to receiving something from Him, even though it was something spiritual and good. As I praised with pure devotion, I began to realize that much of our repeated *asking* is belittling to the Lord. He has already freely given us all things in Christ! As we praise and believe, we do receive that which is in His order and will for us moment by moment, just as the plants draw from the sun all they require, and can utilize no more. There is a greedy spirit in most of us, and that greed can be diverted from material things to spiritual things if we are not careful. I saw that pure praise brings about a greater purification of our hearts.

The other day the Holy Spirit spoke to my heart so directly that I took my pencil and wrote down the words, and now I feel to share them with others: *"The Beloved languishes and thirsts for your praises. Give Him a special offering of praise. What I say unto you, I say unto all—'Praise!'"*

Show forth your love for Him by lauding Him. Lift up your voices with strength, be not afraid.

Span heaven and earth with an Arch of Triumph. Triumphant praise! Tunnel through the rocks; make dry paths through the seas; water the deserts with praise. It has great power! *"Behold what manner of love the Father has bestowed upon you—that you should be called the Praisers of God."* As I meditated upon these words and felt the impact of them upon my heart, I was stirred to recall some words from one of Wesley's hymns: *"Till we cast our crowns before Thee, lost in wonder, love and praise."* We do not need to enter into physical death to be lost in wonder, love and praise. It can become a present reality.

Over and over again the words of the Psalmist were brought to my mind: *"Blessed are they who dwell in Thy house, they will be still praising Thee."* Then I was aware that an adaption of these words was being given to me in the form of a little song:

> Blessed are they who dwell in Thy house,
> They will be always praising Thee.
> They will be singing of Thy glory,
> And lauding Thy name unceasingly.
> Blessed are they who dwell in Thy house;
> They will be always praising Thee, in joy or pain,
> Through loss or gain, they will be always praising Thee.

I sang and sang this little song. Then I was given a strenuous exercise to teach me how to *live* it, and I learned that the praise that ascends during times of pain and loss is more costly and fragrant to God than that which we can offer in times of joy and gain.

I am learning many new lessons in this school of Praise. One of the most precious is this: Praise not only perfects the fruit of our lips and brings it forth in delicious ripeness, but it greatly assists in perfecting all the precious fruits of the Spirit: Love, Joy, Peace . . . , etc. Yes, these thrive and develop in an atmosphere of praise, but are often blighted when we become depressed and doubtful. Longsuffering (a fruit lacking in many of us), gentleness, goodness, faith—yes, all these are brought to perfection in an atmosphere of pure praise. I saw that it was like the warm summer sun that comes to ripen the fruits. We have sown in tears, watered the seed with prayer, have known much testing and exercising of faith. Then we are brought into a higher realm—a realm where praise and thanksgiving flourish constantly and all the precious fruit of our lives is greatly benefited by our living on this higher plane. I know that of a truth,

> "Faith has caught the joyful sound
> The song of saints on higher ground."

Just think what pleasure it would give to the Father if only there were one person on this earth who would manifest constant thanksgiving to God—in every attitude, thought, word and deed! We know that Jesus was such a one and that in everything He did thank and praise the Father. If we obeyed His Word more fully and allowed His grace to operate in us more perfectly, we would find the same pattern being wrought in us. We would breathe out thanksgiving with every breath. We would be overflowing with "the great grace of gratitude." From morning until night this would be our theme. I am striving to become such a one, but have found that there is much in my nature that opposes it. I seem to be dull, unresponsive, lacking in appreciation. I find that it is not easy to be actively thankful at all times, for such a state leaves no place for the self-life to hold sway. But I still strive to fit into this beautiful picture the Spirit has taken the pains to paint for me.

The Lord has been trying to teach me that thanksgiving and praise is the way to victory in every situation. Recently I had an impressive lesson along this line. One of the Lord's dear ones was permitted to greatly tax my patience by coming to me in a strange spirit of animosity and taunting. I felt a current of negative feelings rising within me, particularly because this one seemed to be discrediting and doubting the Lord, as well as me. But suddenly I remembered that PRAISE is the way. So I began offering the Lord inward praise, offsetting everything that was being said by lauding Him and thanking Him. Outwardly a sweet serenity settled over me, while within strong praise was being wrought. In a very short time the whole situation changed. The other person began to take back the cruel things that had been said and before our meeting ended, love and faith and praise to God were flowing from both our hearts. It could have been just the opposite, so I want to remember this lesson—Praise is the way to victory.

The Holy Spirit impressed me about the House of David—and the special Praisers whom he chose. There were 4,000 out of 38,000 Levites, who were to do *nothing* but PRAISE the Lord, play on instruments, and celebrate and recount His glories and victories. For several months now the Spirit has told me to seek out these Davidic praisers. (1 Chronicles 23:5)

After living for days in a spirit of praise toward the Lord, I suddenly found that I had a strong aversion to praise. The words in Romans 7 came to me, paraphrased to meet my need: *"I delight in the law of PRAISE, in the inward man, but I find another law in my members."* I realized then that my old nature, my carnal nature which is not subject to the law of God, was opposing the praise I had been fervently offering, with all my soul, spirit, mind and body. There was a real conflict between the creature and the Creator within my being! And a question arose as to why God should *desire* so much praise. As I prayed earnestly about this, and waited on the Lord, the Spirit instructed me clearly that God does not ask for our praise because of *His need*, but because He has formed us for His praise, and as we truly worship we are raised to our highest degree of communion and awareness of Him. Praise is ennobling, elevating, energizing, and even *creative*—for as we praise we behold Him, and as we behold Him we are changed into the same image.

The cherubim and seraphim who worship at the throne,
Exalt the Lord our God forevermore.
They lift their "Holy, Holy, Holy" in such adoring tone,
And worship their Creator as of yore.
These cherubim and seraphim are sending help to earth,
And from on high they come to teach us here.
O may we learn this worship and bring it to full birth,
Distilled from love and reverential fear.

NEW EXPERIENCES IN PRAISE

"The living, the living, he shall praise you as I do this day."

I do believe that this word of PERFECTED PRAISE is the "saving word" for us at this time. This Word seems to fill me of late, and praise is springing up from my innermost being. Oh how I praise Him for His revelation unto us, and for the manifestation of His wonderful plan. I thank the Lord over and over that we can praise Him without any limitation. I keep seeing Him as the King of Beauty. O may it be said of me that I am one of "the babes" in whom He "perfects praise."

Recently the Lord whispered these words to me: "I want you to become *praise personified.*" How this thought took possession of me! To become an *embodiment of praise in the earth*—a temple filled with His glory by day and by night. I saw that heaven is indeed filled with His praise and glory. It is here on earth that praise is lacking, His glory limited. It seems that above all things He desires *habitations of praise,* pure praise, true praise, fervent praise. "Now I can *be* His praise," kept coming to me. Not only to offer praise, to practice praise, but to BE praise! What more wonderful calling could be given to a mortal? And what would be more fitting, in view of the great redemption He has wrought in us? I rejoiced with all my heart in "the hope of His calling." Yet, at the same time, I was made to realize, as never before, the qualifications required of one who aspires to fulfill it. I saw how far short I was in every way—for perfect praise cannot be manifest in us until there is a perfecting of *all* the fruits of the Spirit. This means utter death to self and a maturity in Christ far beyond that which I have attained. A high calling indeed! And although many may be called to it, few fulfill it as He desires. I long to be one of the few, and I have presented myself unto Him for that express purpose.

No sooner did I begin to live praise in earnest—not just spasmodically as heretofore—than I was beset with a series of most severe trials. Strange new difficulties developed in almost every realm of my life. My body was afflicted with various aches and pains, all clamoring for attention and inviting alarm. I found it a real battle to ignore these things and just keep on praising in spite of them.

Sometimes, especially during the night, the battle would go on for hours at a time. I could not praise aloud, because of the family; so I had to praise intensely, though silently, in order not to give way to doubts and fears and oppression. Annoyances and distractions multiplied during the day. It seemed impossible to keep on rejoicing, trusting, and praising.

My difficulties entered into the realm of the Spirit also; the enemy was trying to dishearten me in every way, trying to get me to cast away confidence and to cease praise.

I have known of the power and subtlety of the enemy for many years; but never have these been so openly manifest as since I began this way of continual praise. It is indeed revealing.

Not only is God revealed in praise, but Satan also is revealed. He is determined that praise be smothered, and wherever the flame begins to leap and dance, he is quick to rush in and put out the altar fire, if he can. I can see that *living* praise, day after day, hour after hour and especially night after night, is going to be a far greater struggle than I had anticipated. But this is what the Lord has asked of me and, by the grace of Jesus, I expect to obey Him.

(Note: We have had similar reports from many others. It is to be expected that Satan will especially attack praise. Lucifer's fall was brought about through a jealousy of the worship of JHVH. And Satan has been trying to extinguish His worship ever since, or if that is impossible, to *corrupt* it.)

The Holy Spirit has been speaking to me in various ways, and especially in the Scriptures, about the "Throne-praise" of God coming down into the earth. He has given me a new revelation of the purity, beauty, perfection, and glory of the praise that is offered by the Cherubim, the elders, the angels, and the saints who worship at the throne of God. It seems that we are to be attuned unto this higher praise, at least at certain times, and that we are to be like an antiphony in the earth, answering to and blending with the highest types of praise. The very thought of it is most exalting and refining. I have had rare experiences like this, and I yearn to participate more and more in this supernal worship.

The word concerning the call to the Mount of Praise has certainly taken hold of me! Yesterday, as I was sewing and felt that I had to get it done, the Lord spoke to me, telling me to stop. As I obeyed, the Spirit really began a work in me. I experienced a "call" from the Lord similar to the call to the ministry when I was in the "church order." That call was very plain, but this seemed to be much *greater* than that. I felt this down to my very toes, so to speak; it has gripped me as nothing else has. The holy fear of God has settled down over me and I feel I must *arise* and obey this call. I *know* it is from the Most High Himself.

"The glorious company of the Apostles praise Thee. The goodly fellowship of the Prophets praise Thee. The noble army of Martyrs praise Thee." And my own heart and voice are joining in with them! More and more I am aware of the fellowship of "the spirits of just men made perfect" and of the holy angels, as portrayed in Hebrews 12:22. Although I have been about forty years on this highway of rejoicing and praise, I feel more and more like a child in the Fathers House. With Abraham I embrace His promises and give thanks, being fully persuaded that He is able to perform them.

Recently the Holy Spirit enabled me to spend almost an entire day in praise, as I went about my tasks. Toward evening I began to feel the tide of the Spirit rising higher and higher, until, by bedtime, it became a veritable *flood-tide!* A sea of high praises rolled, boomed and broke! And I was lost, swallowed up in a rapturous ecstasy of love, worship and adoration—swept out of myself and into the depths of God's being. Floods of most exquisite, intense, penetrating joy enveloped me.

These waters seemed to be a cleansing, purifying, ennobling, sublimating, powerful force. Tears of joy flowed with exultant praises. Over and over I called the Lord my All in All. This title was deeply impressed upon me, and I was given a revelation of Christ as my perfect ALL which has remained with me ever since.

New fountains, new rivers, have been opened to me. Floods to swim in! My God, my All! Who is like unto Thee! My soul doth magnify Thee in a new and greater way.

As a few of us were gathered to offer praise to God, I suddenly felt a strong moving in my body. I seemed to have become a trumpet, and out of my mouth came trumpetings! Then, as we continued to worship, my body seemed to become other instruments, each giving forth its own unique and significant sound. I had an inward vision of David, leading forth the singers, dancers and players-on-instruments before the Ark. And I realized as never before the part praise played in restoring the Ark to Israel. In these latter days of restoration, praise is again playing a vital part in bringing up "the Ark," the awesome, miracle working presence of God!

I lift my voice to sing Thy praise, O Lord Most High,
And join the hosts that glorify Thy name,
Who send their anthems ringing through the earth and
sky
To offer Thee their hearts' acclaim.
My heart shall praise Thee, my lips shall praise Thee,
My tongue shall praise Thee, Lord, eternally.
For Thou art great and greatly to be praised, O Lord,
And Thy glory all the world shall see and every knee shall
bend
While fervent prayers ascend,
And every tongue shall then proclaim Thy name.
For Thou are great and greatly to be praised, O Lord,
And worthy of all power and fame.

REVELATIONS & ILLUMINATIONS

"I will praise Thee; for I am fearfully and wonderfully made; marvelous are Thy works."

As a few of us were gathered unto the Lord, the Spirit began to move upon us in earnest, fervent praise. Very soon I saw, in the Spirit, a high mountain, and was given to understand that it symbolized the "High Order of Praise." A herald stood on the very peak or top of the mountain, blowing a trumpet—sounding a reveille or call to ascend this Mount of Praise. When the trumpet began to sound, I heard the words, "Ascend, ascend, ascend! Leave the lowlands; make haste and ascend the Mount!" This was repeated, with variations, several times.

It was revealed to me that the "lowlands" represented the state or condition of each one who was being called—that state wherein we come short of this high calling. And I saw there must be a clean breaking away from all that ensnares us or hinders our ascent—anything, everything that does not pass His holy scrutiny and sanction—whether it be in the realm of the world or the flesh or Satan.

As I listened to the clear, certain tones of this-trumpet, I KNEW the summons was IMPERATIVE: that it was not from man, to be taken lightly, but a call from The Highest Himself—authoritative and commanding. I also knew it was URGENT: calling for immediate attention; and that the Lord was very weary of our vacillation, and grieved with our procrastination.

Furthermore, the call was DECISIVE: it was time for us to rally all the forces and faculties within us—our affections and interests, our wills and ways, our time and talents, ALL—for His glory and for His praise. I saw clearly that if we were to continue in this "high calling" we must "BE HIS PRAISE, LIVE HIS PRAISE" in everything.

The Spirit called for "pure praise" without the admixture of self, or of desire for blessings or favors in return, but praise which arises from the motive of pure love from a purified heart. Moreover, this praise He desired was "holy praise" or consecrated praise, which is offered unto God alone, and offered in the true spirit of praise, and not from the force of habit into which it is easy to fall. Only this high and holy praise will be acceptable unto Him who is High and Holy, who "dwells between the Cherubim!"

It was also disclosed that this lofty praise is a "glad and joyous praise" which springs from glad and grateful hearts, because it is our glorious privilege to praise Him who is Love! Although the heathen worship their gods with great sincerity and frenzied devotion, spending hours in their fanatical rituals, they are never inspired with holy, joyful praise such as that which we are privileged to offer unto our loving God. TO KNOW HIM is to LOVE HIM, and to love Him is to PRAISE HIM!—with joy and gladness!

I saw that when we could praise God with "perfect praise," it would become "projected praise"—powerful and effective in His hands to the tearing down of the strongholds of the enemy, the casting down of imaginations and every high thing that exalted itself against the knowledge of God, and for the deliverance and salvation of multitudes of captives! I heard the words, "I will work as My people praise Me," and "When will My people learn to praise Me?" This revelation and experience has moved me to a deeper heart-searching, and to a greater purpose and resolve to ascend this holy Mount of High Praise, the dwelling place of our God.

I feel strongly that the glory of God is at stake. It seems He has put it within our power to protect His glory and to advance His fame. In view of this, how sinful is our neglect! It seems that this old nature of ours is actually competing with God for honors. We were made for *His* glory, not our own. The Lord has given me a little glimpse of the horribleness of our old nature, the leaven of which is trying to work its way into the Holiest. It must be a pure offering we bring. It is holiness unto the Lord or nothing. I am overwhelmed with the thought of His glory. He has offered us a tremendous privilege. I tremble at this word from Him! I can feel His heart yearning and desiring this high praise; it seems that it is even broken and bleeding, waiting, waiting, for this heavenly praise.

Last night I could see the heavenly ones praising Him according to His heart's desire. But it seemed that He had not yet found those on earth who could praise Him this way. I saw a circuit, and the Lord was waiting for some on earth to complete the circuit so the heavenly glory could flow from above to earth. Then I saw His glory flashing from east to west in the midst of those on earth who arose and answered the call. I am so glad to have had this word. I feel that I have been visited by the Most High. By His grace, I want to obey and meet you at the top of the Mount.

As I was engaged in worshiping the Lord when a great thankfulness swept through my entire being. It seemed to originate in the Holy Spirit and I felt that He was rejoicing in our praise unto the Lord. I was so very thankful to be called into this ministry of glorifying the King.

Then I uttered these words, *"My heart is inditing a great and glorious matter. For great is the Lord and greatly to be praised!"* I had a glimpse of the angels and saints in heaven, and they too were rejoicing in the praise of mortals. Soon another picture passed before me: I saw myriads of souls seeking the Lord, praying, crying, sighing, moaning, beseeching Him with tears and doleful petitions. There was so little praise! I was greatly grieved at the neglect of praise. I longed to praise Jesus in some great outstanding way so that I might make up for this lack. And I cried out within myself, recalling the years I spent in crying and beseeching Him, giving very little praise: O to be expendable in praising God! O to expend myself in His praises!

During the night I was suddenly awakened, and I heard an inward voice speaking to me. My heart was so touched and stirred that I knew it was the voice of My Beloved Lord. And this is what He said, "You little realize the realm into which you could be taken if *everything* but praise were silenced and subdued within you." Then He gave me a glimpse of this realm . . . *a realm* so creative, supernatural, peaceful, and positive that I was amazed. It was truly beyond the limits of my own imagination. As I have pondered this revelation, I have realized more fully than before that much of our thought-life, feelings, attitudes, and words are tinged with negative and even destructive power. They are impure because they are mixed. Therefore they are subversive in their effect. On the other hand, what great creative power we could manifest in Christ if in everything we gave true and fervent praise and thanksgiving.

All my Christian life I have recognized the importance of prayer, but for some reason the importance of praise had never been brought to my attention. One day as I was quietly waiting upon the Lord in prayer, the Spirit moved in a most unusual way. For several hours His presence lingered, and I was given a revelation about the *ministry* of praise. I am not able to put into words what I experienced and saw, but it is all confirmed in Scripture. Actually there is far more in the Bible about praising God, rejoicing in Him, and singing to Him, than there is about praying. As I searched the Scriptures, I found more than four hundred references to praise. (These did not include a number of synonyms, words such as extol, sing, glorify, etc.) The references to prayer are fewer. But the two go together, as we know, and the two are the two "wings" that lift us Godward. *The strange thing is that praise is so neglected.* In this revelation, I felt the Lord's great desire was that I and others enter into a life of high praise, continual praise. It seemed that there would be limitless power and fruition manifested in any who obey Him in this ministry. I also saw that it is the highest and most heavenly of all ministries.

WHAT THE SPIRIT IS SAYING

"He who has an ear, let Him hear what the Spirit is saying."

Do not underestimate the power and purpose of praise. Satan seeks to *divert* My people from giving Me fervent, pure, and continuous praise. Praise is a *life* to be lived, a *battle* to be fought, and a *way* to be followed. It is a *key* to many hidden mysteries of the Kingdom, and a *power* few men have discovered or learned to use. It is a *vocation* to be pursued, and a *calling* to be obeyed. It is an *art*, an *exercise*, and a *practice*. My Praisers are FEW; there is need that MANY rise up swiftly to render high and effectual praise unto Me. Search the Word and wait upon the Spirit, that you may be instructed in PRAISE, the *everlasting ministration* of the saints.

The failure to give the Lord the glory due His name is the most shameful among all the failures of the people of God. Even those who do praise Him the most frequently and fervently fall far short of the high and holy praise He desires and requires—a praise worthy of His great glory. Earthly kings and leaders receive far more praise and demonstration of honor than the King of Heaven. It is His desire that the praise of the heavens shall come down into the earth, and that He be praised on earth as in heaven. Indeed, *not until His praise is resounding throughout all the earth shall His open glory be made manifest.* He reveals Himself in the midst of praise!

Revelations, prophecies, and teachings about praise—as good as they are—are not the principal thing: it is the *performance of praise*—both in the life and on the lips—that is vital. It is better to receive one word from the Spirit and obey it, than to have an abundance of revelations which go unheeded. There is much talk about praise, but little praise! It is easier to say, "Praise ye the Lord," than to say, "I do praise Thee, my Lord." *"Be ye doers of the Word, and not hearers only, deceiving your own selves."* (James 1:22) Praise is not complete until it is *expressed.* It is not enough to say, "I have the thought of praise in my heart." *Praise must be enacted, given a form, made manifest.* Our God is a God of action and performance. He desires that we perform our vows, and make His praise glorious.

The radius of Christ's circumfulgence toward us is increased as we praise Him in Spirit and in truth. This was impressed upon me in the form of a spiral. It began with a small circle at the bottom, but as it went up it enlarged with each "round" of praise. We ascended in praise, spiraling up and up into the heavens until our praise was resolved into angelic tongues and a new song sprang from our lips.

Render unto the King free, joyful, radiant praise. Let it be varied (not monotonous) as His works are varied; glorious as His power is glorious; colorful, as His creation is colorful; rich, new, fluent, and eloquent. Sing it, speak it, dance it, shout it, act it, write it, breathe it, think it, radiate it, live it, express it in a hundred ways. He is worthy of your best and highest praise!

The praisers go before the Ark, preparing the way of the King. Praise wakens the slumbering, heals the wounded. It evaluates in heavenly terminology the boundless graces and mercies for which we have no words or comprehension. It spans differences and distances. It unites all who love the Lord in truth.

Praise affirms that God is; God can; God will; and God has! Praise is the power God gives us to wield. Praise is the victory. It is a powerful magnet, drawing the Beloved One to the praiser, and vice versa. Praise God, and He will draw nigh unto you. It draws others to Him with the assurance and reassurance of His love and response.

Praise is our insurance and assurance. It is faith's fulfillment, hope's fruition, love's coronation. There is something of a consummation—two-way—about it. Praise defies defeat, implies faith, denies the flesh, applies wisdom, supplies strength. It is an art—the beginning of wisdom. The secret of the Lord is with them that praise Him, and He will show them His covenant. Praise gives form or substance to the things which are to come. It makes way for God's plan to be fulfilled.

His praise shall continually be in the heart and mouth. Praise is a sowing or a planting; it is a watering; it is a gathering of flower and fruit; it is a life after death. Praise is beauty expressed; song rendered; glory revealed. It is an act of love. It is like the bloom on the first-fruits. It is sweet music's overtone! It is the blossom's fragrance; fire's glow; heart's warmth. Praise is active. It is the activation-motivation of love for God in bloom. It is like a live wire that no one but the life-giving Spirit can touch. It is armored love, plus fortified faith; Praise covers a multitude of faults. Cover with praise all that is unseemly, unlikely, unpleasant and ungodly. True praise does not depend upon feeling, but upon obedience. True praise gives freely, unquestionably, unconditionally, and receives immediate audience. Praise prepares the way for the Lord and, in turn, for the saint and for the sinner. It is like blending or combining faith and devotion. It seems to be the divine partaking of humanity, as it passes through human channels. It is the shortest distance between the saint and the King of the saints.

Praise is like sweet incense, like the God-essence that man takes out of himself and pours back on God. It is often like taking out your very hearts and offering them to Him, as you offer the sacrifice of praise.

PRAISE is a fragrant flower which springs forth from good soil—the planting of the Lord.

PRAISE withers amid thorns and briars (a sharp, critical spirit.)

PRAISE fades upon rocky earth (hardness of spirit.)

PRAISE dies upon wayside ground (uncultivated spirit.)

PRAISE flourishes in good ground (a mellow and tender spirit.)

PRAISE blossoms in rich soil (the generous spirit.)

PRAISE flowers in the sunshine (a glad, cheerful spirit.)

PRAISE multiplies abundantly when cultivated and watered.

PRAISE does not grow like weeds (without care.)

PRAISE is sweet incense which rises from a purified-by-fire heart.

PRAISE is the perfume of love's devotion.

PRAISE is the essence of sorrow's tears.

PRAISE is like a cloud of glory which fills the Temple.

PRAISE is like the holy anointing oil compounded of myrrh, cinnamon, cassia, and the oil olive (a combination of ingredients.)

The everlasting praises of the Eternal One mount up into heaven; they go down into the depths. He that dwells in the heights shall hear it and be glad. He takes sweet refuge in the mountains of His praise. (Zion!) These habitations of praise, these spiritual skyscrapers of glorification, are His desired haven. Praise Him in the heights. Magnify Him in the depths! Earth and heaven, make His praise glorious!

The entrance of His praise also brings light. Blessed are they which sow praises beside all waters: The waters of affliction (Marah), humiliation, and persecution; as well as beside the waters of blessing.

There is a divine secret in the high praise of God. It releases His power. Praise resembles helium, causing us to rise above the earth. It also enables us to parachute His power to far distant lands. It is a secret weapon and no man knows what may be accomplished by practicing the praise of the Living and only true God.

The Beloved languishes and thirsts for your praise. What I say, I say unto you all, "Praise!" Lift up your voice with strength, be not afraid; span heaven and earth with a triumphant bridge of His praises. Tunnel through the rocks, make paths through the seas; irrigate the arid wastes.

Love delights to see the Beloved arrayed as becomes His excellence! She weeps as she sees Him in the garments of humiliation. She rejoices to behold Him in the vestments of His exaltation. Our precious Christ can never be made too much of. Heaven itself is but just good enough for Him. All the pomp that angels and archangels, and thrones, and dominions, and principalities, and powers, can pour at His feet *is* too little for Him. His people can never extol Him enough.

Praise unlocks heaven's portals;
Praise causes doubts to cease;
Praise brings precious blessings;
Praise leaves the sweetest peace.
Praise breaks all bands asunder;
Praise sets the captive free;
Praise lightens every burden;
Praise is the master key;

Praise changes circumstances;
Praise establishes the heart;
When praise becomes perpetual,
Praise is a Holy Art.

Deafen your ears to the din of this world, and attune your hearts to the music of the spheres, the music of the heavenly realms, the music of the winds, the seas, the trees. It is the voice of the Lord that shakes the trees of the forest; the voice of the Lord that whispers in the winds, that roars in the seas. Be deaf to the voices and the din of this world, that you may be alert to His voice, His music! There is music all around you. Make music unto the Lord!

Sing unto Him and make melody in your hearts unto Him. You know not the mystery of this music, the power of this singing. He has not called you to make a clamor unto He has said, "Sing! Sing! Sing unto Me!" And this song must not be neglected, this song must not cease, no matter how heavy your heart may be, nor how weak your body; no matter how much there may be to trouble your mind—Sing! Sing! Sing unto the Lord! Speak unto Him and unto yourselves with psalms and hymns and spiritual songs. How heavenly is this concourse! How rich and rare are the true songs of the Spirit! Yet how few are they in the earth! The Lord has a listening ear! Do not try to catch the ears of men, nor attract their attention. Sing unto the Lord! His ear is open to your song! And when you sing unto Him out of the depths of your heart, He will cause your voice to be heard on high. Yes, far above the range of mortal ear. How foolish to desire to be seen and heard of men! Such desires have the Pharisees. "Let *Me* see thy face; Let *Me* hear thy voice."

Praise cannot dwell with bigotry or abide with self. No true praise emerges from a mouth whose heart is filled with resentment or self-pity. *Praise is completely divorced from condemnation.* The Lord wants a bona-fide praise. He does not want fair-weather praise. Be instant in praise, in and out of season. Give extraordinary praise. He has done extraordinary things.

Continue in praise, offering thanksgiving in small things—in all things. Let no man forbid thee to praise or despise thy song of glad thanksgiving in the earth. Ephemeral creature, praise Him while it is light, for the night cometh soon.

Highly favored and most blessed are they who find and follow the way of high and holy worship. Yea, blessed are they who learn here in the earth the way of heavenly worship that leads into the presence of the Most High. They shall arise and be freed from the binding ties of the earthly. They shall put on wings and escape like a bird out of the snares of the enemy, flying straight home to God's own heart whence the spirit came. For the spirit descended from God Himself and must return unto Him. Does not thy spirit within thee beat its wings like a caged bird, seeking escape, seeking its homeward flight? Do not wait for the hour of death to come and release your spirit unto Him. Let your spirit be freed now, while there is yet breath in your nostrils, while your heart is still beating strongly and you are clothed upon with this body of earth. It is true that when death comes your body shall return unto dust and your spirit unto God who gave it; but it pleases the Lord that even now, while still living in this body, your spirit shall rise often, seeking the Father in holy worship, dwelling in His presence with song and praise.

Worship, worship, worship and glorify
His name, His sacred name,
His holy name, His unspeakable name!
Let the earth be shaken!
Let the mountains be cast into the heart of the sea!
Let the heavens themselves bend down before Him!
Let every star flame out to His glory!
Let every sphere whirl, whirl, whirl in space
In perfect order, in perfect beauty,

In perfect array, in perfect grace!
All creatures great and small, the Lord calls on them all.
Let everything that lives, let everything that breathes,
Let everything that has life, glorify Him, exalt Him!
Pay tribute to the Creator of heaven and earth!
And let the saints most of all, excel in this worship.

Out of the Temple shall come forth the voice of praise. Yes, and the VOICE shall speak from the Temple—the VOICE of the ALL HOLY. Even as He speaks from the Throne, so shall He speak from His Temple on earth! Everything in His Temple shall cry, "Glory, glory, glory!" The vessels of the Lord shall be cleansed and purged by fire, polished and restored to the Temple of the Lord. And they shall be called "The people of the Purging Fire," for by them shall the God that answers by fire purge the earth. They shall be the bearers of the sacred fire. They shall take it from the Altar and scatter it in the earth. By fire shall the Lord purge the earth. (Psalm 29:9; Malachi 3:1)

His praise shall rise like a fountain.
And flow like a river
Until it becomes a mighty sea of everlasting glory.
It shall ascend unto the highest heights
And blend with the songs of the blest;
It shall stoop to the deepest depths
And bring peace to the imprisoned and oppressed.
It shall be a balm to the wounded
And a wine to the fainting heart,
An oil of joy for the head,
How wonderful is praise like this!
It shall run with the speed of light
To all the dark hidden places;
It shall destroy every evil thing,
It shall conquer in every field,
And live throughout the ages to come.

Summon *all* the powers of your being! Summon all the powers of your being . . . your being's ransomed powers, the powers that you know not of, the powers that are hidden within you, to praise the Lord. I have not permitted man to know all the powers that are latent and locked within his being, for those he has discovered he has used to his own destruction. But I say unto you, call forth, summon all the powers of your being and devote them to this praise, the high praise. Oh, devote all the powers that are latent within your *soul,* the powers within your *heart and its affections.* Summon the *vital energy of your body of flesh*, the body I have created for My glory. Summon all your powers and do not dissipate them on vanity. Do not waste breath—it is *life!* Do not waste thought—it is powerful, both to destroy and to create. Do not waste words, for the time shall come when you shall be held accountable for every word you utter. Your words shall become impregnated with power. Praise Me unceasingly!

"He has given a banner to them that fear Him, that it may be displayed because of the truth." He has given them a trumpet to be blown because of righteousness. He has given them an armor of light to put on, and a shield to be lifted. With the high praises of God in our mouths and a two-edged sword in our hands, we rise to follow our Conquering King who rides forth for Zion's war.

> "Then onward from the hills of light
> Our hearts with love aflame,
> We'll vanquish all the hosts of night
> In Jesus' conquering name!"

O Lord, many are Thy crowns! We would exalt Thee and crown Thee *now* with *praise!* Here, in Zion, we would give Thee Thy first dominion. We should be the *first* to bring back the King! Thou hast been in the midst of Thy people as their Servant—Lord, their accommodating God and helper—answering their petitions, doing unto them according to their needs and desires. Now Thou art coming forth in the midst of Thy people to be their Ruler and to perform *Thine own pleasure.* Man's ways shall be brought to a sudden end. Thine own ways shall be established, and Thy people shall be a broken, willing people, in the day of Thy power. They shall serve Thee with newness of heart and mind, newness of devotion, and with an eye single to Thy glory and pleasure. Our Suffering-Servant has become our Glorious King! (Psalms 2, 110)

> We went out weeping, we went out weeping;
> We have come back rejoicing, we have come back rejoicing!
> Laughter has filled our mouths; joy has crowned our hearts.
> Praise be to the One who turned our mourning into dancing!
> We have sown in tears, we shall reap with joy.
> We went out empty, we have come back full.
> Our lips are fragrant with praise,
> Our voices vibrant with song—
> The singing people of the Singing God.
> We are His singing sons.
> The heavens shall be filled with song,
> And the earth shall respond with music;
> The spheres shall sing,
> And every star shall voice its melody.
> And the Lord of the Heavens shall rise
> And go forth in the midst of song,
> He shall go forth in the midst of music.
> We shall sing the songs we learned in our night of sorrow!
> We shall sing the songs we learned in the wilderness!
> We shall sing the songs we learned on our bed of pain!
> We shall sing the songs we learned in this barren land!
> We shall sing the songs we learned on our pilgrimage!
> We shall sing the songs we learned on Zion's hill!
> We shall sing the songs we learned in His Chamber!

We shall sing the songs we learned in the banqueting house!

O, Solomon had a thousand and one songs,
And a song above all songs!
But our King has ten thousand times ten thousand times
Ten thousand times ten thousand times as many songs—
And a Song of Songs. A Song of Songs!
A song no one can learn unless He teach it to him.
The Song of Songs! A Song for the chief singers,
A canticle of canticles, an anthem sublime!

O, the day of the Lord breaketh—and it is a terrible day! It is a day of darkness and strife, a day of bitterness and enmity, a day when Satan too comes down with great power to work his works and to deceive men. How shall ye escape unless ye shall mount up—far above all—on the wings of praise? He will deliver the soul that praises Him; that one shall mount up far above all, far above all, to dwell in His presence. Yes, He will manifest His victory to the one who believes; and if any man *believes* he will *rejoice* and give *praise,* for *faith cannot be silent.* Faith has a song! Hallelujah! Sing the song of faith! Sing the song of love! O keep holy day before Him, for the day of the Lord is a holy day to His saints, and a terrible day to His foes. Keep holy day, for I say to you that, Zion in that day shall be filled with praise and glory; and whosoever will go up into the City of God must go with songs of pilgrimage, entering His gates with thanksgiving. There is no other way to enter the gates of that strong city, and if any man would enter and dwell in His courts, let him continue to praise, praise, praise!

By *My own arm* will I bring deliverance! By My own arm will I bring salvation, and no man shall be able to glory in that day, or say, "See what deliverance we have wrought by *our* prayers and *our* works!" I say unto you that by My own arm, by My own power, by My own strength, I will work My works. Wherefore, let all the house of Israel magnify

Me. Let all the house of Israel shout unto their God and praise Him; and let the house of Aaron praise Him without ceasing. Yes, let Israel rejoice, for the Lord in the midst is mighty. He will save. He will rejoice over them as the bridegroom rejoices over the bride. It is fitting to give thanks unto Him and to exalt Him. It is fitting to rise up out of the dust and go before Him with singing. It is fitting to be radiant, overflowing with thanksgiving and praise. O, put off your sackcloth and put on thy beautiful garments of praise, and anoint your face with oil and adorn yourself as a bride prepared for her husband, and go forth to meet Him. Is He not at the door? Go forth to meet Him!

Strike the loud timbrel! Clash the loud cymbals! The Lord Jehovah hath triumphed gloriously. He hath made a way for the redeemed to pass over. *He hath made a way of praise for the redeemed to pass over.* He hath rolled back the sea. Israel praised the Lord on that great day when the horse and his rider were cast into the sea. They sang together and rejoiced before the Lord. But how soon their song of praise died down! O that Israel *had praised* the Lord! O that men *would* praise the Lord! O that His people had praised Him by the waters of Marah! O that they had praised Him in the wilderness! Their pilgrimage would have been cut short! O that men would rise to glorify Him in *this* day! We would soon see His power.

In the midst of praise, O Lord, Thou wilt show forth Thy presence. Thy presence and Thy praise dwell together. You will meet him who rejoices, Hallelujah! Thy praise is sweet to our lips; it is honey to the tongue; it is as wine to the palate. Thy praise is a luscious fruit, reviving the faint. Thy praise, O Lord, is better than wine. We offer unto Thee, O Lord, a living praise! It is a well-ripened fruit. It has been watered with tears in the valley of affliction; it has grown in the sunshine of grace; now it has ripened and is a fit offering for Thee, O our King! We kiss the Son and offer Him the harvest of the fruit of our lips.

Like the sound of many waters, O Lord, is Thy voice; and the praise of the saints shall ascend unto Thee like the tumult of the sea. Thy praise shall be so great and so loud and so high that it shall fill all the earth and heaven. From Thy throne, Thou shalt reply, and shall pour forth THY praise and blessing upon Thy people, and every man—as Thou has said—shall have praise of God. Blessed are they who have praise *for God.* In that day they shall receive praise *from* God. (1 Corinthians 4:5)

Thou art the God our fathers praised, the God our mothers praised! Our God! Be praised as a King is worthy to be praised! Be praised with a praise exceeding the praise the heathen give to their idols! Be praised in beauty! Be praised in strength! Be praised in glory! Let Thy people bring forth a praise worthy of Thee, worthy, worthy, worthy! We would not bring Thee an offering that costs nothing. Our father David despised such an offering. I will not offer that to the Lord which costs nothing. I will bring a *costly* offering. Bring a costly offering. Be prepared to pay a price for it—a great price. Bring a costly offering unto the King.

Come ye, come ye; stir up that which is within thee; put on the armor prepared for thee. Put on thy helmet and prepare to ascend. You need special *light* for this special way, for the path is dark, stony and thorny. This new way is not a way of delight and ease. It is not a casting of thyself upon a cloud of glory; it is a difficult way, a way that bruises—but He bindeth up again and again. *This new way is the praise way.* Great must be the praise of My people. This High Way (highway) has not yet been trodden in the earth, but it is traversable, for it is marked by the blood of the Lamb. Behold, the Spirit leadeth thee in the new praise path. It is My hand that guideth thee and not another's. This is My praise way. Arise, arise, put on strength, O daughter of Zion! Ascend to the peak of peaks where standeth the holy angels, the immortal saints, awaiting thee. Come ye who know the Lord, ye who love His name and dwell on High. Praise "opens the gates that you may enter. Arise this very hour. Tread upon scorpions; push down the enemies by the power of praise. Let the weak say I am strong. Take the shield of faith and the sword in thy hand and hasten toward the goal, for the time is short. This is the hour. Possess the peak of peaks. This is My land, a land flowing with the richest of milk and the sweetest of honey. Possess the land and breathe the pure air of the Spirit. And bless the name of thy God forever and even forevermore.

Give praise unto the Lord with all your hearts. Speak of His wonderful kindness and goodness in the midst of the Assembly. Lo, He has dealt with you in abundant mercy and abounding grace. So let your thanksgiving abound toward Him. Do not praise Him grudgingly nor of necessity, but liberally and joyfully offer the sacrifice of praise unto Him, even when your hearts have cause to be heavy and oppressed. Look not upon the things that are seen, which are external and passing. Set your hearts and your eyes upon the things that are unseen, which are eternal and unchanging. If you walk by sight and feeling, you shall be depressed. And if you praise only when you feel like praising, or have some special cause for praise, you will be miserly toward the Lord. Be not silent, but break forth into singing and shouting. For the dead praise not the Lord, neither they that go down into the pit. But let everything that lives and has breath Praise the Lord and sing aloud unto Him. For the Lord most high is magnificent in all His ways and magnanimous in all His acts.

Sing unto the Lord even by the waters of Babylon! In all places, in all conditions, sing unto the Lord! Let the song of the Lord be heard among all nations! For the song of the Lord is mighty. The Lord Himself is your strength and song. And He is a singing God. In the midst of His church, Jesus sings aloud and all His sons are singing sons. The song of the Lord is a weapon mightier than sword or spear. When the Israelites began to sing and praise the Lord, He sent an ambush against their foes and gave His people the victory. Learn how to sing in the storms as well as in the sunlight.

"To Thee, O Lord, we give thanks. Though our mouths were full of song as the sea, and our tongues of exultation as the multitude of its waves, and our lips of praise *as* the wide-extended firmament; though our eyes shone with light like the sun and the moon, and our hands were spread forth like the eagles of heaven, and our feet were swift as deer, we should still be unable to thank Thee and to bless Thy name, O Lord our God and God of our fathers, for one-thousandth or one ten-thousandth part of the bounties which Thou hast bestowed upon our fathers and upon us. Therefore the limbs which Thou hast given us and the spirit and breath which Thou has breathed into our nostrils, and the tongue which Thou hast set in our mouths, lo, they shall thank, bless, praise, glorify, extol, reverence, hallow, and assign kingship to Thy name, O our King! For every mouth shall give thanks unto Thee, and every tongue shall magnify Thee: every knee shall bow to Thee and whatsoever is lofty shall prostrate itself before Thee; all hearts shall fear Thee, and all the inward parts and reins shall sing unto Thy name, according to the Word that is written, All my bones shall say, "Lord, who is like unto Thee? Who can be compared with Thee, O God, great, mighty and awful, most High God, possessor of heaven and earth? We will praise, laud and glorify Thee, and we will bless Thy holy name. Thou art God in Thy power and might, great in Thy glorious name, mighty forever and awesome by Thy awesome acts, the King who sitteth upon a high and lofty throne.

"In the assemblies also of the tens of thousands of Thy people, the house of Israel, Thy name, O our King, shall be glorified with joyous cries in every generation; for such is the duty of all creatures in Thy presence, O Lord our God, to thank, praise, laud, glorify, extol, honor, bless, exalt and adore Thee, even beyond all the words of song and praise of David, the son of Jesse, Thy servant and anointed."

—Hebrew Prayer

Let all the house of David now rejoice,
And sing unto the Lord;
Let them begin with happy voice
To magnify Him in accord.
Let them bring forth the harp and the timbrels,
Let them clash the highly sounding cymbals;
Let the instruments now be attuned!
Let all the house of David now rejoice,
And sing unto the Lord;
For it is time they made sweet melody
And brought forth heavenly harmony
For the pleasure of Zion's great King!
Let all the house of David now rejoice
And sing, sing, sing!

PERFECTING PRAISE

Frances Metcalfe

INTRODUCTION

At Resurrection Time, 1974, the blessed Holy Spirit spoke to us about perfecting our praise in the reverential fear of the Lord. Since then He has given further instruction and inspiration to us regarding the ministry of praise. And we shall share herein some of these precious truths which various members of our Fellowship have experienced. In the Greek, the word for perfecting is *epiteleo.* It means to fulfill, to consummate, accomplish, complete or finish. "To bring to full fruition" is implied. In English, the meaning of perfecting is "to bring to the highest possible degree of excellence." It also means to complete, mature or finish. We also made a study of the Hebrew and Greek words which are translated praise in the King James Version and we are including this, hoping it will bless you as much as it blessed us.

PERFECTING PRAISE

One of the first things He impressed us to do was prayerfully to review LIVING THE LIFE OF PRAISE and MAKING HIS PRAISE GLORIOUS. Also to read any other books we have along this line. We have sent forth these teachings far and wide for the past twenty-five years, and yet it is possible that we shall ourselves fall short of all that the Lord desires in our own praise and worship. He also revealed that in praising the Lord we should turn to the various verses about praise in the Psalms, in Isaiah, and in The Revelation, and incorporate these verses in our own praise and songs to the Lord. He impressed us not to wait just for our meetings to pour out praise, but to do this alone each day.

When we assemble, He urged us to really "break the alabaster box" and pour out its entire contents—to really give of our utmost in praise, song, and worship and to let it be a real "drink offering" unto Him. He showed us not to stint our praise in any way, but to give of our best and most fervent praise each time, not holding in reserve something for the future. When Mary broke the alabaster box and lavished all its contents on Jesus, she was anointing Him for His burial.

But now we are anointing Him for His appearing and His great latter day manifestation. The hymn says that He is clothed in splendor and girded with praise. Let us anoint and gird Him with our most precious praise!

He revealed that the Lord really thirsts for our praise, even as our souls thirst for Him. So, His satisfying drink is the pure, loving, fervent worship and praise of His people.

He showed us that He is leading us into a higher praise, a higher worship, and also into a higher, more heavenly walk. Even though we are in the midst of the earth, we have also been raised up and placed, even planted, in heavenly places in Christ. (Ephesians 2:6) *"Whoso offereth praise glorifieth Me, and to him who ordereth his conversation (walk and talk) aright, I will show the salvation (the great reserved fulness of the endtime salvation) of God."* (Psalm 50:23) The Hebrew word for glorify is *kabad*. It means to make numerous, rich, honorable or great. The English word means, to elevate to celestial glory; to shed radiance and splendor upon; to magnify, adore and exalt.

He told us to "summon all the powers of our being" to enter into this praise at this time. *"Let all that is within me bless His holy name."* He dealt with us about the word glory, and about giving Him glory continually. He made it so clear that we, His people, are His glory on the earth. (John 17:10) And He also showed us that He had preserved us on earth for this purpose. Heaven abounds with His glory. But on earth there is so much to dishonor Him. O, may we be a glory people, giving God glory all the day long!

It is not possible to give glory to God outwardly at all times, as we know, but there can be an inward glorying in the Lord at all times, in all places and in all circumstances. Even in our small circle, we had opportunity to give inward glory to God while in such unlikely places as the hospital, the dentist's chair, the unemployment office, and a court of law. We were encouraged to give "inward glory" in the home, the office the shop, and on the highway. It seems it particularly pleases the Lord to be praised and glorified in difficult, unlikely places and circumstances.

"Whether, therefore, ye eat or drink, or whatever ye do, do all to the glory of God." (1 Corinthians 10:31) Each meal time should be a feast with the Lord. And we must truly learn to discipline ourselves not to eat for self indulgence, but for the glory of God. Many Spirit-filled Christians do not seem to realize that gluttony is a sin. He reminded us again that He wants a lively, living praise from us and not a dead, formal, ritualistic praise and worship. He wants us to praise Him as those who are alive from the dead—in newness of life, with gladness of heart.

He has indeed turned our mourning into dancing. He has put off our sackcloth and girded us with gladness. No matter what the conditions around us are, no matter how we feel, the Holy Spirit will enable us to give Him vital living praise. *"Thou hast turned for me my mourning into dancing; Thou hast put off my sackcloth, and girded me with gladness; to the end that my glory may sing praise to Thee, and not be silent. O Lord my God, I will give thanks unto Thee forever."* (Psalm 30:11, 12)

One of our members shared this experience: "This worthy exercise in praise unto our God has been upgraded. I feel finally that I've reached a plateau. This giving of perfected (mature) praise to the Lord has been pondered. *'The fear of the Lord is clean, enduring forever.'* (Psalm 19:9) *'The fear of the Lord is the beginning of wisdom.'* (Proverbs 9:10) So the fear of the Lord is the good soil, the productive soil for praise that is pure, true and mature from which to spring out. It is living in this attitude and giving this practical praise unto our God at all times, in all things, that causes the real conflagration (in the Spirit) when we come together to praise our God."

Let nothing or anyone dampen or hinder our praise to the Lord. I must discipline myself to praise—for this is my joy offering to the Lord. The sacrifice of praise! The sacrifice of joy! *In everything give thanks!* He gives us the garment of praise for the spirit of heaviness. (Isaiah 61:3) I felt led to look this up in the Hebrew. The word "heaviness" in Hebrew is, *kahah*, meaning weakness. While we offer praise to the Lord, according to this verse, it is health to cure or cover our weakness. The word garment is, *maateh*, a covering or wrapping, to wear praise as a covering or wrapping and reveals that we can't keep our praise unto God all inside and unvoiced. I pray to be fully covered, wrapped in this garment—mind, soul, spirit, body, and heart. None of the fiery darts of Satan can penetrate this covering. When his subtle attacks have penetrated, could it be that some area of our being wasn't fully covered with this wrapping? Yes, it could be!

The following anointed prayer came forth in one of our night praise times: "Praise waiteth for Thee, O God, in Zion, waiteth for Thee and on Thee. Praise waiteth on and ministereth unto Thee, O Lord, in ways that we do not yet fully understand. There is a ministry and a mystery in worship. There is a ministry in praise. There is a harmony, a unity with Thee, as we praise. O Lord, Thou hast taught us these holy ways. *'Blessed is the one (man) whom you choose and cause to approach You, that he may dwell in Your courts. We shall be satisfied with the goodness of Your house, even of Your holy Temple.'"* (Psalm 65:4)

Thank You, Lord, for choosing us and causing us to come into Your courts, for You have said that we enter into Your courts with praise, into the courts of the Living God; and that we may dwell in Your holy Temple, that Temple not made with hands, eternal in the heavens. You have said that we may have access, O Lord, into the Holy Place of the Most High.

One night the Holy Spirit gave us this little chorus. The melody is, "All Over the World the Spirit is Moving." Here is the chorus: "All over again, the Spirit is moving, All over again, to stir out hearts to praise. All over again, He is giving revelations of how to worship the Lord, in holy, heavenly ways."

One verse was strongly impressed. It is found in Psalm 54:6: *"I will freely sacrifice unto Thee; I will praise Thy name, O Lord Jehovah, for it is good."* And the sacrifices He impressed on us are as follows:

The sacrifice of joy when feelings and circumstances seem to be contrary. (Psalm 27:6)

The sacrifice of thanksgiving always and in all things. (Psalm 107:22)

The sacrifice of a broken spirit and contrite heart. (Psalm 51:17)

The sacrifice of praise. (Hebrews 13:15)

Another wrote: "This morning I was struck with Romans 12:1, *'Present your bodies a living sacrifice . . . which is your reasonable service.'* Many of the translations render 'reasonable service' as 'spiritual worship.' In the very consecration of our bodies in the act of fully yielding our lives to Jesus, in that act of total consecration is the very highest form of worship and praise! For that reason it is called 'spiritual worship!'"

I will be glad and rejoice in Thee, O Lord, No matter how I feel. I will praise and thank Thee with all my heart for I know that Jesus is real. Thy Word is real and Thy love is Oh, so real! So I will be glad and rejoice in Thee, O Lord, No matter how I feel. *"Let the high praises of God be in their mouths."* (Psalm 149:6) The Holy Spirit stirred our hearts to call upon the Lord that the high praise of God come forth in us in all its fullness and beauty. We caught a new vision of such praise. But we were also shown that it would indeed be costly, and that there must be much more refining done in us to bring it forth.

The Holy Spirit has given us several songs of praise, but most of them are Scripture portions set to music by Him. We do feel led to share this one which came with a blessed anointing. The melody is, "The Comforter Has Come."

"With all the saints below And all the saints above Our voices we will raise To praise the Lord we love. We'll sing His holy name And offer our acclaim, The King of Kings is He! The King of Kings is He! The King of Kings is He! His Kingdom shall be spread From sea to shining sea. And every knee shall bow And every tongue confess That Christ is Lord of all."

One night, as we worshiped, the Holy Spirit spoke the words in Psalm 9:14: *"That I may show forth all Thy praise in the gates of the daughter of Zion. I will rejoice in Thy salvation."* The word just preceding this says, *"Thou hast lifted me up from the gates of death."* How wonderful! We know the Lord has healed and delivered us from death many times during our lifetimes, even beginning when we were small children. And, of course, He has delivered us all from the gates of spiritual death. Instead, we are placed in the beautiful gates of the daughter of Zion. And there we are to show forth not some praise, not just part of His praise but ALL of His praise.

What a vision He gave us as we meditated! The word about rejoicing follows. And the Spirit impressed us again that rejoicing plays a big part in our worship. We are to rejoice in and with the Lord heartily, as befits the inhabitants of Zion.

Another time, the Holy Spirit began to sing a portion from Isaiah 51:3. Only He sang it this way: *"For the Lord has comforted Zion, He has comforted all her waste places, He has made her wilderness like Eden, and her desert like the garden of the Lord; joy and gladness shall be found in it, thanksgiving and the voice of melody."* Over and over the Spirit impressed us with the beauty and ministry of the voice of melody in praising the Lord. Singing melody alone, without words, is a type of praise that pleases the Lord. Humming or whistling can also enter into this type of worship. And whether in our special praise times or as we go about our tasks, we can minister to the Lord in lovely melodies.

In Ephesians we find well loved words: "Be filled with the Spirit, speaking to yourselves in psalms and hymns and spiritual songs, singing and making melody in your heart to the Lord. Giving thanks always for all things unto God and the Father in the name of our Lord Jesus Christ." (5:18-20) Here, again, melody is coupled with thanksgiving. The words in Colossians 3:16 also were brought with new emphasis: "Let the word of Christ dwell in you richly in all wisdom; teaching and admonishing one another in psalms and hymns and spiritual songs, singing with grace in your hearts to the Lord." Singing in the Spirit is thus shown to be a beautiful evidence of being filled with the Spirit and letting the word of Christ indwell us richly.

One of our number was undergoing very fiery trials and a sudden attack came upon her. The Spirit dealt with her to laugh loudly in the face of the enemy. He impressed her that laughter is another form of praise, and that the Lord truly wants to fill our mouths with laughter as well as engage our tongue with singing. *"Then was our mouth filled with laughter, and our tongue with singing; then said they among the nations, the Lord hath done great things for them."*

(Psalm 126:2) As she looked to the Lord for further confirmation in the Word, He led her to 2 Kings 19:21: *"This is the word that the Lord hath spoken concerning him (referring to the King of Assyria, a type of our enemy); the virgin, the daughter of Zion, hath despised thee, and laughed thee to scorn; the daughter of Jerusalem hath shaken her head at thee."* For several days she was led to laugh in the midst of all the pressures and attacks from the enemy. When she related all this to us, the Spirit came upon her and some of us also in holy laughter. Job 8:21 also came into focus: *"Till He fill thy mouth with laughing, and thy lips with rejoicing."* Yes, holy laughter is indeed a form of praise

MAKING HIS PRAISE GLORIOUS

We'll laugh and shout and sing, Making His praise glorious. We'll magnify our King, Making His praise glorious, We'll live through all our days, Making His praise glorious, Giving Him glorious praise.

This song, given so many years ago by the Spirit was revived again in our midst. I looked up glorious, and it means in the original Greek—copious, great, magnificent, resplendent, and illustrious.

The Holy Spirit continued to deal with us about the importance of rejoicing heartily day by day as well as in the meetings. Many Scriptures came to mind, but we still felt weak and unable in ourselves to really rejoice—meaning to be glad, to joy in, and to be cheerful and happy, in the Greek. In the Hebrew, the meaning is to exult, jump for joy, triumph in, shout aloud, brighten up, be merry, glad and blithesome. As we considered all this, we felt utterly unable to continue on a path of constant rejoicing and praise. Our many problems, physical condition and age—just everything—seemed overwhelming. We really cried to the Lord for His enabling. For we realized more than ever before how utterly supernatural such a walk must be. We knew we were being pressed into God as never before. And we praise Him for this. Then He spoke so comfortingly, *"You are rejoicing in hope."* (Romans 12:12) And you are *"looking for the blessed hope and the glorious appearing of the great God and our Savior, Jesus Christ."* (Titus 2:13) Let us live daily rejoicing in hope—and remembering always, *"Christ in us, the hope of glory."* (Colossians 1:27)

The Lord spoke to several of us about His great triumph, and about His desire that we triumph always in all circumstances, through our Lord Jesus Christ. He gave a little vision of a saint, radiant with joy and victory in the midst of many severe trials—a real overcomer and conqueror—*"more than conqueror"* (Romans 8:37 puts it.) A triumphant saint is a special praise and glory to God. Just before this verse in Romans, Paul was speaking about tribulation, distress, persecution, famine, nakedness, peril and the sword—yes, even about martyrdom. So surely the grace of Christ is sufficient for the trials and troubles we encounter from day to day.

We wish we could put into words how beautiful and meaningful the word triumph was made to us, as the Holy Spirit moved. We found that in the Hebrew it means: with a shout of joy, a proclamation, a rejoicing, to glory in, to sing aloud, and to be victorious. The Scriptures He quickened to us are: *"Shout unto God with the voice of triumph!"* (Psalm 47:1); *"The Lord hath triumphed gloriously!"* (Exodus 15:1); *"Now thanks be unto God, who always causeth us to triumph in Christ."* (2 Corinthians 2:14) The word here in the Greek means, a procession or pageant of triumph. Moffatt translates it: *"Wherever I go, thank God, He makes my life a constant pageant of triumph in Christ."* The Amplified reads: *"But thanks be to God, Who in Christ always leads us in triumph—as trophies of Christ's victory—and through us spreads and makes evident the fragrance of the knowledge of God everywhere, for we are the sweet fragrance of Christ (which exhales) unto God."* As we live in victory and joyful praise, what a fragrance is going up to God! Meanwhile, however obscure we may be in the world, all the unseen world of demons, angels and saints are viewing our daily life as a "pageant" either of defeat and dejection or of triumph and glory to God. Also the saved and unsaved alike are witnessing our daily lives and inhaling whatever "fragrance" we are breathing out.

Speaking of our lives being like a pageant, we will share with you a vivid dream one of us had. In the dream she was being urged by a dear friend to take part in a chorale and play that was being given in our village. (As a young girl she loved being in choirs, choruses, plays, pageants, etc.) This friend was telling her that it was such a shame that the public could not hear her voice and enjoy her talents. There was a bit of flattery in this, of course, and for just a moment she hardly knew what to say. Then the Holy Spirit spoke through her saying, "Why, every day multitudes hear your voice lifted up to the Lord in singing and praise." When she woke up, she realized that it was true.

We may feel that we are all alone. But in the book of Hebrews we are told that we are surrounded by a "cloud of witnesses." It is certain that angels and demons are everywhere, and that when we sing and praise in the Spirit, our voice is truly heard on high, as well as here on earth. We are God's spectacle, as in 1 Corinthians 4:9: *"For we have become a spectacle to the world—a show in the world's amphitheater—with both men and angels (as spectators)."* (Amplified) The Greek meaning of "spectacle" is theatrical. And one of these days God is going to make us His actors in the greatest "spectacular" the world has ever witnessed. Right now He is training us and preparing us to show forth His grace and glory throughout all the earth and heavens.

One was given: *"Take with you words and turn to the Lord, say unto Him, Take away all iniquity and receive us graciously; so will we render the calves of our lips."* (Hosea 14:2) Before we praise, our minds should be cleansed and under the Blood of Christ. We know that we are not to offer praise merely in obedience, which is basic, but with an overflowing gratitude, love, appreciation and joy. This praise breaks down barriers, and tears away partitions. Its holy vibrations shatter evil forces, and scatter the powers of darkness.

Praise is the highway, the elevator, the way to "Come up higher," as He is calling us. Jesus said that praise is perfected out of the mouths of babes and sucklings. So must we become childlike and fearless in praises. In Psalm 8:2 we read, *"Out of the mouths of babes and sucklings hast Thou ordained strength."* So, perfecting praise links us with ordaining strength. And truly the joy of the Lord is our strength—strength of mind, spirit, soul and body.

Another wrote: "The Lord wants from us a constant praise. Our spirit can be in constant praise and communion, even though our brain, at times, must be occupied with our daily tasks and work. This makes for a continual communion in the Spirit. And we can ask the Holy Spirit who dwells in our spirit to help us in this. He is so willing and eager to help each and every one to be in continual praise. May our minds and spirits work together with the Holy Spirit as we yield our will to Jesus Christ, for His glory. *"Wherefore gird up the loins of your mind, be sober, and hope to the end for the grace that is to be brought unto you at the revelation of Jesus Christ."* (1 Peter 1:13)

As we were worshiping, one had a vision of a rainbow around the Throne of God. It was in a complete circle, extending beneath the Throne into the earth. The heavenly throngs were praising Him and making up that part of the rainbow in beautiful, colorful praise. It was our responsibility to make up the bottom pan of the rainbow in beautiful, colorful glory.

It can be comparatively easy to praise God with others, since their praises encourage our praises. But to praise God when all alone and in difficult tasks is another thing. In 1 John 2:27 we read, *"But the anointing (charisma) which ye have received of Him abideth in you, and ye need not that any man teach you."* Neither can any individual offer our praise, nor live our lives for us. This can only be done by The Christ, the Anointed One, who lives within us.

One morning this week, I awakened with the thought of the Anointed and the anointing. The word "anointing" in the above verse is *charisma* (Psalm 51:6) *Charisma* in the Greek means a free gift, grace, favor, kindness of God. How great is this free gift! And how grateful should our response be in praise.

In a dream, one was ministering the Word of God in a rather large meeting, in which there was much moving of the Spirit. When she awakened, the Holy Spirit was singing this song:

In His temple everyone speaks of His glory! (Psalm 29:9) In His temple everyone sings of His grace!

In His temple there is worship and thanksgiving, There is honor and blessing and praise.

We had a strong moving one night of lauding and applauding the Lord for quite an extended period of time. His many mighty works in heaven and earth were held before us in a vast panorama. Then this stirring word came forth: "Yes, Lord, we laud You and applaud You and rejoice in all Your mighty acts, in all Your performances from the beginning of time until now. Yes, we laud and applaud You! Encore! Encore! As we continue to applaud You unceasingly, You shall again appear and throughout the whole earth Your performances, Your acts shall increase. Encore! Encore! O Lord, appear here in our midst too, for we know that You have kept the best for the very last."

In the Old Testament there are at least eight different Hebrew words that are translated "praise" in the King James Version. Each of these is most interesting. A study of them is sure to enrich our praise to the Lord, and to inspire us to worship and praise Him more pleasingly and perfectly.

The first mention of praise in the Bible is in Genesis 29:35, *"And she (Leah) conceived again, and bore a son; and she said, Now will I praise the Lord; therefore she called his name Judah, and ceased bearing."* The Hebrew word is *yadah*, meaning to revere or worship with extended hands. Also to confess, praise and give thanks. Literally it means to make use of the hands in praise, not just to extend them, or raise them, but to move them. Often the Spirit will lead us to move our hands in beautiful, graceful gestures. And every movement has a meaning, just as in sign language. So let us be free in using our hands in praise. Notice that the name Judah itself means praise or celebrate. So the beautiful name of Judah is taken from the Hebrew word *yadah*. This word occurs in 2 Chronicles 20:21; Psalms 7:17, 33:2, 99:3 and in other places in the Scripture.

In Leviticus 19:24, we find the word *hallul*, meaning a celebration, a feast of praise, merry praise, holy joy and laughing. It is connected in this Scripture with an offering of fruit unto the Lord. And truly all our praise and worship involves offering to God the fruit of the Holy Spirit—"love, joy, peace, long-suffering, gentleness, goodness, faith, meekness and temperance". (Galatians 5:22, 23) *"For the fruit of the Spirit is in all goodness and righteousness and truth."* (Ephesians 5:9) This word, *hallul*, is closely related to *hallel*, which is used in Judges 5:3; 2 Chronicles 8:14; Nehemiah 12:24 and in some of the Psalms. It means also to show forth, to shine, to sing praise, to be prepared for marriage and to give in marriage. What a beautiful word! When we praise the Lord in this way, we are often in close union with Him.

Ephesians 5:19 speaks of *"Psalms and hymns and spiritual songs, singing and making melody in your heart to the Lord."* So too, in Colossians 3:16, we are instructed to thus sing unto the Lord and one another.

Another precious word is *Barach*, meaning to bless abundantly, to congratulate, salute, kneel as an act of adoration and to thank. This word is used in Judges 5:2, Psalm 103:1, and in numerous other places, translated in the English as "bless." It implies a hearty well-wishing and affection.

The Lord desires praise on stringed and other instruments as well. The Hebrew word *zamar*, means to strike with the fingers or play upon a musical instrument, accompanied by the voice. It implies both singing and playing. It means to celebrate in song, to give praise and to sing Psalms. It can be found in Psalms 57:7, 138:1 and other places. In its root meaning it also indicates "to trim a vine." We are truly living branches in Christ, the Vine. And worshiping the Lord in this way does accomplish a pruning or trimming of our branches, as the self-life is put to the cross.

In Psalms 63:3, 106:47, 147:12 and other places the word *shabach* is used. This means to address or praise in a loud tone, to get so loud your enemies stand silent or flee! To praise in authority is implied, and also to triumph, glory in and adore. Often the Holy Spirit leads us into this strong praise. Shouting can be one form of "shabaching" the Lord.

Another Hebrew word occurs in Proverbs 27:21. It is *mahalal*, and it means fame or praise. It is closely related to *hallel*, which has a wide range of meanings. In the Amplified version this verse reads: "As the refining pot for silver and the furnace for gold (bringing forth all the impurities in the metal), so let a man be in his trial of praise (ridding it of all that is base and insincere) for a man is judged by what he praises and of what he boasts." Graham Truscott, in commenting on this verse, says that it means that "entering fully into God's praise places us in the refining fire of the Holy Spirit." Truly the Lord puts us through many fiery trials to purify our praise of Him.

The word *todah* is used in Psalm 42:4 and in other places, it is translated "thanks." It refers to a choir of worshipers, the praise of a throng, joyful rejoicing or a sacrifice of praise. It is also the Hebrew word for "thanks," implying appreciation and gratitude. True appreciation and gratitude are important elements in our praise of the Lord.

The first mention of praise in the New Testament is in Matthew 21:16. Here the Greek word is *ainos*, meaning to laud, commend or praise. This is also used in Luke 18:43 and Romans 15:11. It is closely related to *aineo* which is found in Luke 19:37. In John 9:24, 12:43 and 1 Peter 4:11, we find the word *doxa*, meaning glory, honor, magnify, praise and worship.

The word *epaineo* occurs in Romans 2:29, 13:3 and Ephesians 1:6. This means to laud, applaud, commend and praise. When Jesus speaks of singing praise in Hebrews 2:12, the Greek word is *humneo*, meaning to hymn, to sing a religious ode or psalm, to celebrate in song. Where it speaks of giving the Lord the sacrifice of praise, in Hebrews 13:15, the Greek word is *ainesis*, meaning, "a thank or praise offering."

One night, while worshiping, the Holy Spirit moved upon us in a strong way and brought forth a portion of the Word in Exodus: *"And the LORD descended in the cloud, and stood with him (Moses) there, and proclaimed the name of THE LORD."* (In the Hebrew, YHVH, pronounced with the accent on the last syllable, according to Strong's Concordance, *Yehovah*. Others, as we know, pronounce it *Yahweh*, or *Yahvah*. It means, The Eternal Self-existent One—literally, *(The I AM that I WAS that I WILL BE!)*

"And the LORD passed by before him, and proclaimed, Yehovah God, merciful and gracious, longsuffering, and abundant in goodness and truth." (Exodus 34:5-7)

Often in our meetings we would sing out the various compound names of the LORD, as found in the Old Testament and this seemed to please Him very much indeed. For days afterward the Spirit kept moving in us about these compound names, filling us with rejoicing that all of them find their fulfillment in *Yahshua*, our Lord Jesus Christ. *"Therefore, My people shall know what My name is and what it means; therefore they shall know in that day that I am He who speaks; behold I AM."* (Isaiah 52:6, Amplified) *"Who hath ascended up into heaven, or descended? Who hath gathered the wind in his fists? Who hath bound the waters in a garment? Who hath established all the ends of the earth? What is His name, and what is His Son's name, if you canst tell?"* (Proverbs 30:4)

Yehovah-yireh: The Lord my provider (Genesis 22:13, 14)
Yehovah-rapha: The Lord my healer (Exodus 15:26)
Yehovah-nissi: The Lord my banner (Exodus 17:8-15)
Yehovah-mkaddesh: The Lord my sanctifier (Leviticus 20:7, 8)
Yehovah-shalom: The Lord my peace (Judges 6:24)
Yehovah-raah: The Lord my shepherd (Psalm 23:1)
Yehovah-ori: The Lord my light (Psalm 27:1)
Yehovah-tsidkenu: The Lord my righteousness (Jeremiah 23:6)
Yehovah-sabaoth: The Lord of Hosts (Isaiah 54:5)
Yehovah-shammah: The Lord is present (Ezekiel 48:35)

Several of us were moved to "extol Him by His name YAH!" (Psalm 68:4) We found a special anointing upon us as we sang forth, spoke forth or shouted these sacred names revealed in the Old Testament. We know that all of them apply to Jesus, and that He has been given a name above every name. HalleluJAH! (Ephesians 1:20, 21; Philippians 2:9, 10)

During this time we were also led into a study of His Sacred Name, Jehovah. Psalm 83:18 was especially blessed: "That men may know that Thou, whose name alone is Jehovah, are most high over all the earth." The following is a partial list of Scriptures defining our relationship to the Name.

The Lord's name is to be:

Blessed: Job 1:21; Psalms 72:19, 103:1
Called Upon: 1 Chronicles 16:8; Psalms 80:18, 99:6, 105:1; Isaiah 12:4
Confessed: 1 Kings 8:33-35; 2 Chronicles 6:26
Declared: Psalms 22:22, 102:21; John 17:26
Exalted: Psalm 34:3; Isaiah 12:4
Extolled: Psalm 68:4
Feared: Psalms 61:5, 86:11, 102:15

Given Thanks: 1 Chronicles 16:35; Psalm 106:47
Gloried in: 1 Chronicles 16:10, Psalms 29:2, 86:12, 96:8
Honored: Psalm 66:2
Loved: Psalms 5:11, 69:36
Magnified: 2 Samuel 7:26, 1 Chronicle 17:24
Manifested: John 17:6
Mentioned: Isaiah 26:13
Praised: 1 Chronicles 29:13; Psalms 7:17, 44:8, 135:1
Proclaimed: Exodus 33:19, 34:5
Rejoiced In: Psalm 89:16
Remembered: Psalms 20:7, 45:17, 119:55
Sought: Psalm 83:16
Sung To: Psalms 66:4, 68:4, 69:30
Trusted: Psalm 33:21
Waited On: Psalm 52:9

In His Name we are to:

Bless Others, Burn Incense (Offer Praise), Lift Up Our Hands, Minister, Set Up Our Banners, Walk before Him. (See Deuteronomy 21:5; Malachi 1:11; Psalms 44:5, 118:10; Psalm 63:4; Deuteronomy 18:5; Psalm 20:5; Micah 4:5.)

One day as we were worshiping the Lord, someone saw a very large arena and in the center of it a great performance was going on—mighty acts of healing, deliverance and salvation. There were many men and women through whom the Lord was performing these acts. But the only Performer she could identify was Jesus! It was Jesus who was performing all the mighty acts of deliverance, healing and salvation. As she gazed on this in wonder, the Holy Spirit prompted her to say: "Lord; where are we in the midst of all this?" (referring to our company of believers and worshipers) His answer surprised her.

He said, "Why, you are in the rooting section!" Then she saw a great company of praisers, singers, and worshipers all attired in special garments, sitting in a special place in the grand stand. At a signal they would all rise and shout, sing, or praise the Lord in other ways. They were like a great choir. It seemed that as they applauded, the Lord would be cheered on, girded with greater strength and zeal. And just as the rooting section plays a special part in stirring a football team on to victory, so the Lord seemed to be greatly pleased with His rooting section.

MISCELLANEOUS EXCERPTS

The Golden Candlestick

The following are collected excerpts of various teachings, prophetic words, and poems from the journals, missionary notes and newsletters of the Golden Candlestick—primarily from Frances Metcalfe. Some are in bits and pieces as the original copies are very old and corrupted, making a perfect translation impossible. In fact, some of the mimeographs are no longer extant. Still, I believe in order to be "complete" these collected works would require the inclusion of the following.

—James Maloney

It is a good and excellent thing to sing praises unto Him. Pour out your songs and praises as a drink offering. Pour out your soul before Him for He is the Lover of your soul, spirit and body. He is a True Husband who loves His wife even as His own flesh, His own spirit, His own soul. Great is this Love. And He desires us to be ever more closely knit together with His own body, soul and spirit. It is a good and pleasant and delightful thing to pour out love and praises unto Jesus our Beloved. He loves our bodies and is going to change them. He spent much of His ministry on earth healing the sick, and He never wasted His time.

As high as the heavens above,
So great is God's mercy and love,
And as far as the east is from the west
He has removed the sins we have confessed.
So magnify Him, magnify Him
And join with the hosts above,
So magnify Him, magnify Him
And sing of His grace and love.

Magnify, magnify! Make bigger! It is His people that are to magnify Him and make Him bigger! With some of us He is a mighty small God. How should we magnify Him and make Him bigger because we can't make Him big enough.

And may He forgive me for me, for everything in me that has been irreverent, or is irreverent. I want to revere Him and to be reverent at all times. Recently I have just been permeated with that word *reverence.*

My mouth shall speak the praise of the Lord,
My mouth shall speak the praise of the Lord,
My mouth shall speak the praise of the Lord,
And let all flesh bless His Holy Name forever.

I will praise Thee, O Lord, with my whole heart. You are a very personal God, very personal, as well as universal, very personally ours, Lord! And how You love us and cherish us and prize each of us in a very personal way.

With the high praises of God in our mouth,
And a two-edged sword in our hand,
With the high praises of God in our mouth,
We will go forth at His command,
To execute His righteous justice
And to overcome the enemy,

To overcome the enemy on every hand.
Yes, to overcome His enemies on every hand.

Clap your hands, all ye people! Clap your hands, all ye nations! For He comes! He comes! He comes! to reign in the earth. He shall appear to our joy! And the meek shall have a great increase of joy. "I will see you again," He said, "And your sorrow will be turned into joy." (John 14:20) His hour of joy is near. It is a day for the world to weep and lament, the day of His coming in judgment and power. But it is a day of jubilation and exultation for His own. He shall appear to our joy. It shall be a time of great reward for those who have continued with Him in His tribulations. From tribulation to jubilation! How quickly He turns our sorrow into joy! So let Him deal with you now as He wills. Be an instrument in His hands, and let Him "play" upon you as it pleases Him. Do not be afraid to let Him tune you, stretching your heart-strings tightly—a higher melody is being born! Yet in the highest notes of praise we can hear the undertone of weeping and sorrow. Was not the foundation of His music laid in death and blood and tears? And listen! In the very highest notes you can detect the undertones that lend beauty and strength to the theme! Learn to listen for the overtones and the undertones in His music. Learn to hear the whole symphony, the full sweep of the diapason, the consummate concord of His anthems. Let Him play all His notes upon you, from the lowest to the highest.

THE SON RISES!

As You once rose up from the tomb,
Bursting all death's cruel bands,
So rise up in us, dear Lord,
And of our beings take command.

As You then showed Yourself alive—
Triumphant over all Your foes,
Show Yourself again in us,
And unto men Your life transpose.

As You to them in love appeared
Amazing all Your chosen ones,
O risen Lord, appear in us
Unto Your daughters and Your sons.

Rise up and work Your mighty works,
Walk with us, IN us, Lord, we pray,
As You once walked within Your saints
In the Church's early day.

Take up Your life again in us,
Nor ever lay it down, dear Lord,
Let US be no more seen or known,
Display Yourself, the LIVING WORD!

With great power
The Disciples gave witness of His resurrection.
With great power and authority,
And many signs and wonders were done.
And we too, O Lord,
Will bear witness of the resurrection.
Your people will carry this word
To every nation—to all the nations.
We shall go forth bearing witness
Of His resurrection life.
The Lord is risen! The Lord is risen!
The Lord lives and His people live.
He is the God of the living,
The living shall praise You,
As we do, O Lord, this day.
My dead men, He said, shall live,
And shall sing unto Me.
O to every nation, and to all the heavens
We shall bear witness—
Witness of His resurrection.

The Lord is in His Holy Temple. The Lord is in His living Temple. Let all the earth keep silence before Him. He is in His sanctified ones, His living Temple. Let all flesh be silent before Him. For He shall suddenly visit His Temple with overwhelming power. Yes, He shall visit His temple, and all shall be astounded at His mighty act. All shall be astounded! Zion shall tremble, shall tremble before the Mighty One. He shall come down in His might and Zion shall be astounded. All things shall be exposed and brought to light. "All things are naked and opened unto the eyes of Him with whom we have to do." (Hebrews 4:13) O prepare your heart, prepare your heart. Prepare, prepare, for the Lord shall suddenly come to His temple. In a new and astounding way He shall come. He shall arise in Zion and SHOW HIMSELF ALIVE, by many, many, many infallible proofs. Yes, Lord, those who once were blind shall see, those who once doubted shall no longer doubt, those who once were deaf shall hear. And out of the mouths of babes and sucklings You shall ordain strength. You shall confound Your enemies. Your "babes" And Your sons shall be manifested—they shall manifest Your fulness and Your authority. Yes, Your absolute authority shall be upon Your anointed ones.

O behold the empty tomb, the empty tomb!
It is not a place of death and gloom—the empty tomb!
O hear the song of the empty tomb,
Telling, witnessing, resurrection.
It rings with the voice of angelic ones,
"He is not here, He is risen!"
How it sings!
The silent tomb the singing,
The empty tomb is ringing—Angelic voices singing,
"He is not here! He is not here!"
O death is swallowed up in Life.
He is not here, He is risen
A rolled away stone, a broken seal,
Testifying, witnessing, singing
Of resurrection glory and power!

You said to Your Disciples, "Why are ye so fearful? How is it that ye have no faith?" (Mark 4:40) We remember how often You spoke to them about this matter. And we remember the Centurion and the faith You found in him. In these Gentiles You found faith that was honoring to God. (Matthew 8:10-13) And so on these latter days You are moving among the Gentiles as well as the Jews, bringing forth this mighty army equipped with all this armor of God which You have provided. We do want to please You and have the faith that flourishes and increases and matures. We want to please You in both love and faith.

"Now faith is the substance of things hoped for, the evidence of things not seen. For by it the elders obtained a good report." (Hebrews 11:1,2) We too want to obtain a good report. The faith of our fathers! The faith of our mothers! The faith of the Apostles! And, we thank You, Lord, that You are changing us and perfecting our faith, not only in our own precious Body of Believers here, but in all the Body of Christ throughout the whole earth. You are purifying Your Body in the Earth, Lord, that we may bring forth the fruit that is wrought by faith. Your Word is still saying to us, "according to your faith, be it unto you."

"Seeing is believing,"
The world has said to thee;
But Jesus changed the order,
"Believe and thou shalt see."
"Believe and thou shalt see."
This is His Word to thee.
The glory of the Lord
Shall be revealed,
Believe and thou shalt see.

We would come to You with pure hearts, believing hearts, without doubt or fear, hearts that have faith in You and Your Word, Lord. For we know that You and Your Word are one, "In the beginning was the Word was with God and the Word was God." (John 1:1) And we want to be true believers and receivers, believers and receivers, of all that You have provided in Your Covenant. You said that You would teach us all that is in "the deep, inner meaning of Your Covenant," (Psalm 25:14, Amplified) that great salvation which You said is to the uttermost. And You said that You are our Great High Priest, ever living to intercede for us, wherefore You are "able also to save to the uttermost all those who come unto God by You." (Hebrews 7:25) we want to be "saved to the uttermost"—in body, soul and spirit. O Lord, that every part of our beings shall truly belong to You and be Your holy ground, and that there be no place, no room, no ground for the enemy, no place for any other spirit but the Holy Spirit. You said, "neither give place to the devil" (Ephesians 4:27) and we don't want to give any place to him in our mind. Our minds, our beings belong to You, Christ the Lord, and You have promised us "the spirit of power and of love and of a sound mind." (2 Timothy 1:7) A sound mind! We want our thoughts as well as our words to speak forth the truth that is in Your Word. We want to be in agreement with the Living God. Let all that is within me agree with the Living God and His Word. Let all that is in me being in harmony with the Truth as it is in Christ Jesus. O Lord, I don't want to have distrust or have any place left in my being for self or the evil one to hold dominion. Let Jesus be Lord in me, and my whole being. This is our cry! Let all that is within me not only bless His holy Name, but let all that is within me believe His Holy Word. Hallelujah! Let all that is within me believe the Word of the Living God!

WHAT THE SPIRIT SAITH

O Lord, we praise You for the "faith once delivered to the saints," the faith, the faith once delivered to the saints. And You said that we were to "contend," contend for that faith once delivered to the saints. (Jude 3,20,21) We want that true faith, that pure faith, that faith that Paul preached and taught, and that Peter preached and taught, that faith that all the Apostles taught and lived, yes, the True Faith. And we know, Lord, You said that when You come, would You find faith in the earth? (Luke 18:8) You will be looking, Lord, for that faith, that true faith, that pure faith, that living faith. And You are purifying us, Lord, that this faith may come forth in us as gold, as pure gold tried in the fire. Hallelujah!

O Lord, that we may be found in that glorious company in the True Faith once delivered to the saints and delivered also to us. Hallelujah! O Holy Spirit, You are the Spirit of Faith, and we have the Word, the Words of Faith, the Logos and the Rhema. Hallelujah! for the Logos and the Rhema! Hallelujah! for the True Word of Faith, that we may be purged of all that is of error, that we may be purged of all that is darkness, of all that is of our human spirit, or any other spirit. O Lord, that we may be purged to come forth strong in THE Faith. O this wonderful faith, Lord, which You first planted in us, and now are perfecting and bringing to maturity! By this faith great things shall be wrought. By faith mighty works shall be done. By faith, You said, that kingdoms shall be subdued. By faith even the dead shall be raised. By faith! By faith! By this pure and living faith. (Hebrews 11:33-35)

O Lord, You said to Your own, even after Your resurrection, "Be not faithless, but believing!" (John 20:27) Be not faithless, but believing! Believing! Believing! And even then some of them did not believe, even after You were raised from the dead. O Lord, there is in us, as human beings, evil hearts of unbelief. And only by Your power can doubt and unbelief and all that is opposing this faith be cleansed and purged from us. O Lord, we would not be among the fearful and unbelieving, the doubting and the wavering; for You said that the man that waivers shall receive nothing from the Lord. (James 1:6-9)

You told us that this is a way of "faith that worketh by love." (Galatians 5:6) O we thank You, Lord, that in each of us this faith is living, this faith that worketh by love. We thank You and praise You, Lord, that even as it was said of the Thessalonians that their faith was growing exceedingly (2 Thessalonians 1:3), so may it be that this faith shall grow, not just sparingly, but abundantly, that we may have faith to stand in the latter days, the evil days which are even upon us; that having done all we may stand, having always that shield of faith whereby we shall be able to quench all the fiery darts of the evil one, and having in our hands that sword of the Spirit, which is the Word of God. (Ephesians 6:16,17)

We remember that woman to whom You said, "O woman, great is thy faith, be it unto thee even as thou wilt." (Matthew 15:28) She wasn't even in the holy family of the Israelites, but she was commended for her faith. You commended her. We want to please You also. We don't want to covet anything You don't want for us; but we want to have that faith that You can commend, so that You can say, "According to your faith be it unto you," (Matthew 9:29) for it will be Your Word of Faith in our hearts and in our mouths.

Keep your eyes fixed steadfastly on the things which are unseen, the eternal verities of God. It shall be given you at times to touch the ultimate, and to glimpse the consummate perfection of those elect souls who in this life are subjected unto the Lord in all things.

How great is the gulf lying between the newly-born child of God and the fulness of Grace and Truth which shall be manifest in that one when mature and perfected he shall stand faultless before the Presence of God with exceeding great joy! How small is the capacity of the immature. Growth, development, perfection—all a work of grace by faith—can progress only as there is complete and continuous submission to the will of God and the operations of the Holy Spirit. At times discipline, suffering, pain, separation, toil, privation, rejection all play their part in your perfection. Every faculty must be sensitized and exercised to respond to the impulse of the Holy Spirit. Every thought and imagination must be captivated and brought into complete subjection to the mind of Christ. Every affection must be firmly reined by His own heart strings. Every desire and longing must be purified until all self-motivation is completely abolished. Only the truly purified and refined soul is able to comprehend with all the saints what is the length and depth and breadth and height of the knowledge of God, and know the constraining love of Christ that surpasses all knowledge. When you do perceive, at rare moments, the infinite nature of God and the fulfillment of His purpose for you, then your heart is flooded with gratitude that He so relentlessly exercises you and prepares you for that crowning day. (Hebrews 5:7; 12:5-11)

Be of good cheer, and in nothing be dismayed or doubtful. Stand firm and immovable. Stand, I say, and lift high the standard given you, which is in your hand. "When the enemy shall come in like a flood, the Spirit of the Lord shall lift up a standard against him." (Isaiah 59:19) He would try to dishearten you and to make you careless and off guard, feeling there is little for you to do. But each one has a particular part to play in that which I am bringing forth in the earth, and each one is facing many odds and trials. It is so important that not one go down in defeat, even for a day. It is not a time to be at ease, but to STAND and WITHSTAND. Be faithful in battle and also remember all the saints scattered abroad, and all the saints assembled on high, as you intercede and worship before the Throne. "Blessed be God in His Saints"! (Isaiah 59:16-21)

I am girding you with new strength so that you shall be able to stand in the midst of the evil hour which is breaking upon all the world. There shall be no fear in your heart, and no doubt in your mind, for you shall be clad in the armor of light. Strength and honor shall be your clothing, and you shall rejoice, greatly rejoice in the time to come. Out of weakness shall you be made strong. Blessed are they who partake of My weakness, saith the Lord, for they also shall share in My strength. I was crucified in weakness; I was RAISED IN POWER. Therefore, drink the cup of weakness that I may give you the cup of divine strength—a potent wine for you to quaff. I am the Lord Jehovah in Whom is everlasting strength.

O Lord, You said the glory of the Lord shall be revealed and all flesh shall see it together, for the mouth of the Lord hath spoken it. We praise You that You shall be in Your people and You shall shine forth, that all people shall see the glory of the Lord. For You said You have called many sons to glory. "Christ in us the hope of glory." (Colossians 1:27) Everyone You justify You also shall glorify. (Romans

8:30) you have already done this, although it is not yet visible. One of these days it shall be visible. You even said that You gave us Your glory, for You gave Your glory to Your disciples. Your very own glory, the glory You had with the Father before the world was, that it might be upon Your disciples. The Holy Spirit is the Spirit of Glory and of Power. And He rests upon us and is in us and He shall be manifest. From glory to glory You are changed us. All we beholding as in a mirror the glory of the Lord are being changed into the same image, into the same glory, "from glory to glory." (2 Corinthians 3:18) And it shall shine forth. Your words will be heard to the ends of the earth. Your works will be wrought! And Your people's hands will be Your hands extended healing and in power. Your people's faith will be Your faith in which You move and walk in the earth. And Your people's voices will be Your voice as You speak Your words.

Your word says, Lord, that "As He (Jesus) was, so are we in this present world." (1 John 4:17) O that we might manifest Him in this present world! For You have called us to be witnesses. You have placed us here to bear witness to *all* that Christ is! You have called us to bear witness of *all* the fulness of salvation! You have chosen us for full salvation, not just a partial salvation, but full salvation for spirit, soul and body—that we might manifest it to the world!

Long ago, before the world's foundation,
The Father chose us in Christ for full salvation.
And He has made us in Him a new creation,
To the praise of the glory of His grace.

To the praise of the glory of His grace!
To the praise of the glory of His grace!
He has made us in Christ a new creation,
To the praise of the glory of His grace!

Beloved in THE BELOVED,

Once more we are approaching the season of Passover and Resurrection. Maybe hallowed to you in a special way! Yet these are everyday realities to those of us who are dwelling in Christ, partaking of His precious body and blood, joined to Him as one spirit, by the Holy Spirit who lives in us. And, indeed, "we are members of His body, of His flesh and of His bones." (Ephesians 5:30) How wonderful and intimate is this communion! At the beginning of 1976, the Lord gave me a precious verse in Psalm 25:14, the Amplified version: "The secret (of the sweet, satisfying companionship) of the Lord have they who fear—revere and worship—Him, and He will show them His covenant, and reveal to them its (deep, inner) meaning."

Since that time, those in our fellowship have been passing through some very fiery trials indeed. We are sure the Lord is seeking to perfect our faith and love, as well as our praise, that we might be like the Thessalonian Church, to whom Paul wrote that their "faith groweth exceedingly, and the love of everyone of you all toward each other aboundeth." We are in this processing, and the Holy Spirit is faithful to perfect and prepare each one of us to present us faultless (Jude 24) to our Heavenly Bridegroom, the Lord Jesus Christ. It seems there is much suffering involved in this preparation. Also there is vigorous spiritual warfare. Ephesians 6 is our handbook for this. And we constantly look to Jesus who is

Victor over self, sin and the devil. "For this purpose the Son of God was manifested, that He might destroy the works of the devil." (1 John 3:8) Also 1 John 4:4 is consistently held before us: "Ye are of God, little children, and have overcome them, because greater is He that is in you, then He that is of the world."

In the midst of our battles, as there have been some wonderful victories, and for these we praise and magnify the Lord. One of our number was quite literally brought back from the very gates of death. A few have said that they have been aware of the presence of angels, upholding, strengthening and protecting them. Hallelujah!

We greatly appreciate your letters and requests for booklets. And we are especially thankful for your prayers for us. Forgive us if at times we are a bit slow in answering. We do faithfully take your prayer requests to the Lord. My husband, Marian, and I are all presently undergoing strong attacks against our physical bodies. It is only by grace and faith that we can rise each day to continue on in the Lord. I know you will hold in faith for the Lord's full victory in us, spirit, soul and body.

We are rejoicing by faith in the great and glorious Victory of Jesus Christ on the cross of Calvary. We know that there "(God) disarmed the principalities and powers ranged against us and made a bold display and public example of them, in triumphing over them in Christ and in it (the cross.)" (Colossians 2:15, Amplified)

Marian and all the saints here join me in sending you love and blessing. Yours, rejoicing in our Resurrected Lord!

Signed,
Frances Metcalfe
Marian Pickard

PASSOVER-RESURRECTION 1976

At first there were but twelve who,
In the Upper Room,
Sat down with Jesus at the Paschal Feast.
But now we come in myriads
To sup with our Beloved—
So greatly has His "little flock" increased!

Once more He lifts the Cup
Vintage red and bittersweet,
And we hear Him say,
"This is My Blood," again.
Then we in turn receive it
With thanksgiving, as did they.
That we may taste His passion and His pain.

And when He breaks the Bread
And speaks the Holy Words
That bless it and transform it to our need;
Again Christ stands revealed—
ALIVE forever more!
As the Bread becomes His Body indeed!

—F. M.

O Lord Paraclete, O Lord Paraclete, we honor You. Yes, we honor You, Holy Spirit. Spirit of Truth and of Light! Spirit of Life, we honor You! We bless our Father God, for You are the Promise of the Father. And we praise our Lord Jesus Christ, for He prayed for You to descend upon Your Church. And we know that in this dispensation You have been very active, but in this latter-day You shall be manifest more and more, and more and more. O Holy Spirit, we rejoice in Your latter day work! We rejoice in Your latter day power! We rejoice in Your latter day Victory! And we honor You, Spirit of power! Spirit of Fire! Spirit of burning! Burn in our hearts. Burn in us in a new and greater way, O flaming Spirit of the Most High God!

The works of the flesh avail nothing. Only that which is wrought by the Holy Spirit lives on. We should be faithful unto the Holy Spirit, for he that soweth to the flesh shall of the flesh reap corruption; but he that soweth to the Spirit shall reap everlasting life. We want to sow abundantly, sow to the Holy Spirit. We know You said that if we walk in the Spirit, we shall mortify the deeds of the flesh. We desire to honor the Holy Spirit more and to a holy walk with the Spirit, the Holy Spirit.

I saw the Holy Spirit descended like a tornado, a twister. It was as a ball of fire and it was the Holy Spirit. He began to speak to me about been baptized and the Holy Ghost and fire and He began to reiterate that, "it shall be very tempestuous about Him." We know the Word says that "a fire devoureth before Him and it shall be very tempestuous round about Him." We have been baptized in this fire of the Holy Spirit. It is a Consuming Fire and it only consumes the works of the flesh. He appeared to Moses in the burning bush. And He will fan the flames in our hearts and new fire shall leap up upon the altar of our hearts. How precious and glorious to be swept into this great Fire and purifying of the Holy Spirit. We shall be endued with His power. Thank You, Lord, for this mighty outpouring of Your Spirit, the Holy Spirit. How we bless You!

Lord Paraclete, tonight we bow
To offer thanks just now;
For all the Spirit has taught us to us
And shown us JESUS!

Chorus:
Blessed, blessed Lord,
Who interprets His Word,
Eternally.

Blessed Lord, Remembrancer,
Recalling to us His Word,
Holy, Heavenly Teacher;
Spirit of our Lord!

He promised the Comforter would come
And now we know He's REAL!!!
Great Spirit of the Living God,
You're on our hearts a seal!

Chorus:
The Word and Spirit agree;
What Blessed Witnesses
Find response in you and me
The Bible says!

I will sing of mercy and lovingkindness
And justice, O Lord, to You will I sing.
I will sing of mercy and lovingkindness,
O Lord, to You will I sing.
I will behave myself wisely
And give heed to the blameless way.
O Lord, when will You come to me?
I will walk within my house in my integrity
And with a blameless heart,
I will sing to Thee.

I will set no wicked thing before my eyes.
I hate the work of them who turn aside.
A perverse heart shall depart from me.
I will know no evil thing
And with Your help, Lord Jesus,
I shall behave myself wisely in Your perfect way.
(From Psalm 101, Amplified)

I am so happy with Jesus, my Love,
My heart is winging its way up above.
My feet are dancing a rhythm divine
I am so happy for Jesus is mine.

Heavenly joy! Heavenly joy!
Once I was so sad and blue,
Now I am smiling just for joy.
Heavenly joy fills my heart,
Fills my heart to overflowing.
I was so sad but now I am so glad,
For heavenly joy fills my heart.
Heavenly joy! Heavenly joy!

Because of Jesus' love
A bliss I have never known
Has come to me in the love of Jesus.
So divine is this heavenly joy,
I rejoice in heavenly joy. Hallelujah!
I was wandering, lost and cold
In the night of the soul,
But Jesus found me,
Put His arms around me.
What love, what bliss, what joy is this,
Heavenly joy! Heavenly joy!

I asked the Lord to open up the door so He could come in and I felt Him opening big double doors into a new realm and I felt St. Paul and other saints and the angels all around us and that they were going to take us into a new realm.

Jesus Christ is alive and well in my body.
And the Holy Spirit that raised Him from the dead
Lives in me.
And the Father too has taken up His abode.
Jesus Christ is alive and well in planet earth,
And walking in the bodies of His saints.

Blessed is the nation whose God is the Lord! We thank You, Lord, that You indeed have been the God of this nation and You have chosen us for Your inheritance from the birth of this nation. Our founding fathers honored You in this land. And now You are moving in every part of this country, from north to south, from east to west. We thank You for the many who are fasting and praying and for each one who is turning to You with their whole hearts. We thank You too for those who are entering into praise and worship from coast to coast, exalting You in the midst of this turmoil and strife. We are so thankful to be a part of this wonderful nation. You said that the nation that forgets God shall perish and the wicked shall be turned into hell. We want to be in the nation that remembers YOU. We want our nation to remember You in great and mighty ways. We thank You for the ways in which You are coming forth and we expect yet greater movings and manifestations this very year, Lord, mighty movings to the Holy Spirit!

The Beloved is at hand! The Beloved is near! The Beloved is in our midst! O adore Him! O praise Him and give Him your heart's pure love. The Beloved! Our Beloved! The Chiefest among ten thousand times ten thousand times ten thousand. The very fairest in all of heaven. O He has shown you His beauty. He has shown you His love. He has privileged you to draw nigh unto Him and to walk closely with Him. O rejoice and be glad, rejoice and be glad, no matter what is going on around you. He is in your midst!

Today the Holy Spirit moved so sweetly impressing me that The Beloved wanted to be loved in a special way. "This is MY DAY, and even in the midst of warfare I still want to remind you of our intimate relationship, our heart union."

I felt as though I was being born away to the tent of our Beloved in the burning desert. I could hear the cries of battle over the dunes and the sounds of triumph and trumpets blowing, for the Captain of the Hosts was at their head. Then suddenly the curtain drew aside and our Beloved rode in all His might and strength and shook the tent. His heart was aflame with love and He came to our tent to be refreshed. It was a time set apart for love, that we might lavish Him with love. And for the moment all was forgotten but that we might satisfy the longing of His heart, the Majestic and Holy One. He desires our love that He may rise up in strength and go forth as a Mighty Man of War, and that we too may arise and run through a troop and leap over a wall, as we go back into the battle, with the sound of His riding forth triumphantly. His arrows are sharp in the heart of the King's enemies. O this is our Beloved! This is our Ishi!

From nation to nation
This word of salvation
Shall flow like a river
And spread like a fire,
Until all earth's peoples
Both far and near
Shall find in Christ
Their true desire.

The "Desire of Nations" shall come! We hail You, Lord, as the Desire of Nations! May the Word of the Lord have free course and may it run and be glorified. We unite with Your Body throughout the earth and join in praise for all that the Holy Spirit is doing both far and near. We expect Your Church to move on as never before in resurrection life, in unexpected ways and unexpected places, in the power You have given her. And we too await Your appearing. We daily watch for You and seek Your face.

Where the Spirit of the Lord is there is liberty,
Where the Spirit of the Lord is there is liberty,
From the law and all its bondage He has set us free.
Where the Spirit of the Lord is there is liberty.

He will lift up a standard against the enemy,
Through His grace and power we all made overcomers be,
And the Lord will lead us on to certain victory,
Where the Spirit of the Lord is there is liberty.

From our fleshly carnal nature He can set us free,
And by walking in the Spirit we can more than conquerors be,
And His grace and His blessing on every hand we'll see,
Where the Spirit of the Lord is there is liberty.

There is liberty to witness, liberty to pray,
Liberty to live for Jesus every day,
Liberty to praise God—what a Jubilee!
Where the Spirit of the Lord is there is liberty.

How beautiful the love of God the Spirit,
How beautiful the love He freely shares,
He comes to banish sorrow, pain and sadness,
To tell the aching heart He deeply cares.
Throughout the earth He wings in gentle power
Unto the spirits waiting to be healed.
When He converts the soul, making it whole again,
In tender kindness is His blessedness revealed.

Just before I awoke, I was in Jerusalem and noted that Deborah Maude was in the dream. We were in the Mount of Olives Chapel and wanted to worship and draw near to the Lord. But there were a number of anti-Christ people that came in and there was real confusion and an awful atmosphere and we couldn't do anything about it. So we went outside and were having our meeting outdoors, and Debra took off and danced and danced and whirled and whirled and leaped, finally falling down in the presence of the Lord. Some brother came up behind me and laid his hand on my head and said, "Don't be afraid to prophesy." Those that were opposing were right there. Then another brother came and looked right into my eyes and said, "Don't be afraid to prophesy." And then I began to sing, "When the enemy comes in like a flood, do not fear but trust in Almighty God." And then I awoke.—It seemed to have something to do with us, and with this hour we are living in. I felt great victory. The Lord is going to be Victor!

The Lord spoke that Zion is a city under siege and that we are under attack especially because we are pressing on into the fulness of Christ. O Lord our sufficiency is of Thee. All Sufficient! You are sufficient in all things, materially and spiritually. We receive from You. All things come from You, whatever the instrument You use. You are in our midst, the Mighty One, the All-sufficient One—sufficient to bring us into Your fulness.

The remarkable teachings of the

Golden Candlestick continue in

Volumes 2 and 3, coming soon!

Please visit www.answeringthecry.com

for more information!

CPSIA information can be obtained at www.ICGtesting.com
Printed in the USA
LVOW071122280213

321990LV00004B/10/P

9 781449 729226